Externalization

This book explores theoretical issues of the syntax-phonology interface within the Minimalist Program of linguistic theory and proposes an entirely new approach to prosodic categories. Conceptual as well as empirical questions are addressed, concerning how syntactic objects are mapped to the sensorimotor system through the processes of externalization. Elaborating on recent progress in the theories of labeling and workspace-based syntactic derivation, this book further develops a null theory of the prosodic domains, and recasts these as the domains of interpretation that are reducible to more fundamental concepts of linguistic theory. Phonological phrases are characterized by Minimal Search, a third factor principle of efficient computation. Intonational phrases are taken to be reflexes of the termination of syntactic derivation, which is formulated in terms of the workspace to which MERGE applies.

This book explores the new implications this theory has for the general architecture of grammar as well as for linguistic interfaces. It provides a comprehensive review of the development of theories of the syntax-phonology interface from over the past three decades. The book is well-suited for general linguistic readers as well as phonologists, syntacticians, and any linguists interested in interface research.

Yoshihito Dobashi is Associate Professor at the Faculty of Humanities, Niigata University, Japan. He received his PhD from Cornell University in 2003. He has published papers in journals such as *The Linguistic Review*, *Linguistic Analysis*, *Journal of East Asian Linguistics*, and *Linguistic Inquiry*, as well as edited volumes.

Routledge Studies in Linguistics

Conceptual Conflicts in Metaphors and Figurative Language
Michele Prandi

The Language of Pop Culture
Edited by Valentin Werner

Perspectives from Systemic Functional Linguistics
Edited by Akila Sellami-Baklouti and Lise Fontaine

Time Series Analysis of Discourse
Method and Case Studies
Dennis Tay

Heart- and Soul-Like Constructs across Languages, Cultures, and Epochs
Edited by Bert Peeters

Systemic Functional Political Discourse Analysis
A Text-based Study
Eden Sum-hung Li, Percy Luen-tim Lui and Andy Ka-chun Fung

Systemic Functional Language Description
Making Meaning Matter
Edited by J.R. Martin and Y.J. Doran

Rarely Used Structures and Lesser-Studied Languages
Insights from the Margins
Emily Manetta

Externalization
Phonological Interpretations of Syntactic Objects
Yoshihito Dobashi

For more information about this series, please visit: www.routledge.com/
Routledge-Studies-in-Linguistics/book-series/SE0719

Externalization

Phonological Interpretations of
Syntactic Objects

Yoshihito Dobashi

LONDON AND NEW YORK

First published 2020
by Routledge
2 Park Square, Milton Park, Abingdon, Oxon OX14 4RN

and by Routledge
52 Vanderbilt Avenue, New York, NY 10017

Routledge is an imprint of the Taylor & Francis Group, an informa business

First issued in paperback 2021

British Library Cataloguing-in-Publication Data
A catalogue record for this book is available from the British Library

Library of Congress Cataloging-in-Publication Data
A catalog record for this book has been requested

ISBN: 978-0-367-02932-6 (hbk)
ISBN: 978-1-03-208947-8 (pbk)
ISBN: 978-0-429-00115-4 (ebk)

Typeset in Times New Roman
by Apex CoVantage, LLC

Contents

Acknowledgments

In writing this book, I have been helped by many people. I am very grateful to Takamichi Aki, Nobu Goto, Koji Hoshi, Jiro Inaba, Shin-Ichi Kitada, Hisatsugu Kitahara, Hiroki Narita, Kuniya Nasukawa, Kayono Shiobara, Yosuke Sato, Hisao Tokizaki, Changguk Yim, and students in my seminars at Niigata University. Chapter 2 is an extensively revised version of Dobashi (2014). I would like to thank Lisa Selkirk for insightful comments on an earlier version of chapter 2. I would also like to thank audiences at the 3rd Workshop on Phonological Externalization (Sapporo University, September 2016), a workshop at the 153rd meeting of the Linguistic Society of Japan (Fukuoka University, December 2016), Keio Linguistic Colloquium (Keio University, January 2017), the 4th Workshop on Phonological Externalization (Niigata University, February 2017), a symposium at the 89th General Meeting of the English Literary Society of Japan (Shizuoka University, May 2017), the 32nd annual meeting of Sophia University Linguistic Society (Sophia University, July 2017), a workshop at the Linguistic Society of America Summer Institute (University of Kentucky, July 2017), Tokai Area Circle of Syntax (Chukyo University, April 2018), and a workshop at the English Linguistic Society of Japan 11th International Spring Forum (Hokkaido University, May 2018). Thanks also go to participants in an intensive seminar held at Tohoku University, August 2018. I would also like to thank Greg Hadley for encouraging me to write a book, and David Kipler for suggesting stylistic improvements.

This work is in part supported by JSPS Grant-in-Aid for Scientific Research (KAKENHI) Grant Numbers 17K02806 and 15H03213.

Abbreviations

1	first person or class 1
2	second person or class 2
3	third person or class 3
4 *etc.*	class 4
ACC	accusative
AUG	augment
APP	applicative
C	complementizer
CAUS	causative
CL	clitic
DJ	disjoint verb form
FOC	focus
FUT	future
FV	final vowel
GEN	genitive
HAB	habitual
INDEF	indefinite
INDIC	indicative
INF	infinitive
INFL	inflection
LOC	locative
NOM	nominative
OC	object clitic
OM	object marker
PERF	perfective
PL	plural
PRES	present tense
PST	past tense
PRT	particle
REL	relative marker
REM	remote past tense
SM	subject marker
SP	subject prefix

TAM	tense-aspect marker
TOP	topic
PP	past participle
S	(person) singular
SG	singular

1 Introduction

Some phonological rules apply within domains that span word boundaries, and it is generally held that syntax-phonology mapping defines such prosodic domains by relating some syntactic notions to certain prosodic categories. Thus, domains of Spell-Out are believed to correspond to prosodic domains in Multiple Spell-Out Theory (e.g., Uriagereka 1999), and syntactic constituents are assumed to be matched by prosodic domains in Match Theory (e.g., Selkirk 2009, 2011). These theories have been highly successful in describing prosodic phenomena and have added to our understanding of the nature of the syntax-phonology interface. This book aims to deepen this understanding by crystalizing the notion of *externalization* in the architecture of grammar elaborated upon the strict internalist perspective on language (Chomsky 2005, *et seqq.*), where the processes of externalization are ancillary to the generation of a discrete infinity of hierarchically structured linguistic expressions mapped to the conceptual-intentional (C-I) interface. On the premise that linear order is a property of the sensorimotor (SM) interface, I attempt to show that prosodic domains are derived from the linearization procedures that make linguistic expressions interpretable at the SM interface. Specifically, I argue that primes for linearization procedures serve as prosodic domains. Furthermore, the structural organization of prosodic categories, i.e., the prosodic hierarchy, is also derived from the multiple modes of linearization that are well motivated on independent grounds. This book therefore seeks to construct a null theory of prosodic categories and their structural organization in terms of linearization.

Chapter 2 is a chronological overview of some important theories of syntax-phonology relations and prosodic domains. It highlights important issues in the field, including the mismatch between syntactic and phonological structures, cross-linguistic variation, and prosodic categories and their hierarchical organization. A particular focus is developments concomitant with progress in syntactic theory. The discussion starts with the early attempts to relate syntax to phonology: Chomsky and Halle's (1968) readjustment rules and Bresnan's (1971) cyclic approach to stress assignment. The 1980s laid the foundations of the theoretical study of the syntax-phonology connection. First, the several sizes and hierarchical structure of prosodic domains were recognized (Selkirk 1980). The following is an instance of the prosodic hierarchy:

(1)   (   )$_\iota$ Intonational Phrase
        (   )$_\varphi$ (   )$_\varphi$ Phonological Phrase
        (   )$_\omega$ (   )$_\omega$ (   )$_\omega$ Prosodic Word
        Annemarie   can eat   the burger

Second, with the advent of X-bar Theory (Jackendoff 1977; Chomsky 1986b), the mechanism of syntax-phonology mapping is formulated in terms of specific notions in the phrase structure: Nespor and Vogel's (1986) Relation-based Theory exploits syntactic relations holding within phrase structure to account for prosodic domains, while Selkirk's (1986) End-based Theory refers to the edges of syntactic constituents to derive prosodic words and phonological phrases. Third, as the notion of parameter was introduced into the field of syntax (Chomsky 1981), research on prosody also started to take parametric approaches to cross-linguistic variation, by attributing variation to the difference in prosodic domains rather than to phonological rules.

The 1990s saw remarkable theoretical progresses in syntax and phonology, led by the general notion of economy: in syntax, the Minimalist Program revived the cyclic approach to sentential phonology by constructing a phase theory that incorporates Multiple Spell-Out; in phonology, Optimality Theory gave rise to a reformulation of End-based Theory, which was encompassed by Generalized Alignment Theory (McCarthy and Prince 1993), thus allowing us to capture a much wider range of prosodic phenomena and cross-linguistic variation in terms of constraint interaction. End-based Theory then evolved into current Match Theory (Selkirk 2009, 2011), which regards syntax-phonology mismatch as a superficial phenomenon and offers a unified account of the three prosodic categories: prosodic word, phonological phrase, and intonational phrase.

Chapter 3 begins with a brief review of the development of syntactic theory around 2000 and introduces Multiple Spell-Out and phase theory. It recapitulates Dobashi's (2003) theory of phonological phrasing in some detail, to critically evaluate Multiple Spell-Out approaches to phonological phrasing. It also discusses Dobashi's (2013) attempt at unifying prosodic categories in terms of linearization, which forms the basis for the proposed mechanism of phonological interpretations of syntactic objects.

Dobashi (2003) highlights a systematic discrepancy between the prosodic and Spell-Out domains in phase theory. This discrepancy is shown to be resolved by a procedure that defines a linear order between Spell-Out domains. In this theory, cross-linguistic variation in phonological phrasing is largely attributed to syntactic structure: X and Y are phrased together if they are in the same domain of Spell-Out. Further variation results from the restructuring of phonological phrases that apply for purely phonological reasons, such as prosodic weight. Thus, syntax-phonology mapping defines basic phonological phrases, and the phonology restructures them if needed. At the time, this theory was considered to be a null hypothesis because it does not require an independent mechanism that creates phonological phrases. However, from a broader perspective, this theory cannot account for prosodic categories other than phonological phrases. That is, Multiple Spell-Out theory of phonological phrasing is not a true null hypothesis, in that it requires additional mechanisms to account for intonational phrases and prosodic words.

Dobashi (2013) argues that three kinds of linearization procedures must be postulated to linearly order linguistic expressions: Lin(W), linearization of terminal elements of the syntactic objects (i.e., words); Lin(S-O), linearization of Spell-Out domains; and Lin(¬S), linearization based on non-syntactic factors such as prosodic weight (e.g., heavy NP shift in English) and information structure (e.g., topicalized phrases in languages like Chichewa and Italian), which encompasses all remaining linearization procedures not handled by Lin(W) and Lin(S-O). It then proceeds to show that each of the basic units or primes arranged by these linearization procedures corresponds to its own prosodic category: Lin(W), Lin(S-O), and Lin(¬S) yield prosodic words, phonological phrases, and intonational phrases, respectively. Thus, linearization uniformly accounts for prosodic categories, and the Multiple Spell-Out theory of phonological phrasing turns out to be subsumed under this linearization-based approach to prosodic domains.

Chapter 4 examines the internalist approach to language and externalization. Most theories discussed in Chapters 2 and 3 explicitly or implicitly assume a version of the so-called Y-model of grammar, which prevailed from the late 1970s to 2000s (Chomsky and Lasnik 1977). Thus, S-Structure/Spell-Out splits a syntactic derivation into PF and LF branches. However, a strict interpretation of the internalist concept leads us to characterize the basic property of language as a generative procedure that infinitely generates hierarchically structured expressions mapped to the C-I interface (Chomsky 2016). I call this architecture of grammar the I-model since it is a monotonous mapping to the interface. The processes of externalization do not fall within this characterization of language since they introduce linear order and are mapped to the SM interface. They are therefore excluded from the core architecture of grammar, and are hence ancillary operations to language. This view suggests that the operation Spell-Out, in its original form, is not formulable since it bifurcates the syntactic derivation, disrupting the computation to the C-I interface. I suggest that the syntax-phonology mapping instead be recast as an interpretive procedure, in line with Epstein et al. (1998) and Boeckx (2003/2007). On the basis of the traditional observation that content words are visible, while function words are not, in the syntax-phonology mapping (Selkirk 1984; Truckenbrodt 1999), I argue that the phonological component can detect unlabelable elements such as a root R. It then identifies syntactic objects SOs in much the same way as the labeling algorithm (Chomsky 2013, 2015), i.e., with minimal search for unlabelable elements. I show that such SOs correspond to phonological phrases. Furthermore, I argue that they must be linearly ordered with respect to each other, and propose a linearization procedure called Lin(LS) that arranges the linear strings that correspond to the SOs identified by the phonological component. Lin(LS) replaces Lin(S-O), and phonological phrases are therefore reduced to primes for Lin(LS). Empirical materials to be discussed include not only the data examined by Dobashi (2003), but also the complementizer-trace effect and its cross-linguistic variation, the relation between richness of agreement and phonological phrasing, phonological phrasing of topicalized constituents in Chichewa and Zulu, possible intonational boundaries in ECM and simple transitive constructions in English, phonological phrasing in Bantu applicative constructions, case suffixes and their effect on prosody in Japanese, and the distribution of weak pronouns in English.

Chapter 5 recasts intonational phrasing as an interpretive procedure. As minimal search for an unlabelable element identifies a phonological phrase, a similar principle of efficient computation is expected to guide the identification of intonational phrases. I argue that terminated derivations can be detected with zero search in a workspace, and that they are interpreted as intonational phrases. Chomsky et al. (2017) define the termination of a derivation by referring to a workspace of the syntactic computation: a derivation can terminate when a workspace contains a single object. Terminated derivations to be examined include root clauses, (*as-*) parentheticals, non-restrictive relative clauses, vocatives, expletive expressions such as *good heavens!*, nominal appositives, main clauses in slifting and quotative constructions, tag questions, and right-/left-dislocated constituents, all of which are interpreted as intonational phrases.

Independent terminated derivations are not syntactically integrated with their associates. They are related by semantic operations such as function application and coindexation. But they have to be linearly ordered with respect to their associated phrases or clauses to be interpreted at the SM interface. Then, the relevant linearization is Lin($\neg$S), which addresses the linearization not handled by Lin(W) and Lin(LS). Lin($\neg$S) linearly orders terminated derivations by making reference to the semantic information. Consequently, Lin($\neg$S) unifies terminated derivations with shifted heavy NPs and topicalized phrases, as discussed in Chapter 3: all these apparently heterogeneous elements are primes for Lin($\neg$S) and are interpreted as intonational phrases. Note that in the Y-model of grammar, it is impossible in principle for the phonology to look at the semantics, since syntax/ Spell-Out intervenes between them. However, in the I-model, the processes of externalization can look directly into the hierarchical expressions that are (perhaps trivially) mapped to the C-I interface. That is, the I-model allows the phonological interpretation of Lin($\neg$S) to consult the semantics.

The strict internalist perspective on language thus results in an interpretive approach to the processes of externalization, in which the phonological interpretations are formulated as linearization procedures and the primes for linearization serve as prosodic domains.

2 Prosodic domains and the syntax-phonology interface

A chronological overview

2.1. Introduction

In the past three decades, numerous studies have examined the syntax-phonology interface from various theoretical perspectives. The term "syntax-phonology interface" now encompasses a wide range of linguistic study, particularly since the advent of the so-called Minimalist Program (Chomsky 1995, et seq.), which seeks to minimize the theoretical devices in the "narrow syntax" component and attribute to the interfaces what were once regarded as the properties of narrow syntax. Thus, the following are often taken to be subsumed under the study of the syntax-phonology interface: linearization, ellipsis, "movement" operations such as Heavy NP Shift, head movement and clitic placement, morphological phenomena in general, and phrasal phonology.[1] Since this book is concerned with the prosodic domains that are sensitive to syntax, greater focus will be put on phrasal phonology, or more specifically, phonological phrase and intonational phrase in the prosodic hierarchy, which will be clarified in the following discussion in this chapter.

Below are some of the research questions and issues often discussed in this field.

2.1.1 Mismatch

One of the phenomena that motivated the study of the syntax-phonology interface is the mismatch between syntactic and phonological structure. In perhaps the best-known example, from Chomsky and Halle (1968: 372), syntactic structure does not match intonational structure:

(1) syntax: This is [the cat that caught [the rat that stole [the cheese]]]
    phonology: (this is the cat)(that caught the rat)(that stole the cheese)

Two problems emerged: the syntactic boundaries do not match the phonological ones, and syntactic phrase structure is right-branching, while the phonological structure is flat.[2] How do we resolve these syntax-phonology mismatches?

2.1.2 Direct reference or indirect reference

Another issue, which is related to the first, is the nature of the relationship between syntax and phonology. More specifically, the question is whether phonology can directly refer to syntactic information. If it can, what is visible and what is not? If it cannot, then what algorithm do we need to relate syntax and phonology?

2.1.3 *Cross-linguistic variation*

As in syntax, prosodic domains show cross-linguistic variation. For example, a verb is phrased with its direct object in some languages but not in others, and such phrasing is optional in yet others. How do we capture this variation? Does it arise from the mapping algorithms? Is it a matter of phonology? Is it a reflex of syntactic variations? Or is there any other way to explain it?

2.1.4 *Prosodic categories*

Several kinds of prosodic domains, such as the intonational phrase and phonological phrase, have been proposed. What kinds of prosodic categories, and how many of them, do we need? How do we differentiate these categories? How are they organized?

2.1.5 *Mapping direction*

Is mapping unidirectional – from syntax to phonology – as is often assumed in minimalist syntax literature? Or is phonological structure present in parallel with syntactic structure, as argued, for example, by Jackendoff (1997)? Also, is it possible for phonology to affect syntax?

2.1.6 *Information structure*

Topic and focus often affect prosodic domains. How can such effects be accounted for?

These and other issues have been considered from various theoretical standpoints in the framework of generative grammar. Among these, this chapter will be particularly concerned with the mechanisms of syntax-phonology mapping that have been proposed to account for the mismatch, cross-linguistic variation, and organization of prosodic categories.[3] In what follows, I will chronologically summarize some of the important theories in order to sketch a general overview of developments in the field of the syntax-phonology interface.[4]

2.2. 1960s–1970s: classical approaches to the syntax-phonology interface

2.2.1 *Mismatch between syntax and phonology*

In this section, I will briefly review earlier attempts to account for the syntax-phonology mismatch.[5] As we have seen in (1), and in (2) below, the three noun phrases here do not correspond to the intonational structure of the sentence:

(2) syntax: This is [the cat that caught [the rat that stole [the cheese]]]
    phonology: (this is the cat)(that caught the rat)(that stole the cheese)

Chomsky and Halle (1968: 372) attribute this particular mismatch to a read-justment rule that "flattens" the multiply embedded part of the structure and turns it into "a conjunction of elementary sentences," where each sentence S is preceded by an intonational break. They argue that this readjustment rule is a matter of performance and does not belong to the theory of competence, as seen in the analysis of self-embedded constructions discussed in Chomsky (1965).

Another readjustment rule discussed by Chomsky and Halle concerns the defi-nition of (phonological) word. They introduce *boundaries*, symbolized as #, into the surface structure, which are grammatical formatives that are elements of the terminal string. The following convention inserts boundaries # into the structure:

(3) The boundary # is automatically inserted at the beginning and end of every string dominated by a major category, i.e., by one of the lexical categories "noun," "verb," "adjective," or by a category such as "sentence," "noun phrase," "verb phrase," which dominates a lexical category.

(Chomsky and Halle 1968: 366)

Thus, for the sentence in (4), boundaries are inserted as in (5):

(4) the book was in an unlikely place
(5) $[_S \# [_{NP} \# [_D \, the]_D \, [_N \# book \#]_N \#]_{NP} \, [_{VP} \# was \, [_{PP} \# [_P \, in]_P \, [_{NP} \# [_D \, an]_D$
     $[_A \# un \, [_A \# likely \#]_A \#]_A \, [_N \# place \#]_N \#]_{NP} \#]_{PP} \#]_{VP} \#]_S$

Then, they define the notion of the *terminus* of a word, as in (6):

(6) $_S[\# X [\#$
     $\#] X \#]_S$
     $\#] X [\#$

(Chomsky and Halle 1968: 367)

Here, S is the category *sentence* and X contains no segments, and a word is defined as follows:

(7) Suppose that we have a string . . . Y . . . = . . . $Z [\# W \#] V$, where $Z [\#$ and $\#] V$ are termini as defined in [(6)], and Y contains no other termini. Then $[\# W \#]$ is a word.

(Chomsky and Halle 1968: 367)

In (8), the underlined characters highlight termini of (5), and (7) defines three words for (8), as in (9):

(8) $[_S \# [_{NP} \# [_D \, the]_D \, [_N \# book \#]_N \underline{\#}]_{NP} \, [_{VP} \# was \, [_{PP} \# [_P \, in]_P \, [_{NP} \# [_D \, an]_D$
     $[_A \# un \, [_A \# likely \#]_A \underline{\#}]_A \, [_N \# \underline{place} \#]_N \#]_{NP} \#]_{PP} \underline{\#}]_{VP} \#]_S$

(9) a. # the # book #
     b. # was # in # an # un # likely #
     c. # place #

Notice that the word in (9b) is not a constituent, given the structure (5)/(8). In the framework of Chomsky and Halle (1968), this is problematic because the word-level phonological rules are assumed to apply to constituents. Therefore, the structure must be readjusted so that words will be constituents. The following readjustment convention is therefore suggested (Chomsky and Halle 1968: 368):

(10)   Suppose that we have a string . . . $W\,X\,[_\alpha\,Y\,Z\,]_\alpha$ . . . , where $[_\alpha$ and $]_\alpha$ are paired brackets, $X\,[_\alpha\,Y$ is a word, and W contains no units. Then this will be readjusted, by convention, to . . . $[_\alpha\,W\,X\,Y\,Z\,]_\alpha$ . . . . Similarly, a string . . . $[_\alpha\,X\,Y\,]_\alpha\,Z\,W$ . . . , where $Y\,]_\alpha\,Z$ is a word and W contains no units, will be adjusted to . . . $[_\alpha\,X\,Y\,Z\,W\,]_\alpha$ . . . .

Note that (10) needs to be applied three times to make (9b) a constituent:

(11) $[_{VP}$ # was $[_{PP}$ # $[_P\,in]_P\,[_{NP}$ # $[_D\,an]_D\,[_A$ # un $[_A$ # likely # $]_A$ # $]_A$
      $\rightarrow[_{VP}\,[_{PP}$ # was   # $[_P\,in]_P\,[_{NP}$ # $[_D\,an]_D\,[_A$ # un $[_A$ # likely # $]_A$ # $]_A$
      $\rightarrow[_{VP}\,[_{PP}\,[_{NP}$ # was   # $[_P\,in]_P$ # $[_D\,an]_D\,[_A$ # un $[_A$ # likely # $]_A$ # $]_A$
      $\rightarrow[_{VP}\,[_{PP}\,[_{NP}\,[_A$ # was   # $[_P\,in]_P$ # $[_D\,an]_D$ # un $[_A$ # likely # $]_A$ # $]_A$

As a result of multiple application of (10) to (5)/(8), *was in an unlikely* is a constituent that belongs to the category A, as shown in the bottom line of (11). Consequently, *was*, *in*, and *an* are analyzed as proclitics to the adjective *unlikely*.

So far, we have briefly reviewed Chomsky and Halle's readjustment procedures. Notice that readjustment is basically the reduction of complex surface structures to simpler ones that serve as inputs to the phonological component. Roughly put, this is a linearization procedure whereby hierarchically structured expressions (e.g., the first line in (11)) are flattened or given a linear property (e.g., the bottom line in (11), where all the terminal elements are conjoined within A). In Chapter 3, I will explore the idea of attributing syntax-phonology mapping to linearization, which is a fundamental property of externalization, in an attempt to account for prosodic domains and their hierarchical organization in terms of linearization procedures within the framework of the Minimalist Program.

Non-linear phonology developed rapidly after the publication of Chomsky and Halle (1968), especially since the 1970s, and it is now recognized that the "junctural" properties of sentences that had been captured by boundary symbols # should be accounted for in terms of prosodic domains that are represented suprasegmentally, without recourse to the readjustment rules (McCawley 1968; Pyle 1972; Rotenberg 1978; see Scheer 2008 for critical discussion). In particular, Selkirk (1980) shows that three kinds of phonological rules are sensitive to prosodic domains: domain span, domain juncture, and domain limit rules.[6] A domain-span rule applies throughout a domain, a domain juncture rule applies between prosodic domains within their superordinate prosodic domain, and a domain limit rule applies at one of the edges of a domain. The following formulations are from Nespor and Vogel (1986: 15):

(12)   a. domain span:
           $A \rightarrow B/[\ldots X \_\_ Y \ldots]_{Di}$
       b. domain juncture:
           i. $A \rightarrow B/[\ldots [\ldots X \_\_ Y]_{Dj} [Z \ldots]_{Dj} \ldots]_{Di}$
           ii. $A \rightarrow B/[\ldots [\ldots X]_{Dj} [Y \_\_ Z \ldots]_{Dj} \ldots]_{Di}$
       c. domain limit:
           i. $A \rightarrow B/[\ldots X \_\_ Y]_{Di}$
           ii. $A \rightarrow B/[X \_\_ Y \ldots]_{Di}$

The domain-span rule in (12a) can be illustrated by *mid tone (M) raising* in Aŋlɔ Ewe (Clements 1978: 47):

(13)   *M-raising*

           $M \rightarrow R/H \_\_ H$

M is raised to an extra-high tone (R) when it is surrounded by high tones (H). Importantly, this rule may apply across a word boundary. Thus, in (14a), H on the last syllable of the first word is followed by M and H on the second word, and the rule applies, raising the M to R. But this rule does not always apply across a word boundary. Thus, as in (14b), the environment appears to be met across the subject and predicate, but the rule does not apply:

(14)   a. /àtyí mēgbé/   → [àtyí mĕgbé]
              tree behind

              [   ]_{Di}
              'behind a tree'
       b. /mí   ā-dzó/   → [mí ā-dzó]
              we   T-leave

              [   ]_{Di} [   ]_{Di}
              'we will leave'

This shows that the rule applies within a particular prosodic domain (designated here as D_i) but not across the domain boundary, illustrating a domain-span rule.

   The domain juncture rule in (12b) can be illustrated by the rule of *Interword Doubling* in Copperbelt Bemba (Kula and Bickmore 2015):

(15)   *Interword Doubling*
       An H on the final Tone-Bearing Unit (TBU) of one word spreads onto the initial TBU of a following word.

This rule, taking the form of (12b-ii), applies across a boundary between smaller prosodic domains D_js within the larger prosodic domain D_i that properly contains D_js (Kula and Bickmore 2015 identify D_i and D_j as phonological phrase and intonational phrase, respectively). Note that this rule is fed by another rule, *Unbounded Spreading*, which, roughly put, spreads the rightmost H tone in a word to the end of the word (see Kula and Bickmore 2015 for details). Consider the following contrast:

(16) a. /ù-mu-limi   tu-ka-pat-a/   → [ù-mú-límí tú-ká-pát-á]
            AUG-1-farmer 1PL-FUT-hate-FV
            [[   ]$_{Dj}$ [   ]$_{Dj}$]$_{Di}$
            'The farmer, we will hate.' (contrastive focus)

      b. /ú-mu-limi   tu-ka-pat-a/   → [ù-mú-límí tù-kà-pàt-à]
            AUG-1-farmer   1PL-FUT-hate-FV
            [[   ]$_{Dj}$]$_{Di}$ [[   ]$_{Dj}$]$_{Di}$
            'As for the farmer, we will hate (him).' (topic)

                                                      (Kula and Bickmore 2015: 169)

In (16a), the object NP receives contrastive focus and it is prosodically phrased with the subsequent verb, belonging to the same prosodic domain D_i. H on the pre-prefix undergoes Unbounded Spreading to the end of the word, and this feeds Interword Doubling, which applies at the D_j-juncture, and places H on the initial TBU of the verb, which in turn feeds Unbounded Spreading to the end of the verb. By contrast, in (16b) the object NP is topicalized, and forms an independent intonational phrase (designated as D_i here), unlike (16a). This intonational phrasing is independently confirmed by the audible pause between the topicalized object and verb. Even though Unbounded Spreading applies to the object, it does not feed Interword Doubling, as we can see from the fact that the verb begins with an L tone. That is, Interword Doubling is a domain juncture rule that applies across a D_j-boundary within the superordinate prosodic domain D_i.[7]

Let us next consider the domain limit rule (which is also called a domain-edge rule), as formulated in (12c). This is exemplified by *Penultimate Lengthening* in Chichewa. This rule lengthens vowels in the penultimate syllable of each prosodic domain (which Kanerva 1990 identifies with phonological phrase; see also Bresnan and Mchombo 1987). Consider (17):

(17) a. /mtengo/   → [mteengo]
              price
              [   ]$_{Di}$
      b. /mtengo uwu/   → [mtengo uuwu]
              price this
              [   ]$_{Di}$
              'this price'

In (17a), the penultimate vowel is lengthened when it is uttered alone. However, if the same word is followed by another word within a prosodic domain D_i, as in

(17b), the penultimate vowel of *mtengo* is not lengthened, but that of the following word, *uwu*, which occupies the domain-final position, is lengthened. That is, Penultimate Lengthening is sensitive to the right edge of the prosodic domain, as in (12c-i).

So far, we have seen that syntax-phonology discrepancies, which were once resolved by the readjustment convention formulated in terms of boundary symbols # in Chomsky and Halle (1968), are now explained by postulating prosodic domains that are represented suprasegmentally. I then reviewed three types of phonological rules that are sensitive to the prosodic domains: domain span, domain juncture, and domain limit rules. Furthermore, Selkirk (1980: 109) argues for a universal repertory of prosodic domain types (such as phonological word, phonological phrase, intonational phrase, and utterance) and claims that these domains are hierarchically structured. Recognition of these structured prosodic categories led to explicit theorization of syntax-phonology mapping, in the 1980s, as we will see in section 2.3.[8] However, before reviewing the theories of the 1980s, let us consider another important issue in the early days of generative grammar: the relation between transformational (syntactic) and phonological cycles. Attention later focused again on this issue, as phase theory developed in the study of syntax in the late 1990s and thereafter, as we will discuss in section 2.4.2 below, and in Chapters 3 and 4.

2.2.2 Transformational and phonological cycles

Early in the development of generative phonology, it was noted that syntactic cycles play a role in sentential phonology. In particular, Bresnan (1971) argues that application of the *Nuclear Stress Rule* (NSR) in English reflects syntactic cycles. Her formulation of the NSR is as follows:

(18) NSR: $\overset{1}{\text{V}} \rightarrow 1 \, / \, [_A \, \text{X} \, \overset{1}{\text{V}} \, \text{Y} \, \underline{\quad} \, \text{Z} \,]$, where Z contains no $\overset{1}{\text{V}}$, and where A ranges over major categories such as NP, VP, S.

(Bresnan 1971: 257)

Here indicates that the word stress is value 1, which is called 1-stress. A "prose version" of NSR, formulated by Gussenhoven (1992: 80), is stated below:

(19) NSR: If there are two or more instances of 1-stress in a phrase or S, assign 1-stress to the rightmost of these.

It is also assumed by convention that any application of 1-stress within a cycle reduces all other values by 1. Thus, in Bresnan's system, the primary stress is determined by demoting other stresses by the convention when the NSR applies. Let us consider the simple transitive sentence "Mary teaches engineering":

(20) $[_S \, [\text{Mary}] \, [_{VP} \, [\text{teaches}] \, [\text{engineering}]] \,]$

Mary	teaches	engineering	
1	1	1	word stress
	2	1	1st cycle (VP): NSR
2	3	1	2nd cycle (S): NSR

At the beginning of the derivation, each lexical item is assigned 1-stress. Then, in the first cycle (VP), NSR applies within VP, and *engineering* maintains value 1 since it is the rightmost element in this domain, and the value of *teaches* is reduced to 2-stress by the convention. Then, in the next cycle, the NSR applies within S, and *engineering* still maintains value 1, and the values of *Mary* and *teaches* are reduced by 1, resulting in the [231] stress pattern.

Bresnan (1971: 258) points out that the NSR cannot give a straightforward account of the following contrast, cited from Newman (1946):

(21)   a. Helen left DIRECTIONS for George to follow.
       b. Helen left directions for George to FOLLOW.

Here and below, constituents with the primary stress are all capitalized. (21a) has the primary stress on *directions* and means that "Helen left directions which George is supposed to follow," and (21b) has the primary stress on *follow* and means that "Helen left directions to the effect that George should follow." That is, *for George to follow* is a relative clause whose head noun is *directions* in (21a), while it is a clausal complement of *directions* in (21b). If the NSR always applied to the final surface structure of the derivation, it would be incorrectly predicted that *follow* receives the primary stress in (21a) as well as in (21b). Bresnan further argues that the following contrasts make the same points as (21):

(22)   a. Mary liked the PROPOSAL that George left.
       b. Mary liked the proposal that George LEAVE.

(23)   a. John asked what Helen had WRITTEN.
       b. John asked what BOOKS Helen had written.

(24)   a. George found someone he'd like you to MEET.
       b. George found some FRIENDS he'd like you to meet.

Thus, it would be necessary to enrich the NSR in some way so that it could account for the contrast between (21–24a) and (21–24b). However, Bresnan (1971: 259) proposes that the addition of just one assumption avoids such an unwelcome complication: "THE NUCLEAR STRESS RULE IS ORDERED AFTER ALL THE SYNTACTIC TRANSFORMATIONS ON EACH TRANSFORMATIONAL CYCLE" (all caps in the original). Given this idea, let us first consider the derivation of (21a):

(25)   [$_S$ Helen left [$_{NP}$ directions [$_S$ for George to follow directions]]]

1	1		1		1	1		1	word stress
					2	2		1	1st cycle (S): NSR
								ø	2nd cycle (NP): Syntax
2	2		1		3	3			3rd cycle (S): NSR

First, 1-stress is assigned to each lexical item (content, but not function, word). Then, in the first cycle (the embedded S), the NSR assigns 1-stress to *directions*, and the stress values of *George* and *follow* are reduced to 2 by the convention. In the second cycle, Equi-NP Deletion (i.e., relativization) applies and deletes *directions* in the complement of *follow*, to derive a relative clause. Note that the NSR does not apply in this cycle since this domain has only one instance of 1-stress, i.e., that of *directions*; another instance of 1-stress was deleted by Equi-NP Deletion. NSR then applies to the third cycle (the matrix S). *Helen, left*, and *directions* have 1-stress within this domain, and NSR assigns 1-stress to *directions* since it is the rightmost of the three, and the convention lowers stress values of all the other lexical items by 1, resulting in [22133].

Let us then consider (21b).

(26) [$_S$ Helen left [$_{NP}$ directions [$_S$ for George to follow]]]

1	1		1		1	1	word stress
			2		1	1st cycle (S): NSR
		2	3		1	2nd cycle (NP): Syntax
2	2	3	4		1	3rd cycle (S): NSR

Unlike (21a), *follow* is an intransitive verb and does not have a complement. Thus, in the first cycle, *follow* is rightmost and receives 1-stress. In the second cycle, *directions* and *follow* have 1-stress, but *follow* is rightmost, maintaining 1-stress, and the value of *directions* as well as that of *George* are reduced by the convention. In the third cycle, again, *follow* is rightmost, maintaining 1-stress, and the values of the other items are reduced by 1.

Thus far we have seen that unification of transformational and phonological cycles successfully accounts for the contrast in (21). Here I will not discuss (22)-(24), which will be accounted for in much the same way as (21). The interested reader is referred to Bresnan (1971). See Berman and Szamosi (1972), Lakoff (1972), and Bresnan (1972) for further discussions about this analysis at the time. See also Adger (2003/2007), Gussenhoven (1992), Kahnemuyipour (2004, 2009), and references cited therein for more recent discussions. See also Chomsky (2000: note 99) for comments on Bresnan's work and its relevance to current syntactic theory. I will briefly review, in section 2.4.2, Kahnemuyipour's approach to stress assignment formulated within the phase theory incorporating Multiple Spell-Out.

In the next section, we will review the two major theories of the syntax-phonology interface proposed in the 1980s. As will be clear from the following discussion, these theories laid the foundations of theoretical and empirical investigations of the syntax-phonology connection. It should be noted, however, that these two theories are representational: they do not reflect syntactic cycles, but rather are formulated on the (S-structure) representation of syntax. Therefore, the formulations of these theories require independent (or in a sense, ad hoc) mechanisms to account for the mapping from phonology to syntax, unlike Bresnan's (1971) theory, which has succeeded in keeping the NSR simple with recourse to syntactic cycles. The 1980s theories did not appeal to cycles, perhaps because of the then-standard grammatical architecture in which syntactic representations (S-structures) are converted to phonetic representations (PF) at a single point of the computation, i.e., the structure of an entire sentence is mapped to phonology at one time (the so-called Extended Standard Theory (EST) model; see Chomsky 1986a: 67ff.). That is, the conversion from S-structure to PF does not reflect syntactic cycles, and cyclic theories like Bresnan's are not formulable in the EST model. Later, the cyclic architecture of grammar was resurrected in the 1990s with the rise of the Minimalist Program for linguistic theory (Chomsky 1993). Cyclic approaches to the syntax-phonology interface have been pursued as the phase theory equipped with Multiple Spell-Out was developed (Chomsky 2000; see section 2.4.2 and Chapters 3 and 4), while representational approaches have thrived, along with Optimality Theory (McCarthy and Prince 1993; Prince and Smolensky 1993/2004; see sections 2.4.1 and 2.5). Let us now move on to the representational era.

2.3. 1980s: the standard theories

This section will briefly recapitulate the two major theories of syntax-phonology mapping: Relation-based Theory (Nespor and Vogel 1986) and End-based Theory (Selkirk 1986 et seq.).[9] Although they are not without problems, especially in light of current theoretical understanding of syntax, most of the present theoretical and empirical issues are rooted in these two theories, and there is no doubt that these theories have laid the foundations for the many investigations in this area. I therefore refer to them as the *Standard Theories*. In this section, we will describe prosodic hierarchy and strict layering, which are adopted by both theories, and review the two Standard Theories, making reference to their approaches to cross-linguistic variation.

2.3.1 *Prosodic hierarchy theory*

Although the number of and names for prosodic categories are matters of debate, the following prosodic categories are often adopted in the study of prosody and are assumed to be hierarchically ordered (Nespor and Vogel 1986; Selkirk 1980, 1986):[10]

(27)   *Prosodic Hierarchy:*

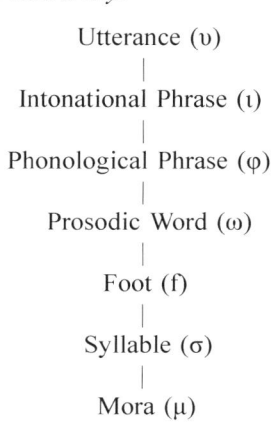

Utterance (υ)

Intonational Phrase (ι)

Phonological Phrase (φ)

Prosodic Word (ω)

Foot (f)

Syllable (σ)

Mora (μ)

Of these, the four top categories are what Ito and Mester (2012: 281) call *interface categories*, formed in terms of syntax-phonology relations; the rest are referred to as *rhythmic categories*, which are intrinsically defined word-internally. These categories are organized to form a prosodic hierarchy, to accord with the *Strict Layer Hypothesis*, which bans recursive structures and level-skipping in this hierarchically ordered set of prosodic categories (Nespor and Vogel 1986; Selkirk 1980, 1984, 1986; Hayes 1989):

(28)   *Strict Layer Hypothesis*: A constituent of category-level *n* in the prosodic hierarchy immediately dominates only constituents at category-level *n-1*.
(Selkirk 2009: 38)

Thus, (29a) is a valid structure while (29b) is not (rhythmic categories are omitted here and below):

(29)   a.   b.

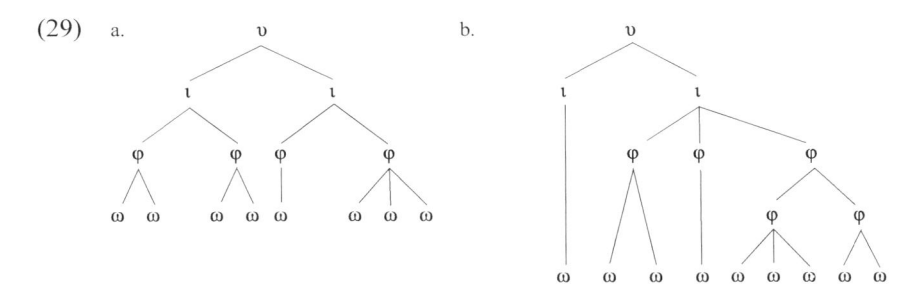

(29b) violates the Strict Layer Hypothesis in two respects: φ is recursive and ι immediately dominates ω, skipping φ. Note that branches can be n-ary, unlike current prevailing syntactic assumptions.

The Strict Layer Hypothesis was considered to be an irreducible principle and played a central role in the study of prosodic categories from its inception until it was recast as a set of violable constraints in Optimality Theory (Selkirk 1996), although its status was soon questioned on empirical grounds, as we will see in section 2.4.

2.3.2.   Relation-based Theory

Let us now review Relation-based Theory. Nespor and Vogel (1986) argue that the domain of a gemination rule, termed *Raddoppiamento Sintattico* (RS), is a phonological phrase, and that it can be defined with respect to syntactic relations found in phrase structure (see also Nespor and Vogel 1982). RS is a phonological rule that applies in central and southern varieties of Italian and is formulated as follows (Nespor and Vogel 1986: 170):

(30)   *Raddoppiamento Sintattico* (RS)

$C \rightarrow [+\text{long}]/[\ldots [\ldots V]_\omega [\underline{} [+\text{son}, -\text{nas}] \ldots]_\omega \ldots]_\varphi$
(where the vowel V bears the main stress of the word)

In (ω_1 ω_2)$_\varphi$, the initial consonant of ω_2 is lengthened if ω_1 ends with a vowel that bears the main stress of the word. They (1986: 167) observe that RS applies to the left of the head of a syntactic phrase within its maximal projection, but not to its right. Thus, RS applies between an auxiliary and a verb (= head), as in (31a), between a quantifier and a noun (= head), as in (31b), and between a copula and the comparative particle *piú*, as well as between *piú* and an adjective (= head), as in (31c). "≈" indicates where RS applies:

(31)   a. Avrá ≈ trovato il pescecane.
          'He must have found the shark.'
       b. È appena passato con tre ≈ cani.
          'He has just passed by with three dogs.'
       c. Il tuo pappagallo é ≈ piú ≈ loquace del mio.
          'Your parrot is more talkative than mine.'

In contrast, RS is blocked (indicated by "//") between NP and AP, as in (32a), between a quantifier and a PP, as in (32b), and between a verb and a comparative adverb, as in (32c):

(32)   a. Devi comprare delle mappe di cittá // molto vecchie.
          'You must buy some very old city maps.'
       b. Ne aveva soltanto tre // di bassotti.
          'He had only three dachshunds.'
       c. Guardó // piú attentamente e vide che era un pitone.
          'He looked more carefully and saw it was a python.'

Given these and other observations, Nespor and Vogel propose the following rules to define phonological phrases. Note that C in (33) is a Clitic Group, which they define as another prosodic category posited between phonological phrase φ and prosodic word ω:[11]

(33)   Phonological Phrase Formation

                                        (Nespor and Vogel 1986: 168)

       a. φ domain
          The domain of φ consists of a C which contains a lexical head (X) and all Cs on its nonrecursive side up to the C that contains another head outside of the maximal projection of X.
       b. φ construction
          Join into an n-ary branching φ all Cs included in a string delimited by the definition of the domain of φ.

First, (33a) identifies what constitutes a domain, and then (33b) constructs a supra-segmental prosodic domain according to which relevant phonological rules apply.

So, this is an indirect-reference theory in which phonological rules do not refer to syntax but to prosodic domains.

Given (33), the syntactic structure of a transitive sentence like (34a), which was widely assumed in the study of syntax in that era, is mapped to the phonological phrases in (34b):

(34)   a. $[_{IP}$ NP$_{Subj}$ Infl $[_{VP}$ V   NP$_{Obj}$ $]]$
       b. (NP$_{Subj}$)$_\varphi$ (Infl   V)$_\varphi$ (NP$_{Obj}$)$_\varphi$

Given that each of the NPs, the Infl (auxiliary verb), and the V correspond to a clitic group *C*, Infl and V are phrased together, since Infl, which is a functional (but not lexical) category, is on V's nonrecursive side, while the NP$_{Subj}$ is not phrased with Infl or V since it is a maximal projection containing a lexical head N that stays outside of the VP. V is not phrased with NP$_{Obj}$ since it is on the nonrecursive side of the NP$_{Obj}$ and because it is outside the NP$_{Obj}$.

As we have seen in (31a) above, RS applies between Infl and V, indicating that they are phrased together phonologically even though they do not form a syntactic constituent. Moreover, the subject is generally phrased separately from the following element as in (35a) below, and the verb is not phrased with its complement as in (35b):

(35)   a. La cecitá // puó essere guarita.
          'Blindness can be cured.'

$\hspace{6cm}$ (Ghini 1993: 44)

       b. Venderá // questo leopardo in dicembre.
          'He will sell this leopard in December.'

$\hspace{5cm}$ (Nespor and Vogel 1986: 173)

That is, Phonological Phrase Formation in (33) correctly accounts for the phrasing of transitive sentences in Italian, as illustrated in (34). Note that this algorithm maps the layered syntactic structure to the flat organization of phonological phrases and also that it captures the mismatch between the syntactic and phonological constituents. Thus, as indicated above, Infl and V form a single constituent in the phonological component but not in the syntactic component.

Although the phrasing in (34b) successfully accounts for basic phrasing facts in Italian, Nespor and Vogel observe, as in (36) below, that the object NP may optionally be phrased with V when it is non-branching (i.e., it consists of only one lexical item), resulting in the phrasing shown in (37). The optional application of RS is marked with "~" in (36):

(36)   Se prenderá ~ qualcosa,   prenderá ~ tordi
       'If he catches something, he will catch thrushes.'

$\hspace{5cm}$ (Nespor and Vogel 1986: 172)

(37) $(NP_{Subj})_\varphi$ $(Infl\ V\ NP_{Obj})_\varphi$

To account for this variation, they propose the following optional rule:

(38) φ restructuring

(Nespor and Vogel 1986: 173)

A non-branching φ which is the first complement of X on its recursive side is joined into the φ that contains X.

Since this restructuring applies to a head and its complement, it does not apply to a subject and verb, even if both are non-branching:

(39)   Papá // mangia
       'Daddy is eating'

(Ghini 1993: 43)

Here, the subject and the verb are non-branching but are not phonologically phrased together, and RS does not apply between them.

Although φ restructuring is optional in Italian, Nespor and Vogel argue that this rule can be extended to account for cross-linguistic variation: such restructuring is forbidden in French and Ewe but is obligatory in Chimwi:ni, even if the complement is branching. Thus, in French and Ewe, a verb and object are always phrased separately, even if the object is non-branching, while in Chimwi:ni (and in some other Bantu languages), a verb and object are always phrased together, irrespective of whether the object is branching. We will examine these examples in Chapter 3.

Thus far we have seen how phonological phrases are defined in Relation-based Theory. Nespor and Vogel argue that intonational phrases are also defined with reference to syntactic relations. They (1986: 188) observe that certain types of constructions form domains of intonation, including parentheticals, nonrestrictive relative clauses, tag questions, vocatives, expletives, and dislocated elements:

(40)   a. Lions [as you know] are dangerous.
       b. My brother [who absolutely loves animals] just bought himself an exotic tropical bird.
       c. That's Theodore's cat [isn't it?]
       d. [Clarence] I'd like you to meet Mr. Smith.
       e. [Good heavens] there's a bear in the back yard.
       f. They are so cute [those Australian koalas].

At a glance, these constructions do not appear to form a natural class, but Nespor and Vogel point out that they share a common property: they are external to the root sentence in some way. Building on Safir's (1985) analysis of nonrestrictive relative clause, Nespor and Vogel argue that constructions that form intonational phrases are linearly represented at S-Structure but are not structurally attached to the sentence tree. Given these considerations, they propose the following rule of intonational phrase formation:

(41)   Intonational Phrase Formation

(Nespor and Vogel 1986: 189)

I. ι domain
    An ι domain may consist of

    a. all the φs in a string that is not structurally attached to the sentence tree at the level of S-structure, or
    b. any remaining sequence of adjacent φs in a root sentence.

II. ι construction
    Join into an n-ary branching ι all φs included in a string delimited by the definition of the domain of ι.

To complete the rough outline of Relation-based Theory, Nespor and Vogel's definitions of other prosodic categories, i.e., prosodic words ω, clitic groups C, and phonological utterances U, are shown below. (43) constructs a prosodic word ω domain consisting of all feet identified by (42). Here, Q is a terminal element of the syntactic tree, and Σ stands for a foot:

(42)   ω domain

(Nespor and Vogel 1986: 141)

A. The domain of ω is Q [= a terminal element of the syntactic tree]
or
B. I. The domain of ω consists of

    a. a stem;
    b. any element identified by specific phonological and/or morphological criteria;
    c. any element marked with the diacritic [+W].

    II. Any unattached elements within Q form part of the adjacent ω closest to the stem; if no such ω exists, they form a ω on their own.

(43)   ω construction

(Nespor and Vogel 1986: 142)

Join into an n-ary branching ω all Σ included within a string delimited by the definition of the domain of ω.

Clitic group formation is given below. Here DCL means a directional clitic. For DCLs, the direction of phonological cliticization is an inherent property of the clitic itself. In contrast, CL is a clitic that can be both proclitic and enclitic, with a host to the right or left:

(44) I. *C domain*

(Nespor and Vogel 1986: 154)

The domain of C consists of a ω containing an independent (i.e., non-clitic) word plus any adjacent ωs containing

a. a DCL, or
b. a CL such that there is no possible host with which it shares more category memberships.

II. *C construction*

(Nespor and Vogel 1986: 155)

Join into an n-ary branching C all ωs included in a string delimited by the definition of the domain of C.

Note that DCLs can ignore syntactic constituency, thereby accounting for syntax-phonology non-isomorphism.

Finally, the definition of phonological utterances U is given below. Here, I is an intonational phrase and X^n is the highest node of a syntactic tree:

(45) I. *U domain*

(Nespor and Vogel 1986: 222)

The domain of U consists of all the Is corresponding to X^n in the syntactic tree.

II. *U construction*

(Nespor and Vogel 1986: 222)

Join into an n-ary branching U all Is included in a string delimited by the definition of the domain of U.

Nespor and Vogel (1986: 223ff.) show, for example, that *Flapping* in American English and *r-Insertion* in British English are domain-span rules sensitive to Us. One might wonder if we really need U, as it seems redundant since it appears to be isomorphic to X^n. However, Nespor and Vogel (1986: 237ff.) show that the prosodic domain U is needed independently of syntax because there are cases in which Us undergo restructuring, which is a non-syntactic operation, so that two Us are combined for pragmatic reasons, extending the domain of U-rule application.

Note that the definitions of prosodic domains here take their immediately lower respective prosodic category (U taking ι, ι taking φ, φ taking C, C taking ω, and ω taking Σ) to form these phrases, incorporating the effects of the Strict Layer Hypothesis.

2.3.3 End-based Theory

Elaborating on Clements' (1978) study of Ewe and Chen's (1987) study of Xiamen, Selkirk (1986) proposes a general theory of prosodic constituency, End-based Theory (or Edge-based Theory). Chen (1987) observes that tone sandhi applies within a tone group (TG) in Xiamen (also called Amoy). The sandhi rule is formulated as follows (Chen 1987: 113):

(46) Tone Sandhi Rule (TSR)
      $T \rightarrow T'/\_\_\_ T$ within a tone group

Here, T is a base tone and T′ a sandhi tone. Consider the tone for *p'ang* 'fragrant,' whose base or citation form has a base tone of HH, as in (47a). If it follows another word in the TG-final position, it shows up with the base tone HH, as in (47b). But if it precedes another word in a TG, it shows up with the sandhi tone MM:

(47) a. p'ang   'fragrant' (base form)
         HH
      b. tsin p'ang   'very fragrant'
         MM HH
      c. p'ang tsui   'fragrant water (perfume)'
         MM HM

Previous analyses suggested that a TG is demarcated at the right end of NP, VP, S (and S′), and sentence AdvP (Cheng 1968, 1973). Chen points out, however, that this formulation is problematic since it is category-specific, and it is not clear why the elements referred to in this formulation form a natural class. Moreover, it is unclear why postlexical phonological rules can be sensitive to syntactic category distinctions. Chen therefore proposes a category-neutral formulation that demarcates a TG at the right edge of every XP (with some stipulation concerning adjuncts, which we will not discuss here). Thus, in (48), the TSR is blocked between the two arguments of a ditransitive verb since the right edge of the indirect object NP marks the right edge of a TG ("//" indicates where the TSR is blocked):

(48) [$_{VP}$ hoo [$_{NP}$ yin sio-ti]   //   [$_{NP}$ tsit pun] ts'eq]
         give   his brother   one CL   book
      'Give his brother a book.'

(Chen 1987: 135)

Selkirk (1986) further generalizes Chen's analysis and proposes End-based Theory, the basic premise of which is that prosodic words and phonological phrases are defined in terms of the ends or edges of certain syntactic constituents. The specification of these ends is parameterized:

(49)   i. a. $]_{\text{Word}}$ b. $_{\text{Word}}[$
       ii. a. $]_{\text{Xmax}}$ b. $_{\text{Xmax}}[$

(Selkirk 1986: 389)

Here, "Xmax" means a maximal projection in the X-bar Theory. (49i) and (49ii) derive the prosodic word and phonological phrase, respectively, from the syntactic phrase structure. Thus, for the ditransitive VP structure in (50), (49ii-a) gives the phonological phrasing in (51a) by deriving the right edges of phonological phrases from the right edges of the VP and the NPs, and (49ii-b) gives the phrasing in (51b) by referring to the left edges of the syntactic XPs:

(50) $[_{\text{VP}}$ V NP NP]
(51)   a. (V   NP$)_{\varphi}$ (NP $)_{\varphi}$
       b. (V $)_{\varphi}$ (NP$)_{\varphi}$ (NP $)_{\varphi}$

Then, the right-edge setting in (49ii-a) accounts for the TGs (referred to as phonological phrases here) in (48). Selkirk shows that the phrasing in (51a) derived by (49ii-a) is not only observed in Xiamen but also in Chimwi:ni (Kisseberth and Abasheikh 1974). Furthermore, she shows that the phrasing in (51b), derived by (49ii-b), is observed in Ewe (Clements 1978). As we have seen in section 2.2, M-raising applies across word boundaries within a phonological phrase in this language:

(52)   M-raising (Clements 1978: 47)   = (13)
              M → R/H __ H

Let us consider (53):

(53)   a. $[_{\text{VP}}$ kpɔ́ $[_{\text{NP}}$ ānyí]]
              see   bee
           'saw a bee'
       b. mē $[_{\text{VP}}$ ná $[_{\text{NP}}$ àtyí] $[_{\text{NP}}$ kōfí]]
           I   gave   stick (to) Kofi'
           'I gave a stick to Kofi.'

In (53a), we have M between Hs across a word boundary, but M-raising does not apply, indicating that there is a phonological phrase boundary between the verb and object. Likewise, in (53b), M-raising fails to apply between the two objects. That is, the phonological phrasing in Ewe conforms to (51b), which can be accounted for by (49ii-b): the left edge of each NP as well as that of VP corresponds to the left edge of a phonological phrase.[12]

As we have seen in section 2.3.2, in the discussion of Relation-based Theory, branchingness may affect phonological phrasing (see (38)), and this needs to be incorporated into End-based Theory. Cowper and Rice (1987) examine branchingness within the framework of End-based Theory and argue that *Consonant Mutation* applies within a phonological phrase in Mende. CM applies to the initial consonant if it follows another word within a phonological phrase. Thus, the initial consonant *p* of the verb *pókɔ̀* in (54a) mutates into *w* in (54b), since it follows the object (the relevant consonants are underscored here):

(54)   a. p̲ókɔ̀   'imitate'
          b. ì   nyá w̲ókɔ̀èlɔ́
              he me imitate   'He imitated me.'

                                      (Cowper and Rice 1987: 189)

They argue that phonological phrases in Mende are formed by reference to the left edge of a maximal projection. Thus, in (54b) above, *nyá* and *wókɔ̀èlɔ́* form a VP, and there is no left edge of an XP between them, as shown below:

(55)   ì [$_{VP}$ [$_{NP}$ nyá] wókɔ̀èlɔ́]

Now, in the following example (56), where an intransitive verb and PP form a VP, as shown in (57), a phonological phrase boundary is inserted between the subject and the verb, blocking Consonant Mutation.

(56)   a. tí   k̲àkpángà ngì má   'They surrounded him.'
              they surround him on
          b. * tì   g̲àkpángà ngì má
                      (Cowper and Rice 1987: 190; see also Conteh et al. 1985: 110)

(57)   [$_S$ [$_{NP}$ tí] [$_{VP}$ kàkpángà [$_{PP}$ ngì má]]]

In contrast, as Cowper and Rice note, Consonant Mutation applies between the subject and verb, as in (58), if the VP is non-branching as shown in (59):

(58)   a. p̲òté   'turn'
          b. ndóláà w̲òtéà   'The baby turned.'
              baby   turn

                                      (Cowper and Rice 1987: 189)

(59)   [$_S$ [$_{NP}$ ndóláà] [$_{VP}$ wòtéà]]

They argue that Mende refers to branching maximal projections (X^{max-b}) in forming phonological phrases and maintain that the reference to branchingness is parameterized: some languages refer to X^{max}, as in Selkirk's (1986) theory, while others refer to X^{max-b}.

Bickmore (1990) extends this idea and argues that the reference to the right or left edge of X^{max-b} should also be parameterized in the following way:

(60)   a. $]_{Xmax-b}$ b. $_{Xmax-b}[$

(Bickmore 1990: 17)

Thus, as we have just seen, Mende chooses (60b), referring to the left edge of X^{max-b}. In contrast, Kinyambo selects (60a), in which the right edge marks the right edge of a phonological phrase. The relevant phonological rule in Kinyambo is *High Deletion*, which deletes the H tone in a word $\omega 1$ if there is another word $\omega 2$ containing H after $\omega 1$ within a phonological phrase φ:

(61) $H \rightarrow \emptyset /[\ldots [\ldots \underline{\quad} \ldots]_{\omega 1} [\ldots H \ldots]_{\omega 2} \ldots]_{\varphi}$

(62a-b) show the lexical tone of each word. In (62c), High Deletion deletes the high tone of *abakózi* since it is followed by *bákajúna* containing H within a phonological phrase. But if the subject is branching, as in (62d), the H of the postnominal modifier *bakúru* is not deleted, indicating that this branching subject NP is followed by a phonological phrase boundary:

(62)   a. abakózi   'workers'
        b. bákajúna   'they help'
        c. abakozi bákajúna   'The workers helped.'
           ($)_{\varphi}$
        d. abakozi   bakúru   bákajúna
           workers   mature   they-helped   'The mature workers helped.'
           ($)_{\varphi}$ ($)_{\varphi}$

Bickmore accounts for the phonological phrasing in Kinyambo by assuming that the right edge of X^{max-b} corresponds to the right edge of a phonological phrase. In (62c), the subject NP *abakozi* is a non-branching maximal projection, so the phonological phrase formation ignores it, and no phonological phrase is formed by reference to the subject NP. In contrast, the subject NP in (62d) is branching, and therefore the phonological phrase formation inserts a right boundary that corresponds to the right edge of the subject NP.

Note that φ restructuring (38) in Relation-based Theory refers not only to branchingness but also to complements. That is, Relation-based Theory predicts that only complements may restructure. However, the End-based approach to branchingness (60) does not mention complements, and any non-branching XP, whether it is a complement or not, is ignored in forming phonological phrases. As the examples in (62) suggest, the reference to complements in Relation-based Theory would be too restrictive. But as we have seen in (39), the subject NP and VP do not undergo restructuring in Italian, even when they are both non-branching, which suggests that the reference to complements is necessary (at least in some languages). I will return to these issues in Chapters 3 and 4.

So far, we have examined the basics of End-based Theory, which is in a sense simpler than Relation-based Theory because syntactic notions like the recursive side or the head/complement distinction need not be mentioned. Although End-based Theory, at this early stage of its development, does not explicitly state how intonational phrases are formed, Selkirk (1984) suggests that they are defined semantically, in terms of the *Sense Unit Condition* (see also Watson and Gibson 2004; cf. Selkirk 2000, 2005).

In this section, we have reviewed the two major approaches to the syntax-phonology interface developed in the 1980s. These two theories are indirect-reference theories: they construct phonological domains according to which relevant phonological rules apply. That is, phonological rules do not refer to syntax at all. Note that Kaisse (1985), for example, proposes a direct-reference theory of the syntax-phonology interface, which refers to c-command (her *domain-c-command*) in syntax (see also Cinque 1993; Odden 1987, 1990, 1996 for direct reference, and Selkirk 1986: 398–400 for criticisms of Kaisse's theory). The debate over the direct versus indirect reference is ongoing. The interested reader is referred to D'Alessandro and Scheer (2015), Kalivoda (2018), Pak (2008), Samuels (2009, 2011), and Scheer (2012a, 2012b) for more recent arguments for direct reference, and to Selkirk (2011) and Bonet et al. (2018), among others, for arguments against it.

2.4. 1990s–2000s

The 1990s saw new developments in the study of generative grammar: Optimality Theory in phonology (Prince and Smolensky (1993/2004) and Minimalism in syntax (Chomsky 1995). These new ideas have had an enormous impact on the field of syntax-phonology interactions. In this section, we will review further theoretical progress in this field. I will review Optimality-Theory approaches to the syntax-phonology interface and then consider phase theory, Multiple Spell-Out, and phonological phrasing in the Minimalist Program.

2.4.1 *Optimality theoretic approaches*

The development of Optimality Theory has resulted in End-based Theory being integrated into the Generalized Alignment Theory (McCarthy and Prince 1993; Selkirk 1996, 2000; Truckenbrodt 1995, 1999, 2007; Gussenhoven 2004, among others). Optimality Theory has violable universal constraints ("soft constraints"), which are ranked in a specific order in a particular language. A generator function *Gen* operates on an underlying input form and produces a set of candidates for the output form by randomly rearranging the input. An evaluator function *Eval* picks one output candidate that optimally satisfies the ranked constraints. Two main features of this theory are (i) that an output may violate constraints and take a marked form as long as it is optimal among candidates and (ii) that cross-linguistic variation results from the difference in constraint ranking among languages.

Generalized Alignment Theory formulates alignment requirements in the form of an Optimality Theoretic violable constraint:

(63)   Align(Cat1, Edge1, Cat2, Edge2) $=_{def}$
          ∀ Cat1 ∃ Cat2 such that Edge1 of Cat1 and Edge2 of Cat2 coincide.
       Where
          Cat1, Cat2 ∈ PCat ∪ GCat
          Edge1, Edge2 ∈ {Right, Left}

Here, PCat and GCat are prosodic and grammatical (morphological or syntactic) categories, respectively. This constraint requires that an edge (right or left) of a prosodic or grammatical constituent of type Cat1 coincides with an edge (right or left) of some other prosodic or morphological constituent Cat2. For example, as McCarthy and Prince (1993) observe in Ulwa, the affix -*ka*- 'his' immediately follows the head foot of the word (a foot is indicated by round brackets below):

(64)   -*ka*- Infixation in Ulwa
       (bás)ka   'hiar'
       (siwá)kanak   'root'

This can be formalized as follows in the form of Generalized Alignment:

(65)   Ulwa -*ka*-
       Align([*ka*]$_{Af}$, L, Ft′, R)

This requires that for every instance of -*ka*- there is a head foot Ft′ such that the left edge of -*ka*- and the right edge of the Ft′ coincide. That is, the left edge of -*ka*- is aligned with the right edge of Ft′.

Note that Generalized Alignment in (63) is designed to be an interface constraint: it relates an edge in some component of grammar (e.g., syntax) to an edge in some other component of grammar (e.g., phonology). The advent of Optimality Theory equipped with Generalized Alignment led Selkirk (1996) to reconsider the traditional formulation of the Strict Layer Hypothesis. The following is a traditional formulation of the Strict Layer Hypothesis, from Selkirk (1996: 189):[13]

(66)   *Strict Layer Hypothesis*
       A prosodic constituent of level C^i immediately dominates only constituents of the next level down in the prosodic hierarchy, C^{i-1}.

She points out that this formulation is "expressed as a monolithic whole," which should be factored out into more primitive constraints (see also Inkelas 1989; Ito and Mester 1992/2003), and suggests that it should be decomposed as follows (here, σ = syllable, Ft = foot, and PWd = prosodic word; see (27) and (29a) for a typical prosodic hierarchy):

(67) Constraints on Prosodic Domination (where C^n = some prosodic category)
   a. *LAYEREDNESS* No C^i dominates a C^j, j > i,
       e.g., "No σ dominates a Ft."
   b. *HEADEDNESS* Any C^i must dominate a C^{i-1} (except if C^i = σ),
       e.g., "A PWd must dominate a Ft."
   c. *EXHAUSTIVITY* No C^i immediately dominates a constituent C^j, j < i-1,
       e.g., "No PWd immediately dominates a σ."
   d. *NONRECURSIVITY* No C^i dominates C^j, j = i,
       e.g., "No Ft dominates a Ft."

(Selkirk 1996: 190)

Selkirk points out that the first two constraints (67a-b) are inviolable. In Optimality Theoretic terms, they are undominated in the constraint ranking of every language. By contrast, EXHAUSTIVITY is violable. For example, Extrametricality in English stress assignment requires that a syllable be immediately dominated by a prosodic word, skipping the layer of foot (Hayes 1982. See also Féry 2017: Ch.3). NONRE-CURSIVITY is also violable, which I will discuss below.

   Given these Optimality Theoretic considerations, the parametric formulation of End-based Theory in (49) is recast in terms of the following Generalized Alignment constraints:

(68) a. ALIGN(XP, R; φ, R): The right edge of each syntactic XP is aligned with the right edge of a phonological phrase φ.
   b. ALIGN(XP, L; φ, L): The left edge of each syntactic XP is aligned with the left edge of a phonological phrase φ.

In addition to these, the following constraint is suggested:

(69) *P-PHRASE: Avoid phonological phrases.

*P-PHRASE has the effect of making (68a) or (68b) inactive. Thus, for the syntactic structure [$_{VP}$ V NP], the ranking ALIGN-XP,L >> *P-PHRASE >> ALIGN-XP,R yields the phonological phrasing (V)$_φ$ (NP)$_φ$: ALIGN-XP,L creates a phonological phrase boundary that corresponds to the left edge of the NP in violation of *P-PHRASE. In contrast, the ranking ALIGN-XP,R >> *P-PHRASE >> ALIGN-XP,L gives the phrasing (V NP)$_φ$: even though the lower-ranked ALIGN-XP,L would create a phonological phrase boundary corresponding to the left edge of the NP, the overriding constraint *P-PHRASE blocks it, and there is no phonological phrase boundary between V and NP.

   Now, let us consider how the ranking among these and other constraints to be introduced below accounts for marked prosodic phrasing and cross-linguistic variation. An interesting consequence of the Optimality-Theory approach equipped with violable constraints is that recursive phrasing is allowed, something strictly prohibited by the Strict Layer Hypothesis. Truckenbrodt (1995, 1999) shows that this is true in the Bantu language Kimatuumbi. He proposes that the alignment constraints interact with the constraint WRAP-XP, which requires that each XP be contained in a phonological phrase φ.

On the basis of observations by Odden (1987, 1990, 1996), Truckenbrodt argues that Kimatuumbi has recursive phonological phrasing. First, he shows that *Vowel Shortening* is sensitive to the right edge of phonological phrases, while *Phrasal Tone Insertion* is sensitive to their left edge. Let us first consider Vowel Shortening, which affects the long vowels in words that are non-final in a phonological phrase:

(70) a. [mpuuɲgá]$_{NP}$ [waabój]$_{VP}$
          (mpuungá)$_{PPh}$ (waabój)$_{PPh}$
          rice   rotted
          'The rice has rotted.'
      b. [mpuɲga wá   [baándu]$_{NP}$]$_{NP}$
          (mpunga wá   baándu)$_{PPh}$
          Rice   of   people
          'the rice of the people'

The long vowel of *mpuuɲgá* is not shortened in (70a), because it occupies the phonological phrase final position, while it is shortened in (70b) since it is the non-final position. Truckenbrodt (1999: 237) gives the following formulation of Shortening:

(71) *Shortening*
      The long stem vowel shortens, except in the prosodic word immediately preceding the right edge of a phonological phrase.

Let us next consider Phrasal Tone Insertion. In contrast to Shortening, Phrasal Tone Insertion is sensitive to the right edge of a phonological phrase. It places an H tone on the last vowel of a word that precedes a phonological phrase:

(72) a. Mambóondo   (in isolation)
      b. [Mambondó]$_{NP}$ [aawíjle]$_{VP}$
          (Mambondó)$_{PPh}$ (aawíjle)$_{PPh}$
          Mamboondo   died
          'Mamboondo died.'

In (72a), the word in isolation does not undergo Phrasal Tone Insertion, because it does not precede a phonological phrase. By contrast, in (72b) the same word undergoes Phrasal Tone Insertion; thus, the final vowel receives an H tone since it is immediately followed by a phonological phrase. Note that the final vowel of *aawíjle* does not receive an H tone, because no phonological phrase follows it.

That is, Phrasal Tone Insertion is sensitive to the left edge of the subsequent phonological phrase but not to the right edge of a phonological phrase containing the word in question. Truckenbrodt (1999: 238) formulates this as follows:

(73) Phrasal Tone Insertion (PTI)
Align (P, L; H, R)
"Align the left edge of each phonological phrase with the right edge of an H tone."
$_P(\rightarrow H \,_P($

Given these two rules, Truckenbrodt examines the following examples:

(74) a. [V   NP   NP   ]$_{VP}$
    ((naampéi   kikóloombe)$_{PPh}$ Mambóondo)$_{PPh}$
    I-him-gave   shell   Mamboondo
    'I gave Mamboondo the shell.'
  b. [N   [P   NP]$_{PP}$ AP]$_{NP}$
    ((kikólombe   cha-asikoópu)$_{PPh}$ kikúlú)
    shell   of bishop   large
    'large shell of the bishop'

Here, the first complements *kikóloombe* 'shell' and *cha-asikoópu* 'of bishop', in (74a) and (74b), respectively, do not undergo Shortening, indicating that they are in the phonological phrase final position and do not undergo Phrasal Tone Insertion, as indicated by the fact that their final vowel lacks an H tone.[14] Truckenbrodt claims that this fact is accounted for by the following recursive phonological phrasing:

(75) Syntax: [X   YP   ZP]$_{XP}$
    Phonology: ((X   YP)$_{PPh}$ ZP)$_{PPh}$
                  ↑
            right edge of a phonological phrase
            with no immediately following left edge of a phonological phrase

The presence of the right edge of a phonological phrase between the first and second complements blocks application of Shortening to the first complement. Because of the absence of a left edge there, however, Phrasal Tone Insertion is not triggered.

He then shows that this recursive phrasing is obtained through the following constraint interaction (Truckenbrodt 1999: 241):

(76) a. WRAP-XP: Each XP be contained in a phonological phrase φ.
  b. NONRECURSIVITY (NONREC): Any two phonological phrases that are not disjoint in extension are identical in extension.
  c. *P-PHRASE: Avoid phonological phrases.
  d. EXHAUSTIVITY: Parsing on every prosodic level is exhaustive.

(77)   WRAP-*XP* and ALIGN-*XP* compel a recursive structure

[X₁ XP₂ XP₃]ₓₚ₁	ALIGN-**XP,R**	WRAP-**XP**	NONREC	*P-PHRASE	ALIGN-**XP,L**
a. ( )	XP₂!			*	XP₂ XP₃
b. ( )( )		XP₁!		**	XP₂
c. ☞(( ))			XP₃	**	XP₂ XP₃
d. (( ))			X₁! XP₃	**	XP₃
e. (( )( ))			XP₃ X₁(!) XP₂	***(!)	XP₂

Crucial here is a newly proposed constraint WRAP-XP. This constraint, ranked below ALIGN-XP,R, serves to exclude candidate (77b), which has a traditional non-recursive structure, in favor of the recursive structure (77c). Both (77b) and (77c) satisfy ALIGN-XP,R, since the right edges of XP1, XP2, and XP3 are all aligned with the right edges of phonological phrases. (77b) violates WRAP-XP because XP1 is not properly contained in a single phonological phrase. In contrast, (77c) satisfies WRAP-XP because each XP has a corresponding phonological phrase that properly contains it. Furthermore, the recursive phrasing in (77c) is allowed since NONREC is ranked below WRAP-XP: the higher-ranked WRAP-XP is satisfied in violation of the lower-ranked NONREC.[15] Therefore, (77c) is selected as the optimal candidate.

Truckenbrodt further shows that the ranking WRAP-XP = NONREC >> ALIGN-XP,R = *P-PHRASE derives the nonrecursive phonological phrasing (X XP XP)_φ for the syntactic structure [X XP XP]ₓₚ observed in the Bantu language Chichewa (Kanerva 1990). In this language, the rule of *Penultimate Lengthening* lengthens a vowel in the penultimate syllable of a phonological phrase. That is, this rule is sensitive to the right edge of a phonological phrase. Thus, in (78), the penultimate vowels of the subject and verb in a simple intransitive sentence are both lengthened, because they belong to separate phonological phrases:

(78)   [XP1   XP2]ᵢₚ   [NP   VP]ᵢₚ
          (   )ₚ(   )ₚ   (kagaálu)ₚ (kanáafa)ₚ
                                   (small) dog died
                                   'The (small) dog died.'

In contrast, there is no phonological phrase boundary between the verb and its complement as in (79); nor is there a boundary between the two complements of the verb, as in (80a-b), unlike Kimatuumbi (cf. (74)):

(79)   [X1 XP2]ₓₚ₁   [V   NP   ]ᵥₚ
          (   )ₚ   (tinabá káluúlu)ₚ
                                   we-stole hare
                                   'We stole the hare.'

(80) [X₁ XP₂ XP₃]ₓₚ₁   a. [V   NP [P   NP]ₚₚ]ᵥₚ
      (   )ₚ   (anaményá nyumbá ndi mwáála)ₚ
                                he-hit   house   with rock
                                'He hit the house with a rock.'
                             b. [V   NP   NP   ]ᵥₚ
                                (tinapátsá mwaná njíínga)ₚ
                                we-gave   chid   bicycle
                                'We gave the child a bicycle.'

The constraint interaction is shown below:

(81) *Chichewa: low-ranking* AʟɪɢN-*XP,R does not insist on the internal p-boundary*

(Truckenbrodt 1999: 246)

[V NP YP]ᵥₚ	Wʀᴀᴘ-**XP**	Nᴏɴʀᴇᴄ	Aʟɪɢɴ-**XP,R**	*P-Pʜʀᴀsᴇ
a. ( )( )	VP!			**
b. (( ))		*!		**
c. ☞( )			NP	*

Here, (81a) is excluded by the undominated Wʀᴀᴘ-XP: VP is not "wrapped" by a single phonological phrase. (80b) violates Nᴏɴʀᴇᴄ because of its recursive structure. (81c) satisfies Wʀᴀᴘ-XP and Nᴏɴʀᴇᴄ in violation of the lower-ranked Aʟɪɢɴ-XP,R: the right edge of NP is not aligned with the left edge of a phonological phrase, but each XP is wrapped, and no recursion is involved. Therefore, (81) is chosen as the optimal candidate.

This approach is highly consistent with the expectations of Optimality Theory: the cross-linguistic variation in phonological phrasing as well as the emergence of marked recursive phrasing is attributed to differences in constraint ranking. Optimality Theory approaches to prosodic domains in this line flourished greatly thereafter in the 2000s, leading to a number of interesting works in the field of the syntax-phonology interface, including Kisseberth and Abasheikh (2011), Kula and Bickmore (2015), Prieto (2005), Samek-Lodovici (2005), Sandalo and Truckenbrodt (2002), Smith (2011a), Yahya (2013), and Zerbian (2006), among many others.

It should be noted here that the recursive phrasing, which was then assumed to be marked, is considered unmarked later for empirical and conceptual reasons. Empirically, recursive phrasing has in fact been found to be prevalent, unlike what the Strict Layer Hypothesis predicts; conceptually, a new theoretical approach has been pursued that recognizes isomorphism between syntactic and phonological constituents (Match Theory). Thus, not just one edge of XP is aligned with an edge of a phonological phrase: both edges of XP are aligned with both edges of a phonological phrase (this theory is further generalized to prosodic word and intonational phrase, as we will see later). That is, a syntactic constituent is matched with a phonological phrase, and recursion in syntax is directly reflected in phonology. The mismatch between syntactic and prosodic structure is handled in the phonological component. Match Theory can be regarded as descended from the ALIGN theory because the alignment of edges is involved directly, but could also be a descendant of the WRAP theory since recursion of phonological phrases results in their corresponding XPs being always contained or wrapped in them, without creating a phonological phrase boundary inside the XPs. We will return to this subsequent development in section 2.5. Before we move on to Match Theory, we will review significant developments in syntactic theory that occurred around 2000: a strictly derivational architecture of grammar is reintroduced, and all three components of grammar (syntax, phonology, and semantics) are assumed to be cyclic, with the computation of these three components proceeding cyclically and in parallel (Chomsky 2004: 107). This reincarnation of a cyclic approach has had a direct effect on the study of the syntax-phonology interface.

2.4.2   *The Minimalist Program and the syntax-phonology interface*

New theoretical devices in minimalist syntax have spurred significant changes in the study of the syntax-phonology interface. Especially influential are cyclic, or multiple, Spell-Out, explored by Epstein et al. (1998), Epstein and Seely (2002), and Uriagereka (1999). Until the mid-1990s, it was commonly held that the syntactic computation splits to Logical Form (LF) and Phonetic Form (PF) at a single point in a derivation (sometimes called the Y-model or the Extended Standard Theory (EST) model):

(82)

To give a derivational account of the "induction step" of Kayne's (1994) antisymmetry theory of linearization, Uriagereka (1999) proposes that Spell-Out applies in a multiple fashion, independently spelling out a complex "left branch" of syntactic structure so that the induction step can be eliminated from the antisymmetry theory. He adopts what he calls a dynamically split model, where a syntactic derivation splits into the interpretive components, in line with Bresnan (1971), Jackendoff (1972), and Lasnik (1972):

(83)

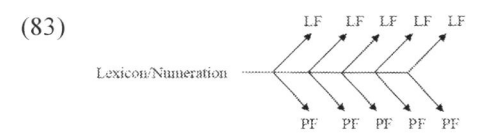

Uriagereka argues that this model not only derives part of the linearization procedure but also provides prosodic domains.[16] He suggests further that the domains of Spell-Out in this model can serve as syntactic islands and semantic domains.

Similarly, Epstein et al. (1998) argue on independent grounds for a strictly derivational, level-free, interpretive architecture of grammar. They suggest that fundamental syntactic relations such as c-command are defined derivationally. It then follows that interpretation by the LF and PF interfaces is also given derivationally. Thus, LF and PF look at each step of the derivation and interpret them step-wise (see Epstein and Seely 2002 for further elaboration of a level-free model; I will return to the interpretive model in Chapter 4):

(84)

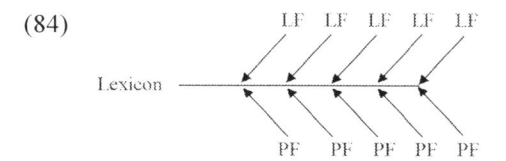

In line with these and many other syntactic investigations, Chomsky (2000, 2001) proposes a phase theory of syntactic derivation that incorporates Multiple Spell-Out. He argues that syntactic derivation proceeds cyclically, phase by phase. In the following phrase structure, CP and vP are taken to be (strong) phases, and the sister of a phase head undergoes Spell-Out:

(85) $[_{CP}$ C $[_{TP}$ NP$_{Subj}$ T $[_{vP}$ v $[_{VP}$ V NP$_{Obj}$]]]]

First the vP phase is constructed, and the CP phase is then constructed. It is assumed that the sister of a phase head undergoes Spell-Out, as the derivation goes on. Thus, the sister of the lower phase head, namely VP, is spelled out first, and then TP, the sister of C, is spelled out.[17]

Given this phase-by-phase derivational model of syntax incorporating Multiple Spell-Out, Kahnemuyipour (2004, 2009), among many others, argues that a domain of phase-by-phase Spell-Out corresponds to a phonological domain. Specifically, he argues that sentential stress (nuclear stress) is assigned in terms of Spell-Out domains. Examining stress patterns in English (SVO word order) and Persian (SOV), he observes (i) that sentential stress always, universally, falls on the object but not on the verb in informationally neutral transitive sentences, regardless of the word order, and (ii) that secondary stress falls on the subject. Here, stress is indicated by underlining, and numbers below the underlines show primary and secondary stress:

(86)   a. English: <u>John</u> saw <u>Mary</u>.   [<u>S</u> V <u>O</u>]
                  2   1   2   1

       b. Persian: <u>Ali</u> <u>ye ketaab</u> xarid.   [<u>S</u> <u>O</u> V]
                   2   1   2   1

           Ali a book bought
           'Ali bought a book.'

(Kahnemuyipour (2009: 117)

To account for this fact, he proposes the following mechanism of sentential stress assignment:

(87)   Sentential Stress Rule:

(Kahnemuyipour 2009: 68)

Sentential stress is assigned at the phase to the highest phonologically non-null element of the spelled-out constituent or the SPELLEE.
$[_{HP}$ [H YP]]: if HP is a phase, YP = SPELLEE.

He further adopts the following two assumptions: (i) the universal order is SVO, and the word order difference results from syntactic movement, as in Kayne's (1994) antisymmetry theory of phrase structure and (ii) the object moves out of VP into the Spec of AspP for Case assignment in the following phrase structure:[18]

(88) $[_{CP}$ C $[_{TP}$ Subj T $[_{vP}$ v $[_{AspP}$ Obj Asp $[_{VP}$ V t_{Obj}]]]]

This is the surface structure of SOV in Persian, and the SVO order in English results from the movement of V to v via Asp. On the assumption that vP and CP are phases, AspP and TP undergo Spell-Out. Regardless of whether V moves to v, Obj in Spec-AspP receives sentential stress when Spell-Out applies to AspP since it occupies the highest position in this SPELLEE, given (87). Likewise, the Spell-Out of TP assigns stress to Subj, which is the highest element in this SPELLEE.

Note that Subj is assigned secondary stress while Obj receives primary stress in both languages, as in (86). Kahnemuyipour argues that his theory is designed to account systematically for the element that receives sentential stress, primary or secondary. Thus, his theory predicts that each SPELLEE has stress, and this is borne out, as in the following examples:

(89)   a. $[_{CP}$ John $[_{vP}$ told Maryam $[_{CP}$ that Jane $[_{vP}$ saw Bill]]]]
                      2   2   2   1

        b.   Ali be Maryam goft ke Mina qazza mi-xaad.
              2   2   2   1

              Ali to Maryam said that Mina food DUR-want.3SG
              'Ali said to Maryam that Mina wants food.'

(Kahnemuyipour 2009: 118)

Kahnemuyipour then suggests that the distinction between primary and secondary stress is made independently of the sentence stress rule in (87). It might be determined phonologically, as primary stress falls on the rightmost constituent in the sentence. It could also be determined syntactically. That is, the first SPELLEE is marked for primary stress. In the bottom-up derivational procedure adopted in this analysis, the first SPELLEE is the most deeply embedded constituent and corresponds to primary stress in (89). This speculation notwithstanding, the phase-by-phase approach to stress assignment seems to successfully assign stress within the domains of Spell-Out.

Kahnemuyipour maintains that his theory accounts for a wider range of data from various languages and is not vulnerable to the theoretical and conceptual problems of the previous analyses of stress assignment, such as Cinque (1993), Zubizarreta (1998), and Legate (2003). The interested reader is referred to Kahnemuyipour's (2004, 2009) original work. For further elaboration of phase-by-phase stress assignment, see Adger (2003/2007) and Grohmann and Putnam (2003/2007), and Kratzer and Selkirk (2007). See also Féry (2011) for an Optimality-Theory account of stress assignment.

So far, we have briefly reviewed Kahnemuyipour's analysis of stress assignment in terms of the phase theory. It should be pointed out, however, that the domains created by Spell-Out that applies to the sister of a phase head do not match the prosodic domains (phonological phrases) predicted by the Standard Theories that we have reviewed in section 2.3. Applied to the derivation of (90a), Spell-Out would yield the prosodic domains shown in (90b), on the commonly held assumption that V moves to v (Chomsky 1995):

(90) a. $[_{CP}$ C $\quad[_{TP}$ NP$_{Subj}$ T $[_{vP}$ V-v $[_{VP}$ t_V $\quad$ NP$_{Obj}$]]]]
　　 b. $($ C $)_\varphi$ $($ $\quad$ NP$_{Subj}$ T $\quad$ V-v $)_\varphi$ $($ t_V $\quad$ NP$_{Obj}$ $)_\varphi$

In contrast, Relation-based Theory and End-based Theory (with the right-edge setting typical in SVO languages) predict the following phonological phrasing:

(91) a. Relation-based Theory: $($NP$_{Subj}$ $)_\varphi$ $($T $\quad$ V $)_\varphi$ $($ NP$_{Obj}$ $)_\varphi$
　　 b. Edge-based Theory: $\quad\quad$ $($NP$_{Subj}$ $)_\varphi$ $($T $\quad$ V $\quad$ NP$_{Obj}$ $)_\varphi$

These phrasings are, of course, largely empirically adequate, as is clear from the fact that much work has been conducted within the framework of the Standard Theories. So, there seems to be a systematic mismatch between the Spell-Out domains and phonological phrases.

As argued by Dobashi (2003, 2009), the linearization procedure among the units of Spell-Out can in fact resolve the mismatch.[19] I will review this approach in detail in Chapter 3.

Multiple Spell-Out approaches to prosodic domains include D'Alessandro and Scheer (2015), Bošković (2017), Fuß (2003/2007, 2008), Ishihara (2003, 2005, 2007), Kratzer and Selkirk (2007), Marvin (2002), Pak (2008), Samuels (2009, 2011), Samuels and Narita (2013), Sato (2009), Scheer (2012a, 2012b), Seidl (2001), Selkirk (2009, 2011), Shiobara (2009, 2010), Simpson and Wu (2002), and Wagner (2005, 2010), among many others. See Downing (2011) for a mixed approach that combines phase and alignment. See also Cheng and Downing (2012, 2016) for a criticism. For a much earlier cyclic approach, see Bresnan (1971), which I discussed in section 2.2.2.

So far, I have reviewed the development of the phase theory with Multiple Spell-Out and its relation to the study of syntax-phonology interactions. In the next section, I will review Match Theory, an evolution of End-based Theory.

2.5.   The 2010s: match theory

The Strict Layer Hypothesis (28), repeated below, has been adopted, often without controversy, as a basic assumption in a wide range of investigations:

(92)   Strict Layer Hypothesis: A constituent of category-level *n* in the prosodic hierarchy immediately dominates only constituents at category-level *n-1*.
(Selkirk 2009: 38)

Conceptually, the Strict Layer Hypothesis was challenged in the context of violable constraints in Optimality Theory, as we saw in section 2.4.1. Selkirk (1996) argues that the Strict Layer Hypothesis can be factored out into LAYEREDNESS, HEADEDNESS, EXHAUSTIVITY, and NONRECURSIVITY, and that each of these is recast as a constraint. Truckenbrodt (1995, 1999) shows that interaction of the constraints ALIGN and WRAP accounts for the (non-)emergence of recursive phonological phrasing.

Empirically, Ladd (1986, 1996), for instance, shows that intonational phrasing can be recursive. Thus, in sentences of the form *A and B but C* and *A but B and C* the *but* boundary is stronger:

(93)   a.   Warren is a stronger campaigner, and Ryan has more popular policies, but Allen has a lot more money.
   b.   Warren is a stronger campaigner, but Ryan has more popular policies, and Allen has a lot more money.
(Ladd 1996: 242)

Under the Strict Layer Hypothesis, we would have the following flat intonational phrasing in both these examples:

(94)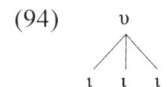

However, the initial peak of the clause after *but* is higher than that after *and*, and the pause before *but* is longer than that before *and*. That is, the same phenomena arise on different scales, depending on where they show up. The following recursive intonational phrasing accounts in an obvious way for the difference in boundary strength:

(95)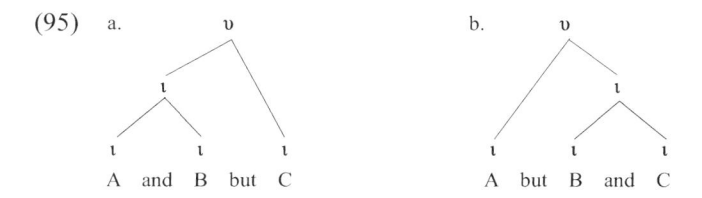

More arguments for recursive phrasing in the prosodic hierarchy are presented by, among others, Booij (1996), Ito and Mester (2007, 2009), Kabak and Revithiadou

(2009) and Zec (2005), for prosodic words, and by Gussenhoven (2005), for phonological phrases.

Given these and other findings, Ito and Mester (2012, 2013) lay out a general model for prosodic structure, Recursion-based Subcategories. They adopt three interface categories: the intonational phrase ι, phonological phrase φ, and prosodic word ω, all of which can be recursive. They assume that utterance υ is in fact the maximal projection of the ι, which accounts for why υ is not recursive:[20]

(96)

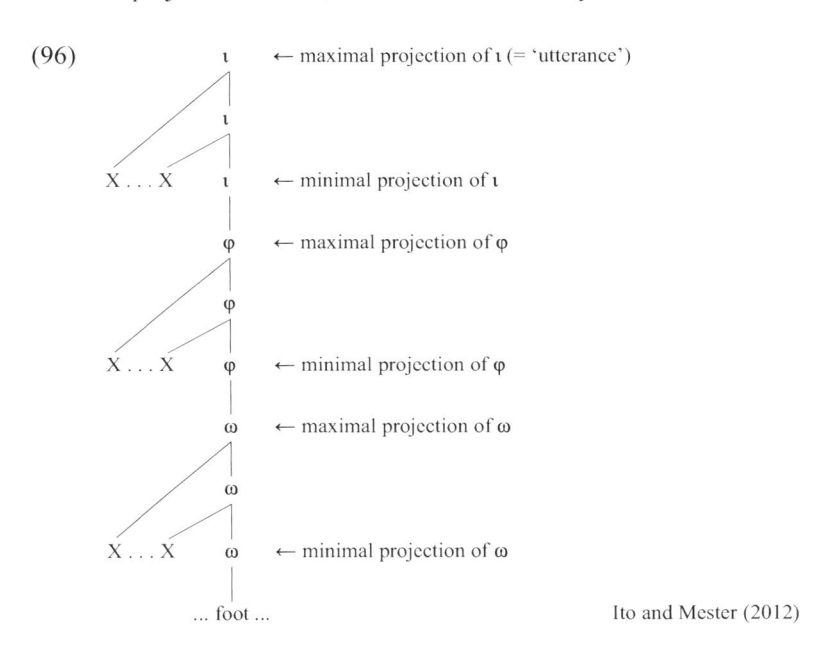

Ito and Mester (2012)

Since this recursive model of prosodic hierarchy is radically different from previous theories, a new mapping algorithm is required for connecting syntax with the recursive prosodic structure. One such theory is proposed by Selkirk (2009, 2011).

In the standard Prosodic Hierarchy theory, reviewed in section 2.3.1, no inherent relationship is assumed between prosodic and syntactic categories. Selkirk (2009, 2011) suggests that the hierarchical relationship among the interface categories (i.e., ω, φ, and ι) is syntactically grounded (see also Selkirk 2005: Section 5). Specifically, she proposes a *Match Theory* of syntactic-prosodic constituency correspondence:

(97) *Match Theory*

(Selkirk 2009: 40, 2011: 439)

(i) Match Clause
A clause in syntactic constituent structure must be matched by a constituent of a corresponding prosodic type in phonological representation, call it ι.

(ii) Match Phrase
A phrase in syntactic constituent structure must be matched by a constituent of a corresponding prosodic type in phonological representation, call it φ.

(iii) Match Word
A word in syntactic constituent structure must be matched by a constituent of a corresponding prosodic type in phonological representation, call it ω.

Note that this is an informal formulation, and it is refined in terms of Correspondence Theory (McCarthy and Prince 1995), to which we will return later. Selkirk argues that the notions of clause, phrase, and word are minimally necessary in any theory of morphosyntax, and the theory of syntax-phonology interaction makes use of these syntactic notions, which have correspondents in phonology. In this theory, ω, φ, and ι are not stipulated phonological entities, but rather syntactically motivated categories.

One of the most salient features of this theory is that recursion and level-skipping in the prosodic structure are taken to mirror recursion in syntax. Thus, the prosodic structure in (98b)=(98c) is obtained from the syntactic structure in (98a), where JP and OP are clauses, other XPs are phrases, and each terminal element is a word:

(98)   a. Syntax

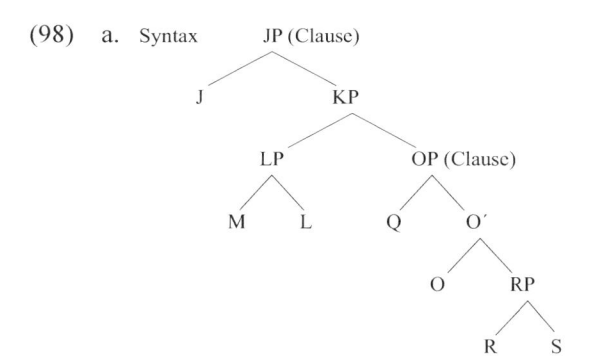

b. Phonology

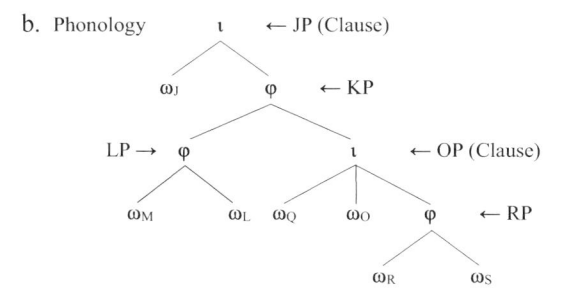

c. $(\omega_J ((\omega_M \ \omega_L)_\varphi \ (\ \omega_Q \ \omega_O \ (\ \omega_R \ \omega_S)_\varphi \ )_\iota \ )_\varphi \ )_\iota$

Here, the φ that matches KP dominates the φ that matches LP, instantiating a case of recursion. The ι that matches JP dominates ω_J, and the ι that matches OP dominates ω_Q and ω_O, instantiating level-skipping. The intonational phrasing is also recursive in that the ι that matches JP dominates the ι that matches OP, even though it does not immediately dominate it.

Given this approach to recursion, let us return to ι-recursion, mentioned above. The relevant examples (93) are repeated here in (99):

(99) a. Warren is a stronger campaigner, and Ryan has more popular policies, but Allen has a lot more money.
  b. Warren is a stronger campaigner, but Ryan has more popular policies, and Allen has a lot more money.

(Ladd 1996: 242)

Here, the *but* boundaries are stronger than the *and* boundaries, and the intonational phrasing of these sentences is as follows:

(100) a. ((A and B)ᵢ but C)ᵢ
  b. (A but (B and C)ᵢ)ᵢ

In section 2.4.1, we saw that recursive phrasing is accounted for in terms of the constraints WRAP and ALIGN: If ALIGN is ranked higher than WRAP, then recursion emerges (see the tableau in (77)). So, it would be expected that interaction of these types of constraints accounts for the recursion in (100). The relevant constraints would be as follows:[21]

(101) a. ALIGN-CLAUSE, R: The right edge of each clause is aligned with the right edge of an intonational phrase ι.
  b. WRAP-CLAUSE: Each clause be contained in an intonational phrase ι.

Truckenbrodt and Féry (2015) show, however, that the interaction of these constraints does not function as we would expect. Let us first consider the phrasing in (100a). Suppose that WRAP is ranked higher than ALIGN. On the assumption that a "clause" in (100) refers not just to each of A, B, and C, but also to the combined clauses, i.e., [A and B], [B and C], and the combination of all three clauses (Truckenbrodt and Féry 2015: 37ff), we would obtain a phrasing where all the clauses are phrased together, as in (102b)/(103b), since WRAP requires all the clauses to be wrapped in an intonational phrase, suppressing the ALIGN requirement. In contrast, if ALIGN is ranked higher, then the phrasing in (102c) is obtained, where A, B, and C are juxtaposed flatly. Note that the correct phrasings (102d) and (103d) are excluded, since they violate a clause-level constraint equivalent to *P-PHRASE, which requires us to avoid the creation of an intonational phrase: (102d) has an extra intonational phrase containing A and B in (102d); (103d) has an extra phrase containing B and C (in bold in the examples). Therefore, the ranking ALIGN >> WRAP would predict, incorrectly, that (102c) and (103c) are optimal candidates.

(102) a. [A   B   ]   C
      b. (   )ₗ   ☞ WRAP >> ALIGN
      c. ((   )ₗ (   )ₗ (   ))ₗ   ☞ ALIGN >> WRAP
      d. (((   )ₗ (   ))ₗ (   ))ₗ

(103) a.   A   [B   C   ]
      b. (   )ₗ   ☞ WRAP >> ALIGN
      c. ((   )ₗ (   )ₗ (   ))ₗ   ☞ ALIGN >> WRAP
      d. ((   )ₗ ((   )ₗ (   ))ₗ)ₗ

So, it can be concluded that the recursive phrasing of the form (100) cannot be obtained by the interaction of WRAP and ALIGN (see also Myrberg 2013; O'Connor and Patin 2015 for further critical discussions about WRAP). Discarding these constraints, Truckenbrodt and Féry (2015: 39) argue that recursion in prosodic structure is a reflex of recursion in syntax. Specifically, the recursive phrasing in (100) is accounted for by the following MATCH constraint suggested by Selkirk (2011):

(104) MATCHILLOCUTIONARYCLAUSE:
      The left and right edges of an illocutionary clause must correspond to the left and right edges of an ɩ.

Here, the illocutionary clause refers to the highest projection of the sentence that determines its appropriateness in a discourse context (Selkirk 2011: 452; Cf. Emonds' (1976) *root clause*, Rizzi's (1997) *ForceP*, Potts' (2005) *comma phrase*).

Given MATCHILLOCUTIONARYCLAUSE, not only each of A, B, and C, but also [A B], [B C], and the entire clause combining all the three clauses, corresponds to its own intonational phrase, reflecting the recursion in syntax:

(105) a. [A   B   ]   C
      b. (((   )ₗ (   ))ₗ (   ))ₗ

(106) a.   A   [B   C   ]
      b. ((   )ₗ ((   )ₗ (   ))ₗ)ₗ

To conclude, recursive prosodic phrasing results from MATCH constraints but not from the interaction of ALIGN and WRAP constraints. Then, recursion in prosodic structure is considered to be unmarked, which is not the case for the theory adopting the constraint NONREC (cf. Ito and Mester 2013).

As suggested earlier, Match Theory is formally recast as a set of violable MATCH constraints within the framework of the Correspondence Theory. If a markedness constraint is ranked above the MATCH constraints, we will obtain prosodic domains that do not match the syntactic structure. That is, syntax-phonology mismatch, a central issue in the field, is reduced to the interaction of the MATCH constraints with markedness constraints. For an illustration, let us examine the phonological phrasing in Xitsonga discussed by Selkirk (2011).

Drawing on Kisseberth's (1994: 157) observations, Selkirk shows that the H Tone Spread in Xitsonga does not apply across the left edge of a branching noun phrase, but can apply across the left edge of a non-branching noun phrase:

(107) a. vá-súsá [$_{NP}$ n-gúlú:ve]
  'They are removing a pig.'
  b. vá-súsá [$_{NP}$ n-guluve y'á vo:n'á]
  'They are removing their pig.'

  (Kisseberth's 1994: 157; Selkirk 2011: 445)

Here, the subject marker *vá-* has an H tone. It spreads across the left edge of the object NP in (107a) but it does not in (107b), where the NP is branching. In the Optimality-Theory formulation of Match Theory, the phrasing is obtained through the interaction of a syntax-prosody correspondence constraint MATCH(Phrase,φ) with a prosodic markedness constraint BINMIN(φ,ω). The former requires syntactic phrases to correspond to phonological phrases, and the latter requires a phonological phrase φ to be minimally binary and to consist of at least two prosodic words (Inkelas and Zec 1990, 1995; Kim 1997; Selkirk 2000). In Xitsonga, BINMIN(φ,ω) >> MATCH(Phrase,φ):

(108)

i.

[[verb [noun]$_{NP}$]$_{VP}$]$_{clause}$	BINMIN(φ,ω)	MATCH(Phrase,φ)
a. ((verb (noun)$_φ$)$_φ$)$_ι$	*	
b. ☞((verb noun)$_φ$)$_ι$		*

ii.

[[verb [noun adj]$_{NP}$]$_{VP}$]$_{clause}$	BINMIN(φ,ω)	MATCH(Phrase,φ)
a. ☞((verb (noun adj)$_φ$)$_φ$)$_ι$		
b. ((verb noun)$_φ$ adj)$_ι$		*

In (108i), where the object is non-branching, (b) is the optimal candidate even though it violates the MATCH constraint, since the higher-ranked markedness constraint BINMIN(φ,ω) is satisfied, while candidate (a), which satisfies the MATCH constraint, is excluded because it violates BINMIN(φ,ω). In (108ii), where the object is branching, candidate (a) satisfies both constraints, mirroring the syntactic constituency while violating the Strict Layer Hypothesis in the standard theory.[22]

So far, we have provided a rough sketch of Match Theory, which argues for isomorphism between syntactic and prosodic structures, thus accounting for the observed non-isomorphism or mismatch in terms of phonological markedness constraints. For further elaboration and extension of Match Theory, see Bennett et al. (2016), Elfner (2012, 2013, 2015), Ito and Mester (2013), Myrberg (2013), Richards (2016), Selkirk and Lee (2015), and papers in *Phonology Vol. 32* (2015), among many others.

2.6.   Concluding remarks

This chapter has sketched the development of theories of the syntax-phonology interface. All the research questions mentioned in section 2.1 are left unresolved, and one hopes that the theoretical tools and conceptual guidelines discussed in this chapter will offer new directions for research. Interestingly, developments in syntactic theory sometimes enable new directions in the study of syntax-phonology mapping: the cyclic approach to syntax in the early days of generative grammar led to Bresnan's (1971) theory of stress assignment; the X-bar Theory in the 1980s has contributed greatly to the Standard Theories (Relation-based Theory and End-based Theory), as explicitly acknowledged by Nespor and Vogel (1986: 165) and Selkirk (1986: 373); and the phase theory in the mid-1990s to 2000s has revived cyclic approaches to syntax-phonology mapping, thereby unifying phonological and transformational cycles (Chomsky 2001: 15). On the other hand, Optimality-Theory approaches to phonology are strongly representational and often completely deny the postulation of cyclic or derivational rule application. Framed within Optimality Theory, Match Theory does not need to depend on the sequential computational processes of syntactic derivation: prosodic domains are defined on the syntactic representation (for related discussion, see Elfner 2015: fn12; Selkirk and Lee 2015: section 3). It remains to be seen whether Match Theory is incorporated into the phase theory (see Selkirk 2009, 2011 for such an attempt), or perhaps vice versa.

In section 2.4.2, we have left open the question of how to account for the mismatch between Spell-Out domains and phonological phrases (see (90) and (91)). In the next chapter, I will show, based on Dobashi's (2003) theory of phonological phrasing, that the process of linearization between Spell-Out domains resolves the mismatch in a principled way, and that cross-linguistic variations in phonological phrasing can be reduced to syntactic differences and prosodic branchingness. It will be also shown, based on Dobashi (2013), that further elaboration of linearization procedures accounts for not only phonological phrase, but also intonational phrase and prosodic word, unifying the three prosodic categories in terms of linearization, which is an essential property of the processes of externalization.

Notes

1 For these topics, see, e.g., papers in Erteschik-Shir and Rochman (2010).
2 See, e.g., Shiobara (2009, 2010) for an approach to the mismatch resolution within a left-to-right derivational framework.
3 For the effects of phonology on syntax, see, e.g., Shiobara (2011), Zec and Inkelas (1990), and Zubizarreta (1998). For information structure, see, e.g., Dehé et al. (2011), Féry and Ishihara (2016), and Frascarelli (2000), Erteschik-Shir (2007), and Kenesei and Vogel (1995), among many others.

4 For overviews of the field, see e.g., Inkelas and Zec (1995), Elordieta (2007), Kager and Zonneveld (1999), Revithiadou and Spyropoulos (2011), and Selkirk (2001, 2011), Scheer (2011), among others.

5 For other earlier approaches that are not discussed here, see Bierwisch (1966), Clements (1978), Downing (1970), Rotenberg (1978), and Selkirk (1972, 1974), among others. See also Halliday (1967).

6 Rice (1990) argues that domain juncture rules can be reanalyzed as domain span rules. See also Vogel (2009a).

7 See Selkirk and Lee (2015: 13ff.) for discussions about Kula and Bickmore's analysis.

8 One school of thought assumes that prosodic domains are defined with reference to the surface phonetic form but not the syntactic structure (e.g., Jun 1998; Beckman and Pierrehumbert 1986; Ladd 1996, among many others), but the debate over this idea is outside the scope of this book.

9 For more papers published around this time, see papers in Inkelas and Zec (1990) and the *Phonology Yearbook* 4 (guest-edited by Ellen M. Kaisse and Arnold M. Zwicky 1987), among many others.

10 An earlier proposal on prosodic organization was made by Halliday (1967).

11 See, e.g., Zec and Inkelas (1991) for critical discussion of the Clitic Group. See, e.g., Vogel (2009b) for arguments for the Clitic Group.

12 We will discuss Ewe in greater detail in Chapter 3.

13 (66) amounts to (28). I use the formulation in (66) here for ease of exposition, along with the formulation of constraints in (67).

14 The long vowel of *naampéį* in (74a) is present for reasons irrelevant to Shortening.

15 The formulation of NONREC here is different from Selkirk's (1996) (see (67d)). Truckenbrodt's NONREC has the effect of choosing (77c) over (77d) since the inner and outer phonological phrases are more similar in the former. That is, the inner and outer phonological phrases in (77c) share X_1 and XP_2 and therefore are not disjoint (in a mathematical sense, i.e., they have no elements in common), and they are nonidentical in only one respect: the outer one has an extra XP_3 as its member, violating NONREC just once. On the other hand, the inner and outer phrases in (77d) share XP_2 and so are not disjoint, but they are nonidentical in two respects. The outer one has an extra X_1 and XP_3, violating NONREC twice. Hence, (77c) defeats (77d). (77d) is ruled out in much the same way, along with an extra violation of *P-PHRASE. See Truckenbrodt (1999) for details.

16 See Revithiadou and Spyropoulos (2009) for a case study of phonological phenomena conducted under Uriagereka's proposal. See also Uriagereka (2012) for further discussion of Multiple Spell-Out. I will also elaborate on the architecture of grammar in a more recent context in Chapter 4.

17 See Chomsky (2001) for timing of the application of Spell-Out. The timing, however, is not relevant to our concern here, so I leave open when exactly Spell-Out applies.

18 See, e.g., Johnson (1991) for the movement of the object. See, e.g., Tenny (1994) for the correlation between accusative Case and aspect.

19 See Fuß (2007, 2008) for another approach to the mismatch within the phase-by-phase Spell-Out framework.

20 Following a suggestion made to them by Shigeto Kawahara.

21 See Truckenbrodt (2005) for the extension of WRAP of XPs to WRAP of clauses.

22 Selkirk (2011: 469) notes that the opposite ranking MATCH(Phrase,φ) >> BINMIN(φ,ω) accounts for the phrasing in Chimwi:ni, German and so on, where branchingness is irrelevant to phrasing.

3 Linearizations and prosodic domains

3.1. Introduction

The linear ordering of linguistic expressions is, in essence, a characteristic property of the phonological component. It is widely assumed in the minimalist literature that the ordering procedures apply to hierarchically structured but unordered expressions of language (i.e., narrow syntax) in the processes of externalization, yielding ordered expressions that are usable at the sensorimotor (SM) interface (Chomsky 1995 *et seqq.*). However, the study of prosodic phonology generally assumes that externalized expressions are not just simple strings of lexical items or segments – crucially, they are also structured in the form of prosodic hierarchy, as discussed in Chapter 2. One such recent attempt to account for the hierarchical prosodic structure is Match Theory (Selkirk 2009, 2011), which regards prosodic structure to be a reflex of syntactic structure. Although attractive and intuitively appealing, Match Theory needs to refer to the notions of "phrases (maximal projections)" and "clauses" in syntax, which are difficult, if not impossible, to define when relying on current syntactic assumptions in the minimalist program. Our task is thus to "explain" what is perceived as a phonological phrase or an intonational phrase at the interfaces, but not to use those unmotivated concepts to analyze observed phenomena. In this chapter, I will review an alternative approach to the prosodic structure that is not based on phrases and clauses but rather on linearization procedures, which are essential to externalization. I hope to construct a null theory of prosodic domains that reduces prosodic structure to indispensable linearization procedures, without recourse to specific mapping algorithms.

In section 3.2, I review the development of syntactic theory from the mid-1990s to the early 2000s, with reference to the syntax-phonology interface. In sections 3.3 and 3.4, I recapitulate Dobashi (2003), with some further elaboration: section 3.3 gives a typological survey of phonological phrasing in SVO, and section 3.4 reviews the attempt to construct a theory of phonological phrasing within the phase theory incorporating Multiple Spell-Out. I show that linear ordering of the domains of Spell-Out accounts for phonological phrasing. In sections 3.5, I discuss other prosodic categories (i.e., prosodic word and intonational phrase), in line with Dobashi (2013), and show that they are also reducible to ordering procedures: all the three prosodic categories are unified in terms of linearization. Section 3.6 concludes the chapter.

3.2.   Multiple spell-out, phase theory, and the syntax-phonology interface

In the pre-minimalist era, it was generally assumed that the grammatical architecture takes the form of the so-called Y-model (or the Extended Standard Theory [EST] model), where the computation goes from D-Structure to S-Structure and then branches to Logical Form (LF) and Phonetic Form (PF) (see Chomsky and Lasnik 1977; Chomsky 1981, 1986a):

(1)

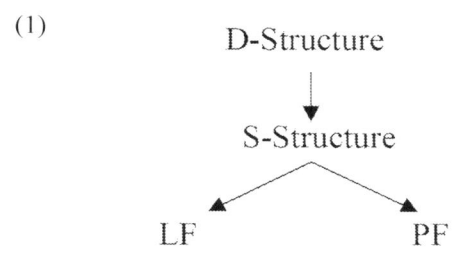

However, in the minimalist program, Chomsky (1993: 2ff.) points out that conceptually necessary linguistic levels are just two interface levels – conceptual-intentional (C-I) and articulatory-perceptual (A-P) (later renamed sensorimotor [SM] to include various modes of externalization such as sign and touch languages: see Chomsky 1998: 116 *et seq.*) – and the internal levels of S-Structure and D-Structure are eliminated from the architecture of grammar. Thus, language constructs pairs (π, λ), π and λ, which are PF and LF representations, respectively. Moreover, along with this elimination of the theory-internal linguistic levels, a new operation, called Spell-Out, is introduced, as shown in (2):

(2)   a.

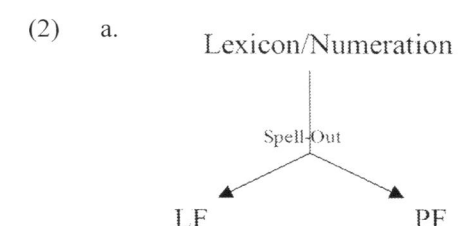

   b. Spell-Out strips away from Σ (the structure already formed) those elements relevant to π, leaving the residue Σ_L, which is mapped to λ by operations of the kind used to form Σ.

(Chomsky 1995: 229)

Chomsky (1993, 1995) assumed that Spell-Out applies to the derivation of narrow syntax just once, probably because the early stage of the minimalist program carried over the traditional Y-model, as in (1). However, as we saw in 2.4.2, subsequent rigorous minimalist investigations have led to the conclusion that a single application of Spell-Out is just a stipulation and that nothing should bar dynamic, multiple application of Spell-Out (Multiple Spell-Out), as argued by Chomsky (2000), Epstein et al. (1998), Epstein and Seely (2002), and Uriagereka (1999):

(3)

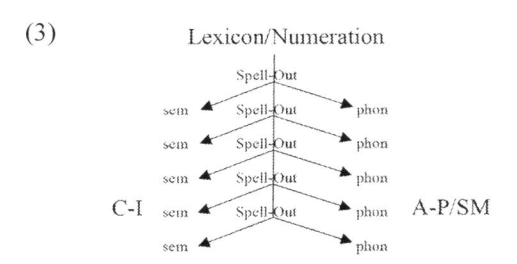

Each application of Spell-Out spells out just part of the derivation, and the structure mapped to the interface levels is not a representation of the whole sentence but its sub-piece, indicated by *sem* and *phon* in (3) (cf. Boeckx 2003/2007). As we will see below, the Multiple Spell-Out model has led to the revival of cyclic approaches to syntax-phonology mapping.

Chomsky (2000 *et seq.*) adopts a version of Multiple Spell-Out, which is incorporated into a phase theory of syntactic derivation. In this theory, the derivation proceeds cyclically, phase-by-phase, reducing computational burden to satisfy a third-factor principle of efficient computation. Specifically, Chomsky (2001: 12ff.) argues that formal features that have been licensed (valued/checked/deleted) are removed from narrow syntax when the syntactic object containing them is spelled-out and transferred to the phonological component. This allows earlier stages of the derivation to be "forgotten," reducing the computational burden. This process is formulated as the *Phase Impenetrability Condition* (PIC). For the syntactic object (6), PIC is formulated as in (7):[1]

(6) $[_{ZP}$ Z . . . $[_{HP}$ α [H YP]]], where ZP and HP are strong phases.
(7)   *Phase Impenetrability Condition*

(PIC: Chomsky 2001: 14)

The domain of H [= YP] is not accessible to operations at ZP; only H and its edge [= α] are accessible to such operations.

(7) entails that elements in YP undergo no further syntactic operations including movement: that is, they are fixed in place. Therefore, the phonological component may interpret or spell-out this domain. Then the following will hold:

(8)   Spell-Out applies to the complement of a strong phase head.

Given this, it follows that Spell-Out applies phase-by-phase, in a multiple way.

So far, we have reviewed the notions of phases and Multiple Spell-Out, which are the basis for the discussion below. Along with these considerations of the computational procedure, the theory of phrase structure has made substantial progress in the minimalist program. Kayne (1994) proposes the Linear Correspondence Axiom (LCA), which seeks to explain stipulated notions such as binarity and endocentricity in the X-bar theory in terms of the linearization of syntactic objects. Chomsky (1995) then introduces Bare Phrase Structure theory, where phrase structure is constructed derivationally by applying the structure-building operation Merge, which applies to lexical items taken from the lexicon. As a result, the phrase structure consists of only lexical items. That is, features that are not intrinsic to the lexical items may not appear in the phrase structure (Inclusiveness Condition: Chomsky 1995 *et seqq.*). Accordingly, phrasal notions such as "maximal projections" or "bar levels" are no longer primitive notions, unlike in X-bar theory (Chomsky 1970, 1986b; Jackendoff 1977), but rather are derivative notions defined on the representation.

In the context of Merge, Collins (2002) further argues that labels and projections should be eliminated from the phrase structure of syntax (for further discussions, see also Chomsky 2004, 2008, 2013; Collins 2017; Fukui 2011; Narita 2012, 2014, among others). Thus, the traditional X-bar schematic phrase structure shown in (9b) should take the form of (9a):

(9)

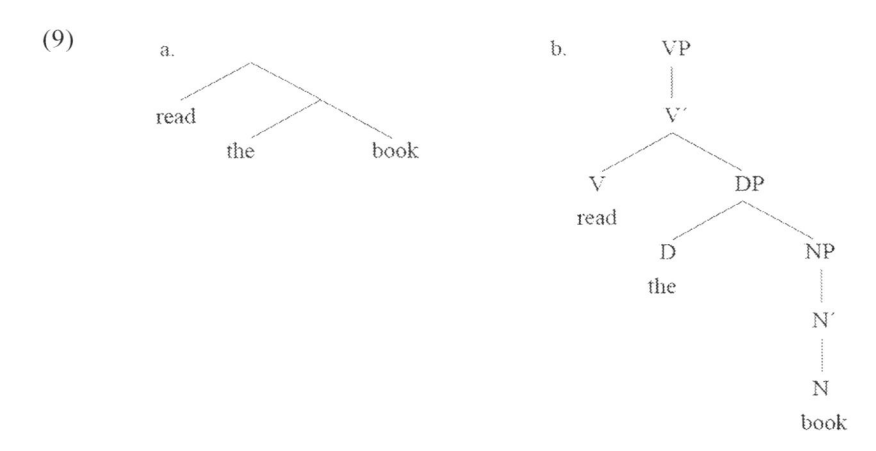

In the label-free theory, phrasal notations such as IP, VP, V′, and V are reduced to the properties of derivation and syntactic relations holding among lexical items. Under this restrictive theory of phrase structure, it is impossible to formulate a theory of grammar that refers to the labels and projections.

Given these considerations of phrase structure, let us consider the formulation of the standard theories of phonological phrasing – Relation-based Theory and End-based Theory – which we have reviewed in Chapter 2:

(10)   *Relation-based Theory:*

    a. φ domain

                                        (Nespor and Vogel 1986: 168)

The domain of φ consists of a C which contains a lexical head (X) and all Cs on its nonrecursive side up to the C that contains another head outside of the maximal projection of X.

b. φ construction

Join into an n-ary branching φ all Cs included in a string delimited by the definition of the domain of φ.

c. φ restructuring

(Nespor and Vogel 1986: 173)

A non-branching φ which is the first complement of X on its recursive side is joined into the φ that contains X.

(11)   *End-based Theory*
    a. $]_{Xmax}$ b. $_{Xmax}[$

(Selkirk 1986: 389)

Both theories (and the Optimality-Theory successors of End-based Theory, i.e., Generalized Alignment and Match Theory) make a crucial reference to projections of phrase structure by referring to maximal projections. These theories are largely successful as descriptive devices, but they are not formulable on minimalist assumptions since they refer to projections.

Collins (2002: section 4) then suggests that in a label-free theory of syntax, phonological phrasing should be accounted for in terms of Multiple Spell-Out. Specifically, he suggests that the phonological string that corresponds to a unit of Spell-Out be marked as a potential phonological phrase. In this way, phonological phrasing can be defined without recourse to maximal projections as long as Spell-Out does not refer to them. Also, it is theoretically desirable to assume that Spell-Out defines a phonological phrase since it is the only independently motivated operation that connects syntax and phonology. Then the simplest assumption about phonological phrasing would be the following, which I take to be a null hypothesis:[2]

(12)   *Null hypothesis:*
    A phonological string that is mapped to the phonological component corresponds to a phonological phrase.

Given these considerations of phases, Multiple Spell-Out, and label-free phrase structure, let us consider the derivation of a simple transitive sentence in English. Let us assume it has the following structure (Chomsky 2000 *et seq.*):

(13) $[_{CP} C [_{TP} Subj\ T [_{v*P}\ t_{Subj}\ V\text{-}v^* [_{VP}\ t_V\ Obj\ ]]]]$

Note that the labels here are just for expository purposes. Obj stays in situ, Subj is base-generated in Spec-v*P and moves to Spec-TP, V adjoins to v*, and t indicates a copy of the moved element. If we assume that CP and v*P are strong phases, Spell-Out first applies to the complement of v*P, namely VP, in the bottom-up derivation. Since copies do not have any phonological content, only the features of Obj are transferred to the phonological component. Given (12), Obj is expected to correspond to a phonological phrase.

(14)   (Obj)$_\varphi$

As the derivation continues, Spell-Out applies to the complement of the strong CP phase. Because the phonological features of Obj have already been transferred/ spelled-out, those of Subj, T (if any), and V-v* are spelled-out and sent to the phonological component. Then, (12) will define the following phonological phrase:

(15)   (Subj T V)$_\varphi$

Combining (14) and (15), the phase theory would predict the following phonological phrasing for a transitive construction:

(16)   (Subj T V)$_\varphi$ (Obj)$_\varphi$

Note that this phrasing differs from that predicted by the standard theories (see Chapter 2). For the phrase structure in (17), which the standard theories usually adopt, Nespor and Vogel's (1986) Relation-based theory predicts the phrasing in (18), and the right-XP and left-XP end-settings in Selkirk's (1986) End-based theory predict the phrasings in (19a) and (19b), respectively:

(17)   [$_{IP}$ [$_{NP}$ Subj] Infl [$_{VP}$ V [$_{NP}$ Obj]]]
(18)   Relation-based Theory:
     a. (Subj)$_\varphi$ (Infl V)$_\varphi$ (Obj)$_\varphi$
     b. (Subj)$_\varphi$ (Infl V Obj)$_\varphi$ if Obj is non-branching

(19)   End-based Theory
     a. (Subj)$_\varphi$ (Infl V Obj)$_\varphi$ Right-XP end-setting
     b. (Subj Infl)$_\varphi$ (V)$_\varphi$ (Obj)$_\varphi$ Light-XP end-setting

A critical difference is that Subj is predicted to be phrased together with V in phase theory, while they are always phrased separately in the standard theories.

Given these predictions, Dobashi (2003) attempted a typological survey of phonological phrasing of subject, verb, and object in SVO languages, which was mainly based on previous studies conducted within various theoretical frameworks. The next section reviews this survey.

3.3.   Phonological phrases: cross-linguistic variation

Studies of phonological phrasing have analyzed diverse constructions in multiple languages, and various proposals for the formation of phonological phrases have been made for particular languages, often without referring to other languages.

But Nespor and Vogel (1986) and Selkirk (1986, *et seq.*) seek to make cross-linguistic analyses of phonological phrasing, thereby laying foundations of parametric approaches to phonological phrasing. However, to gain an accurate theoretical understanding of the architecture of the syntax-phonology relation, cross-linguistic patterns of phonological phrasing should be investigated systematically, with more current syntactic assumptions (see Seidl 2001 for a related discussion). Dobashi (2003) investigates cross-linguistic patterns of phonological phrasing of subject, verb, and object in SVO languages, examining simple transitive and intransitive sentences in particular. These sentences were chosen for this investigation because CP and/or v*P phases are involved, and the phase-hood of these categories is less (or perhaps the least) controversial than that of DP and other categories. I show that there are basically two patterns of phrasing, each of which has two variations:

(20) $(S)_\varphi$ $(V)_\varphi$ $(O)_\varphi$
(21) a. $(S)_\varphi$ $(V)_\varphi$ $(O)_\varphi$
      b. $(S)_\varphi$ $(V$ $O)_\varphi$ if O is non-branching.
(22) $(S)_\varphi$ $(V$ $O)_\varphi$
(23) a. $(S)_\varphi$ $(V$ $O)_\varphi$
      b. $(S$ V $O)_\varphi$ if S is non-branching.

The basic phrasing is $(S)_\varphi$ $(V)_\varphi$ $(O)_\varphi$ as in (20) and (21) or $(S)_\varphi$ $(V$ $O)_\varphi$ as in (22) and (23). (20)- and (22)-type languages disallow modification of these basic phrasings. By contrast, (21)- and (23)-type languages allow modification, depending on the prosodic weight or branchingness (as clarified below). Thus, the basic phrasing in (21)-type languages is (21a), and V and O can be phrased together if O is prosodically non-branching as in (21b); the basic phrasing in (23)-type languages is (23a), and S can be incorporated into a subsequent phrase if it is prosodically non-branching as in (23b).

In what follows, I will recapitulate Dobashi's (2003) survey of the typology in (20)-(23), which will serve as a basis for theoretical discussions in section 3.4.

3.3.1   *Phonological phrasing in Aŋlɔ Ewe and French*

In this section, I examine phonological phrasings in the Aŋlɔ dialect of Ewe and colloquial French. I show that the phonological phrasing in these languages exhibits a pattern in which S, V, and O are phrased separately (as in (20)).

Clements (1978) discusses the phonological phrasing in the Aŋlɔ dialect of Ewe. He shows that mid tone (M) raising applies within a phonological phrase, as we have briefly discussed in Chapter 2. *M raising* is formulated as follows:

(24)   M-Raising: M → R/H __ H

An M tone is raised to an extra-high tone (R) if it is surrounded by H tones. Thus, in (25) the underlying form in (25a) is realized as in (25b):

(25) /àtyí mēgbé/ → [àtyǐ mḛ́gbé]
     tree behind
     'behind a tree'

                                      (Clements 1978: 24–25)

Note that the environment for M raising here is met across a word boundary. The H that precedes M is in the preceding word. Two other rules apply in this example: *R Spread* and *Cadence* (Clements 1978: 25, 49). R Spread spreads an R tone both rightward and leftward until M or L, and Cadence changes an R-R sequence in the domain-final position to R-H. Clements assumes that these rules apply in the following order.

(26) àtyí mēgbé → apply M Raising →
     àtyí mḛ́gbé → apply R Spread →
     àtyǐ mḛ́gbḛ̌ → apply Cadence →
     àtyǐ mḛ́gbé

                                        (Clements 1978: 25)

Given these, let us first see whether the M Raising applies between the subject and the element that follows it. Consider the following:

(27) mí ā-dzó
     we T-leave
     'we will leave'

                                        (Clements 1978: 62)

Here, the M tone is surrounded by H tones. If *mí* and *ā-dzó* belonged to the same phonological phrase, the M would be raised to the extra-high R. However, it is not raised, indicating that the M tone does not satisfy the environment in (24). That is, there is a phonological phrase boundary between the subject and the tense morpheme on the verb, and the environment in (24) is not met within the domain or phonological phrase. Therefore, the subject is not phonologically phrased with the verb.

Let us next consider whether the object is phrased with the preceding verb. Consider (28):

(28) a. kpɔ́ ānyí
        see bee
        'saw a bee'
    b. * kpɔ̌ ǎnyí

                                          (Clements 1978: 24–25)

If *kpɔ* and *ānyí* belong to the same phonological phrase, they would satisfy the environment in (24) since the M is surrounded by Hs; but M is not raised in (28a). As (28b) shows, if M is raised, the result is unacceptable. Therefore, there is a phonological phrase boundary between the verb and the object.

To summarize, the phonological phrasing in Ewe is as follows:

(29) $(S)_\varphi$ $(V)_\varphi$ $(O)_\varphi$

Let us next consider French. Nespor and Vogel (1986: 179) argue that in colloquial French, "Liaison applies in a purely phonological environment." (See Selkirk 1974 for a discussion of Liaison in elevated speech.) That is, Liaison in colloquial speech reflects the basic phonological phrasing in French. Liaison is a phenomenon where the word final-consonant is pronounced if it is followed by the word that begins with a vowel. Let us consider (30):

(30)   a. les enfants
            [lezãfã]
            'the children'
        b. les filles
            [le fij]
            'the girls'

(Selkirk 1984: 333)

In (30a), the determiner *les* ends with a consonant and is followed by a vowel, and the consonant is pronounced. In (30b), the same determiner precedes a word with an initial consonant, and the final consonant of the determiner *les* is not pronounced.

Given these, let us consider the following examples. Here "/" indicates that Liaison is blocked:

(31)   a. Les immigrés/   envoyaient / des lettres /   à leurs familles.
            The immigrants sent   . INDEF.letters   to their families
            'The immigrants were sending letters to their families.'

(Selkirk 1974: 580)

        b. les enfants accouraient
            'The children ran up.'
            i.   [lezãfã akurɛ]
            ii.   * [lezãfãzakurɛ]

(Selkirk 1984: 333)

Here, the verb *envoyait* 'sent' ends with a consonant, and the object *un paquet* 'INDEF.letters' begins with a vowel. However, Liaison does not apply here, indicating that a phonological phrase boundary exists between the verb and the object.

To summarize, the phonological phrasing in colloquial French is as follows:

(32) $(S)_\varphi$ $(V)_\varphi$ $(O)_\varphi$

This is the same pattern seen in Ewe.

3.3.2 *Italian*

In this section, I examine phonological phrasing in Italian. According to Nespor and Vogel (1986: 38), *Raddoppiamento Sintattico* is observed in central and southern varieties of Italian.[3] It is a phonological rule which applies between words within a phonological phrase. In a sequence of word$_1$ word$_2$, the initial consonant of word$_2$ is lengthened (i) if word$_1$ ends in a vowel with the main stress of the word and (ii) if the initial consonant of word$_2$ is followed by a non-nasal sonorant. Thus, in (33), the initial consonant of *banana* 'banana' is lengthened because the preceding word *metá* 'half' ends in a vowel with the main stress and because the initial consonant *b* of *banana* is followed by a vowel:

(33)   La scimmia aveva appena mangiato metá [b:]anana.
       the monkey had just eat.PP half banana
       'The monkey had just eaten half a banana.'

(Nespor and Vogel 1986: 38)

However, even if the above conditions are met, Raddoppiamento Sintattico does not always apply:

(34)   La volpe ne aveva mangiato metá [p]rima di addormentarsi.
       the fox of.it had eat.PP half before of go.to.sleep
       'The fox had eaten half of it before falling asleep.'

(Nespor and Vogel 1986: 38)

Here, *prima* 'before' begins with a consonant *p* followed by a non-nasal sonorant *r* and is preceded by *metá* 'half,' which ends in a stressed vowel, but *p* of *prima* is not lengthened. Nespor and Vogel argue that this is because of the presence of a phonological phrase boundary and propose the following formalization of the rule (adapted from Nespor and Vogel 1986: 170, see also Frascarelli 2000: 20):

(35)   Raddoppiamento Sintattico
       C $\rightarrow$ [+long]/[. . . [. . . V]$_\omega$ [___ [+son, -nas] . . .]$_\omega$ . . .]$_\varphi$
       (where the vowel V bears the main stress of the word)

Given (35), let us consider (36):

(36)   a. Papá   mangia.
          daddy   eat.3SG
          $(Papá)_\varphi$ $(mangia)_\varphi$
          'Daddy is eating.'

    b. La veritá   vince.
      the truth   win.3sg
      (La veritá)$_\varphi$ (vince)$_\varphi$
      'The truth wins.'

    c. La solidarietá   cresce.
      the solidarity   grow.3sg
      (The solidarietá)$_\varphi$ (cresce)$_\varphi$
      'Solidarity is increasing.'

    d. La cecitá   puó   essere guarita.
      the blindness can.3sg be   cure.pp
      (La ceritá)$_\varphi$ (puó essere guarita)$_\varphi$
      'Blindness can be cured.'

In all these examples, the subject ends in a stressed vowel, and the following word (verb or auxiliary verb) starts with a consonant followed by a non-nasal sonorant. However, Raddoppiamento Sintattico fails to apply, indicating that there is a phonological phrase boundary between the subject and verb or auxiliary verb.

    Consider the following examples:

(37) a. Porterá   due   tigri fuori   dalla   gabbia.
         take.fut.3sg two   tigers outside from.the cage
         'He will take two tigers out of the cage.'

      b. Vaccineró   tutte le scimmie entro   due giorni.
         vaccinate.fut.1sg all the monkeys within two days
         'I will vaccinate all the monkeys within two days.'

      c. Venderá   questo leopardo in dicembre.
         sell.fut.3sg   this   leopard   in December
         'He will sell this leopard in December.'

                                 (Nespor and Vogel 1986: 173)

Here, the verbs end in a vowel that bears a main stress of the word, and the object phrases begin with a consonant followed by a non-nasal sonorant, so Raddoppiamento Sintattico would apply if the verb and the object belonged to the same phonological phrase. However, according to Nespor and Vogel (1986: 172–173), Raddoppiamento Sintattico does not apply to the initial consonants *d-* of *due*, *t-* of *tutte*, and *q-* of *questo* in (37a), (37b), and (37c), respectively, indicating that there is a phonological phrase boundary between the verb and object.

    If the object is non-branching or consists of one word, Raddoppiamento Sintattico applies optionally to the initial consonant of the object:

(38) Se prenderá   qualcosa   prenderá   tordi.
      if catch.fut.3sg something catch.fut.3sg thrushes

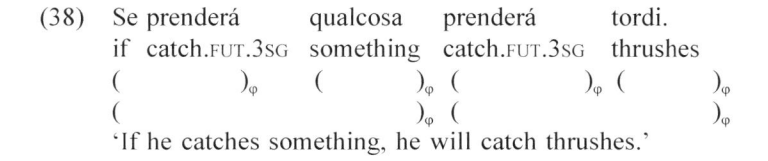

      'If he catches something, he will catch thrushes.'

Here, *q-* of *qualcosa* and *t-* of *tordi* may be lengthened by Raddoppiamento Sintattico.

To summarize, the subject is never phrased with the verb, but the object is sometimes phrased with the verb if it is non-branching:

(39)   a. (S)$_\varphi$ (V)$_\varphi$ (O)$_\varphi$
      b. (S)$_\varphi$ (V   O)$_\varphi$ if O is non-branching

Since the phrasing in (39b) is optional and allowed only if the object is non-branching, I assume, following Nespor and Vogel (1986: 173), that (39b) results from the restructuring of (39a).[4] That is, the basic phrasing is (39a), and the phonological phrase containing a non-branching object, restructures into the preceding phonological phrase, thus resulting in a phonological phrase containing the verb and object. I will return to restructuring in section 3.4.5.

3.3.3   *Kimatuumbi*

In this section, I discuss the phrasing pattern in which the object is always phrased with the verb. Odden (1987, 1990, 1996) shows that a long vowel of a word is shortened (*Shortening*) if the word occupies a non-final position in a phonological phrase in Kimatuumbi.[5] Thus, if there is no Shortening, the word containing the long vowel is in the phonological phrase-final position (see Cowper and Rice 1987; Truckenbrodt 1995, 1999 for discussion):

(40)   a. kịkóloombe
         'cleaning shell'
      b. kịkólombe chaángu
         'my cleaning shell'

(Odden 1990: 260)

(40a) shows that the word for 'cleaning shell' has a long vowel *-oo-* in isolation. In (40b), the long vowel of *kịkóloombe* is shortened because of the presence of the following word. If we assume that *kịkólombe* and *chaángu* form a single phonological phrase, the shortening of the vowel is accounted for since *kịkólombe* occupies a non-final position in the phonological phrase.

Now, let us consider the following example:

(41)   kịkóloombe   shaapúwaanịịke
      shell   broke
      'The shell broke.'

(Odden 1990: 260)

Here, *kịkóloombe* 'shell' is a subject preceding the verb, and the long vowel *-oo-* is not shortened, indicating that there is a phonological phrase boundary between the subject and verb.

Kimatuumbi has another phonological rule, *Phrasal Tone Insertion*, which is sensitive to phonological phrasing (Odden 1987, 1990, 1996).[6] Phrasal Tone Insertion inserts a floating H tone between phonological phrases, and the H tone docks on to the last syllable of the preceding word (Odden 1990: 262). Consider the following:

(42)   a. Mambóondo
           'Mamboondo'
       b. Mamboondó aawįįle.
           'Mamboondo died.'

(Odden 1987: 21, 1990: 262)

(43)   a. kįyógoyo
           'bird (type)'

(Odden 1987: 21, 1990: 262)

       b. kįyógoyó chaatįtuumbuká.
           'The bird has fallen.'

(44)   a. mpųųnga
           'rice'
       b. mpųųngá waabóį.
           'The rice has rotted.'

(Odden 1987: 21)

The (a)-examples in (42)-(44) show that the final vowels of *Mambóondo*, *kįyógoyo*, and *mpųųnga* are tone-less in isolation. In the (b)-examples, they occupy the subject position and the final vowels receive an H tone, indicating that there is a phonological phrase boundary between the subject and verb. The same is true in the embedded clause:

(45)   ngwasa   Mamboondó aatįtuumbuká.
       I-think   Mamboondo he-fell
       'I think that Mamboondo fell.'

(Odden 1990: 263)

Here, *Mamboondo* is the subject of the embedded clause and receives an H tone on the final vowel.

The data for Shortening and Phrasal Tone Insertion indicate that the subject is not phrased with the verb in Kimatuumbi.

Let us next consider the object:[7]

(46)   a. naa-kį-twéetį.
           I-it-took
           'I took it.'
       b. naa-kį-twétį kįkóloombe.
           I-it-took   shell
           'I took a cleaning shell.'

(Odden 1987: 16 (11))

(47) a. naa-ká-laangịte.
          I-it-fried
          'I fried'
      b. naa-ká-langịte chóolyá.
          I-it-took   food
          'I fried food.'

(Odden 1987: 16 (11))

(46a) and (47a) show that these verbs contain a long vowel in isolation. (46b) and (47b) show that the vowels are shortened, indicating that there is no phonological phrase boundary after the verb: the verb and object are phrased together in Kimatuumbi.

Similarly, Shortening also applies to the verb in the embedded clause:

(48) naansájdị [mwaana [ywáakalangịtée ñáma]ₛ]ₙₚ
      I-him-help child   REL-fried   meat
      'I'll help the child who fried the meat.'

(Odden 1987: 17)

Here,[8] -*aa*- of *kálaangite* 'fried' is shortened (cf. (47a)), indicating that there is no phonological phrase boundary between the verb and object in the embedded clause.

Let us now consider whether Phrasal Tone Insertion applies between the verb and object:

(49) tụtanga ywaáwịịlé
      'We know the one who died.'

(Odden 1996: 239)

(50) aatwétịị   mpụụngá noobúuka.
      he-took   rice   and-left
      'He took rice and then left.'

(Odden 1996: 240)

Here, Phrasal Tone Insertion does not apply to the verbs *tụtanga* and *aatwétịị*. The final vowel of these verbs does not get an H tone. Therefore, there is no phonological phrase boundary between the verb and the object.

Odden (1996: 233–234) discusses another phonological rule in Kimatuumbi, *Perfect Tone Loss*. This rule deletes an H tone on the initial mora of the stem of the recent past perfective verb if something follows it within the VP.

(51) a. akáatịte.
          'He cut.'
      b. akatịte kaámba.
          'He cut rope.'

(Odden 1996: 233)

(51a) shows that the initial mora of the verb stem bears an H tone, and (51b) shows that the H tone is deleted because of the presence of the object. Note that Shortening also applies in (51b).

Perfect Tone Loss does not apply in the following examples. The syntactic phrasing is Odden's (1996: 234):

(52) a. [$_{NP}$ [$_S$ [$_{VP}$ ywaábakíye [$_S$ pánga [$_{VP}$ agakáatịté   ]]]]]   awíile.
                    REL-tell-me   that   he-them-cut   he-died
          'The one who told me that he cut them died.'
      b. *ywaábakíye   pánga   agakaatịté   awíile.

(53) a. naankúmbwa [$_{NP}$ [$_S$ [$_{VP}$ ywaámbakíye [$_{VP}$ ugóonjịte]]]]   maláau.
          I'll beat   REL-tell   you-sleep   tomorrow
          'Tomorrow I'll beat the one who told me you were sleeping.'
      b. *naankúmbwa ywaámbakíye ugoonjịte maláau.

The recent past perfective verbs *agakáatịté* 'he-them-cut' in (52a) and *ugóonjịte* 'you-sleep' in (53a) retain their H tones on their first mora of the stem even though they are followed by a word. Those high tones cannot be deleted, as in (52b) and (53b). These examples show that Perfect Tone Loss does not apply because of the mere presence of a word after the verb. Rather, Perfect Tone Loss is sensitive to the presence of a word within a local domain, i.e., the phonological phrase. Therefore, (51b) shows that the verb and object belong to a single phonological phrase.

We have seen that the object is always phrased with the verb in Kimatuumbi. However, all the data I have discussed so far have a non-branching object. Odden does not explicitly discuss the effect of branchingness on phonological phrasing. Thus, it is not clear whether non-branchingness is a requirement for inclusion in a larger phonological phrase in Kimatuumbi, as it is in Italian. However, the phrasing of the verb with the (non-branching) object is not optional, unlike in Italian. Second, although Odden does not discuss branchingness, his data include the following, which indicates that even branching objects are phrased with the verb:[9]

(54) a. naamwéenị % kaapangá kaásị.
          'I saw him while he worked.'

                                                    (Odden 1996: 262)

      b. naammwénii nchéngowe Maliíya.
          'I saw Mary's husband.'

                                                    (Odden 1996: 223)

Here, the relevant phonological rule is Shortening. In (54a), "%" indicates an intonational phrase boundary. Since the intonational phrase properly contains a phonological phrase, the verb *naamwéenị* is in the phonological phrase-final position as well as the intonational phrase-final position in (54a), and the long vowel *-ée-* retains its length. In (54b), which contains the same verb, the object *nchéengo* 'husband' accompanies a possessor *Maliíya* 'Mary's.'[10] If we assume that they form a (syntactic) constituent, (54b) shows that even a branching object triggers Shortening of the long vowel of the verb. That is, a branching object is phonologically phrased with the verb. Note that *nchéngowe* and *Maliíya* also form a phonological phrase, since the long vowel of *nchéengo* 'husband' is shortened. That is, *nchéngowe* is not in a phonological phrase-final position.

Third, a branching benefactive argument in applicative constructions is phrased with the verb (cf. (47)):

(55) a. naan-kálaangjjle.
          'I fried for him.'
      b. naan-kálangjle Mambóondo.
          'I fried for Mamboondo.'
      c. naan-kálangjle ywaápalá kálaanga.
          'I fried for the one who wanted to fry.'

                                                    (Odden 1996: 225)

(55a) shows that the verb has a long vowel *-aa-* in isolation. (55b) shows that the (non-branching) benefactive argument *Mambóondo* triggers Shortening on the verb. Thus, the verb and the object form a phonological phrase in which the verb occupies a non-final position. (55c) shows that the branching benefactive phrase *ywaápalá kálaanga* 'the one who wanted to fry' also triggers Shortening on the verb. Therefore, the branching benefactive argument is phonologically phrased with the verb.

Given these considerations, I conclude that the object, whether branching or not, is always phrased with the verb in Kimatuumbi.

To summarize, Kimatuumbi shows the following phonological phrasing pattern:

(56) $(S)_\varphi$ $(V\ O)_\varphi$

3.3.4 *Phonological phrasing in Kinyambo and Chichewa*

Bickmore (1989, 1990) shows that Kinyambo has a phonological rule that is sensitive to phonological phrasing.[11] The rule, *High Deletion*, is formulated in (57).

(57) High Deletion
          $H \rightarrow \emptyset /[\ldots [\ldots \underline{\quad} \ldots]_{\omega1} [\ldots H \ldots]_{\omega2} \ldots]_\varphi$
      (ω = word, φ = phonological phrase)

                                                    (Bickmore 1990: 9)

The H tone in a word $\omega1$ is deleted if there is another word $\omega2$ containing H after $\omega1$ within a phonological phrase. Application of the rule is illustrated in (58):

(58) a. $[\ [\ \text{o-mu-káma}\ ]_{\omega1}\ [\ \text{mu-kázi}\ ]_{\omega2} \ldots]_\varphi$
                  Chief   old
          'the old chief'

                                                    (Bickmore 1990: 9)

      b. o-mu-kama mu-kázi

(58a) shows the underlying form where both *o-mu-káma* 'chief' and *mu-kázi* 'old' have an H tone. (58b) shows the surface form where the H tone of *o-mu-káma* 'chief' is deleted since *mu-kázi* 'old' has an H tone.

Consider the following examples:

(59)   a. abakózi
           'workers'
      b. bákajúna
           'they help'
      c. abakozi bákajúna.
           'The workers helped.'

(Bickmore 1990: 11)

(60)   a. omukáma
           'chief'
      b. nejákwiija
           'will come'
      c. omukama nejákwiija.
           'The chief will come.'

(Bickmore 1990: 11)

(59a) and (59b) show the words in isolation. Both words have an H tone. (59c) shows that the H tone of *abakózi* 'workers,' which is a subject, is deleted because of the following verb. (60) makes the same point. These examples show that the subject and the verb are phonologically phrased together in Kinyambo:

(61)   (S V)$_\varphi$

However, if the subject is branching, i.e., if it has two (or more) words in it, then the subject is not phrased with the verb:

(62)   abakozi bakúru bákajúna.
        workers mature they-helped
        'The mature workers helped.'

(Bickmore 1990: 14)

Here, the H tone of *abakózi* 'workers' is deleted, but that of *bakúru* 'mature' is not, indicating that there is a phonological phrase boundary after the subject phrase, but no boundary between *abakozi* and *bakúru* within the subject:

(63)   (abakozi bakúru)$_\varphi$ (bákajúna)$_\varphi$
        workers mature   they-helped

Given this, I conclude that the subject is phrased with the verb if it is non-branching in Kinaymbo.

(64)   a. (S)$_\varphi$ (V)$_\varphi$
      b. (S   V)$_\varphi$ if the subject is non-branching.

Note that the branchingness of the verb is irrelevant here – in both cases, the verb is non-branching. Therefore, the difference in phrasing in (64) is solely due to the branchingness of the subject.

Consider the object:

(65)   a. okubón
         see
      b. ómuntu
         person
      c. okubon' ómuntu
         'to see the person'

(Bickmore 1989: 139)

      d. *okubwón' omuntu

(65a) and (65b) show the underlying forms of the words. (65c) shows that High Deletion deletes the H tone of the verb because of the presence of the non-branching object.[12] If the H tone is not deleted, as in (65d), the result is unacceptable. Therefore, the non-branching object is phonologically phrased with the verb.

Let us next consider the branching object. The following example has a branching Indirect Object in the double-object construction:

(66)   a. Nejákwórecha
         'he will show'
      b. omukáma
         'chief'
      c. abakózi
         'workers'
      d. émbwa
         'dog'
      e. nejákworech   ómukama w'ábakózi émbwa.
         he-will-show   chief   of workers dog
         'He will show the chief of the workers the dog.'

(Bickmore 1990: 15)

(66a-d) show the words in isolation. (66e)[13] shows that the H on the verb is deleted by High Deletion, because of the presence of the following branching object, indicating that there is no phonological phrase boundary between the verb and branching object.[14]

I therefore conclude that the object is phonologically phrased with the verb, irrespective of the branchingness of the object.

To sum up, Kinyambo shows the following phonological phrasing:

(67)   a.   (S)$_\varphi$ (V O)$_\varphi$
         b.   (S   V O)$_\varphi$ if the subject is non-branching

   In their analysis of Chichewa, Bresnan and Mchombo (1987) and Kanerva (1990) show that two phonological rules are sensitive to phonological phrase boundaries. *Penultimate Lengthening* lengthens the vowel in the penultimate syllable of each phonological phrase; *Tone Retraction* shifts the tone of the final syllable in the phonological phrase onto the second mora of the long penultimate syllable. Let us first consider the phrasing of the subject and verb:

(68)   a.   mwaná   'child' [lexical form]
         b.   njovu   'elephant' [lexical form]
         c.   (Mwaána)$_\varphi$ (anagoona)$_\varphi$
               child   SM-slept
               'The child slept.'
         d.   (Mwaná anagoona)$_\varphi$
               child   SM-slept
               'The child slept.'
         e.   (Mwaná   wa   njoovu)$_\varphi$ (anagoona)$_\varphi$
               child   of   elephant   SM-slept
               'The child of an elephant slept.'
                                                  (Sam Mchombo: personal communication)

(68a) and (68b) show lexical forms of the words. In (68c) the (non-branching) subject undergoes Penultimate Lengthening and Tone Retraction: The penultimate vowel is lengthened and the H tone on the final syllable is shifted, indicating that a phonological phrase boundary immediately follows the subject. However, as (68d) shows, application of these rules to the non-branching subject is optional. They do not need to apply, and the subject can retain the lexical form. In contrast, these rules always apply if the subject is branching, as shown in (68e). Since *njovu* 'elephant' lacks a lexical H tone, the only relevant rule here is Penultimate Lengthening. The penultimate vowel is lengthened, showing that a boundary immediately follows the subject.
   Let us next consider the phrasing of the verb and object:

(69)   a.   (Mwaána)$_\varphi$ (anaményá   nyuúmba)$_\varphi$
               Child   SM-hit   house
               'The child hit the house'
         b.   (Mwaána)$_\varphi$ (anaményá   nyumbá   ya bwiíno)$_\varphi$
               child   SM-hit   house   of good
               'The child hit the good house.'
                                                  (Sam Mchombo: personal communication)

The object in (69a) is non-branching, while that in (69b) is branching. In both cases, the verb undergoes neither Penultimate Lengthening nor Tone Retraction. If it had, the verb would assume the form *anaméenya*, as shown by Kanerva (1990: 152). So, the examples in (69) show that the object is always phrased with the verb, whether it is branching or not.

The phrasing pattern of S, V, and O in Chichewa is identical to that in Kimatuumbi, as summarized below:

(70)   a. (S)$_\varphi$ (V)$_\varphi$
       b. (S   V)$_\varphi$ if the subject is non-branching
       c. (V   O)$_\varphi$

3.3.5   *Variation in phonological phrasing of SVO languages*

So far, I have discussed the following phonological phrasing patterns:

(71)   (S)$_\varphi$ (V)$_\varphi$ (O)$_\varphi$ Aŋlɔ Ewe, French
(72)   a. (S)$_\varphi$ (V)$_\varphi$ (O)$_\varphi$ Italian
       b. (S)$_\varphi$ (V   O)$_\varphi$ if O is non-branching.
(73)   (S)$_\varphi$ (V   O)$_\varphi$ Kimatuumbi
(74)   a. (S)$_\varphi$ (V   O)$_\varphi$ Kinyambo, Chichewa
       b. (S   V   O)$_\varphi$ if S is non-branching.

Let us consider if the standard theories reviewed in Chapter 2 can account straightforwardly for these patterns. Phonological phrase formation in Nespor and Vogel's (1986) Relation-based Theory is as follows:

(75)   Phonological Phrase Formation

                                                (Nespor and Vogel 1986: 168)

       a. φ domain
           The domain of φ consists of a *C* which contains a lexical head (X) and all *C*s on its nonrecursive side up to the *C* that contains another head outside of the maximal projection of X.
       b. φ construction
           Join into an n-ary branching φ all *C*s included in a string delimited by the definition of the domain of φ.

The basic phrase structure they assume (at the time) is shown below:

(76)   [$_{IP}$ [$_{NP}$ Subj]   Infl [$_{VP}$ V   [$_{NP}$ Obj]]]

When applied to (76), (75) yields the following phonological phrasing:

(77)   (Subj)$_\varphi$ (V)$_\varphi$ (Obj)$_\varphi$

This accounts for (71) and (72a). Moreover, their optional φ restructuring rule, described below, accounts for the phrasing in (72b):

(78)   φ restructuring

(Nespor and Vogel 1986: 173)

> A non-branching φ which is the first complement of X on its recursive side is joined into the φ that contains X.

If this rule is extended so that it always applies whether the complement is branching or not, as Nespor and Vogel (1986: 182) indeed argue, then it accounts for the phrasing in (73). However, since the restructuring rule mentions the complement, it seems to fail to account for (74), where the non-branching subject undergoes restructuring.

In Selkirk's (1986) End-based Theory, the right/left edge of a maximal projection XP defines the right/left edge of a phonological phrase. The choice of a right or left edge yields the following respective phonological phrasings from the syntactic structure (76):

(79)   a. Right: $(Subj)_\varphi$ (V   Obj $)_\varphi$
      b. Left: $(Subj)_\varphi$ (V $)_\varphi$ (Obj $)_\varphi$

(79a) straightforwardly accounts for (73). If the branchingness parameter is introduced so that the right/left edge of a branching XP is referred to in deriving phonological phrases (Bickmore 1990; Cowper and Rice 1987; see Chapter 2), the choice of the right edge accounts for (74), since the right edge of the non-branching subject is ignored when phonological phrases are defined. In a discussion of Ewe data in which the subject, verb, and object are all phrased separately, Selkirk (1986: 391) argues that the left-XP end-setting accounts for (71). Thus, the syntactic structure in (76) indicates that the left edges of the subject NP, VP, and object NP all correspond to the left edges of phonological phrases, as in (71). We would thus expect that the left-XP end-setting accounts for the phrasing in (72a) and that the branchingness parameter addresses (72b). However, Nespor and Vogel (1986: 167) show that Raddoppiamento Sintattico applies between the auxiliary and verb in Italian, as the following example shows (here "≈" indicates the application of Raddoppiamento Sintattico; see Chapter 2 for related discussion):

(80)   Avrá ≈   trovato il   pescecane.
      has.FUT found   the   shark
      'He must have found the shark.'

On the assumption that the auxiliary occupies the position of Infl, which is outside of the VP, the left-XP end-setting would derive the phonological phrasing in (81b) from the syntactic structure in (81a):

(81)   a. $[_{IP} [_{NP}$ Subj] $Infl_{AUX}$ $[_{VP}$ V $[_{NP}$ Obj]]]
      b.   (Subj $Infl_{AUX})_\varphi$ (V $)_\varphi$ (Obj $)_\varphi$

Here, the auxiliary (Infl) and verb are predicted to be phrased separately, and Raddoppiamento Sintattico would not apply between them. So, the left-end setting fails to account for (80), while the right-end setting fails to account for basic phrasing in Italian (72a), where the verb and object are phrased separately.

Viewed cross-linguistically, both standard theories have empirical shortcomings. Then, what about phase theory? As discussed above, (83) is predicted for the phrase structure shown in (82):

(82) $[_{CP}$ C $[_{TP}$ Subj T $[_{v*P}$ t_{Subj} V-v* $[_{VP}$ t_V Obj $]]]]$
(83) (Subj T V-v*)$_{\varphi}$ (Obj)$_{\varphi}$

It appears that phase theory yields the least correct prediction. Subj is phrased with T/V, and V and Obj are always phrased separately. As we will see in the next section, however, phase theory yields better predictions if we consider the linearization process that applies between the domains of cyclic Spell-Out.

3.4. Phonological phrasing and phase theory

In a previous section describing prior studies, I offered a typological survey of phonological phrasing of subject, verb, and object in SVO languages. If we ignore restructuring induced by a non-branching subject and object, the basic phonological phrasing seems to be one of the following:

(84) a. (S)$_{\varphi}$ (V   O)$_{\varphi}$ [Kimatuumbi, Kinyambo, Chichewa]
      b. (S)$_{\varphi}$ (V)$_{\varphi}$ (O)$_{\varphi}$ [Ewe, English, Italian, French]

(84a) is the phrasing predicted by Nespor and Vogel's (1986) mechanism, while (84b) is predicted by the right-XP end-setting of Selkirk (1986). What accounts for this difference? Below, I will show that phase theory incorporating Multiple Spell-Out, along with the independently motivated mechanism of linearization, straightforwardly accounts for (84a) and (84b).

3.4.1 *The assembly problem and assembly process*

Let us now carefully consider how Multiple Spell-Out works. Recall that the syntactic structure of a simple transitive sentence, shown in (82), is:

(85) $[_{CP}$ C $[_{TP}$ Subj T $[_{v*P}$ t_{Subj} V-v* $[_{VP}$ t_V Obj $]]]]$

I assume that Spell-Out defines a linear order among all terminal elements in syntax, with reference to the syntactic information such as asymmetric c-command, in line with Kayne (1994). On the basis of the linear order defined in this way, the phonological features are transferred to the phonological component, phase-by-phase. Thus, when the bottom-up derivation reaches v*P phase in (85),[15] Spell-Out applies to the sister of v*, thus defining the linear order between the copy of V (t_V) and Obj, as in (86):

(86)   Spell-Out (Sister of v*) $\rightarrow$ Linear Order: t_V < Obj

Here "<" indicates precedence. Along with the null hypothesis (12), repeated in (87), the phonological features of Obj are sent to the phonological component, forming a phonological phrase as in (88):

(87)   A phonological string that is mapped to the phonological component corresponds to a phonological phrase.

(88)   (Obj)$_\varphi$

   As the derivation goes on, the next Spell-Out applies to the sister of C, defining a linear order as in (89):

(89)   Spell-Out (Sister of C) $\rightarrow$ Linear Order: Subj < T < t_{Subj} < V-v*

On the basis of this linear order, the phonological features of Subj, T and V-v* are transferred to the phonological component, creating a phonological phrase:

(90)   (Subj T V-v*)$_\varphi$

In this derivation, the units of Spell-Out in (88) and (89) are sent separately to the phonological component. There is no a priori reason to assume that a domain spelled-out later precedes the one spelled-out earlier, because syntactic information such as c-command, upon which linear order is defined, is presumably no longer available in the phonological component, which is an independent module consisting of the outputs of Spell-Out. That is, even if we look at strings (88) and (90), we cannot determine which linear string precedes the other in the phonological component. So, the following two orders are equally possible in the phonological component:

(91)   a. (Subj T V-v*)$_\varphi$ (Obj)$_\varphi$
       b. (Obj)$_\varphi$ (Subj T V-v*)$_\varphi$

Let us call this problem the *Assembly Problem*.[16] To define unambiguously a linear order between two linear strings, consider the following two linear strings:

(92)   a. n < o < p
       b. p < q < r

(92a) ends with *p* and (92b) begins with *p*. Now, we can define the linear order between these two strings by using the following process, called the *Assembly Process*:

(93)   Assembly Process:
       The linear order between two local strings is defined by virtue of the shared member, so that it is consistent with each local string.

For the linear strings in (92), the shared member p acts as a "pivot" of linearization, so that the two strings are linearly ordered with respect to each other, resulting in the following:

(94) $n < o < p < q < r$

Let us now consider the Assembly Problem. An element that can be shared by the two strings is required. Suppose that the leftmost element in each unit of Spell-Out is left behind for the next Spell-Out, so the linearization between the units of Spell-Out is possible:

(95) Spell-Out sends a linearly ordered string to the phonological component Φ, except for the initial element in the string.

That is, when Spell-Out applies to the sister of v, the linear order between t_V and Obj is defined. Then the leftmost element in this linear string (i.e., t_V) is left behind until the sister of C is spelled-out, and only Obj is sent to the phonological component Φ, thus forming a phonological phrase, as in (96a) below. When the sister of C is spelled out, the linear order is defined among Subj, T, V-v*, and t_V, which has been left behind and is still available for linearization. At this point, t_V (defined as preceding Obj and following V-v*) acts as a pivot for linearization, so that the order between the two units of Spell-Out is defined unambiguously, as in (96b). Subj is left behind for the next Spell-Out and is only sent to the phonological component later, when the rest of the structure (root) undergoes Spell-Out, which results in the phrasing in (96c):

(96) a. S-O(Sister of v*)
       i. Linear Order: $t_V < $ Obj
       ii. Mapping to Φ: (Obj)$_\varphi$
     b. S-O(Sister of C)
       i. Linear Order: Subj $<$ Infl $< v < $ V
       ii. Mapping to Φ: (T V-v*)$_\varphi$(Obj)$_\varphi$
     c. S-O(Root)
       i. Linear Order: C $<$ Subj
       ii. Mapping to Φ: (C Subj)$_\varphi$ (T V)$_\varphi$ (Obj)$_\varphi$

On the widely held assumption that the subject is in the Spec-TP, this approach gives a straightforward account of the fact that it is basically phrased alone, in the two language types summarized in (84) and repeated here in (97):

(97) a. (S)$_\varphi$ (V   O)$_\varphi$ [Kimatuumbi, Kinyambo, Chichewa]
     b. (S)$_\varphi$ (V)$_\varphi$ (O)$_\varphi$ [Ewe, English, Italian, French]

Note that the resultant phrasing in (96c-ii) displays the mismatch between syntactic and phonological structure, which is an important issue in the study of syntax-phonology mapping, as discussed in Chapter 2. The phonological phrase consisting of T and V does not correspond to a syntactic constituent, and it accounts for (37) and (80): Raddoppiamento Sintattico is blocked between V and Obj in (37) but applies between T and V in (80). Likewise, the phonological phrase consisting of C and Subj in (96c-ii) does not match a syntactic constituent and accounts for the strong tendency of Subj not to be phrased with a following element (Aux or V). I discuss this phrasing in some detail in 4.5.2.2.[17] Thus, in general, Spell-Out applied at an intermediate phase creates a phonological phrase that does not match a syntactic constituent. That is, the syntax-phonology mismatch follows from the cyclic application of Spell-Out.

Thus far, we have discussed the phrasing of the subject. Then, what about the object? The object is phrased with the verb in (97a)-type languages, and separately from the verb in (97b)-languages. I suggest that this typological variation is attributable to syntactic variation in the present approach.[18]

3.4.2   *Object position and phonological phrasing*

3.4.2.1   English, French, and Italian

In this subsection, I will examine the position of the verb and object in English, French, and Italian. For English, I assume that V moves to adjoin to v^* and Obj stays in situ in English, in accordance with Chomsky (1995) and many others, who adopt the following phrase structure, which I have also assumed in this study:[19]

(98) $[_{CP}$ C $[_{TP}$ Subj T $[_{v^*P}$ V-v^* $[_{VP}$ t_V Obj$]]]]$

In contrast to English, it has been argued that V further moves to T in French (Emonds 1978; Pollock 1989) and Italian (Belletti 1990, 1994, among others). Let us briefly examine Pollock and Belletti's arguments. In French, VP adverbs appear between the verb and the object (Pollock 1989: 367):

(99)   a.   Jean   embrasse   souvent   Marie
                Jean   kisses   often   Mary
           b. * Jean   souvent   embrasse   Marie
                Jean   often   kisses   Mary

Also, the verb precedes the negation *pas* in French:

(100) Jean   (n') aime   pas   Marie
         Jean   likes   not   Marie

Similarly, in Italian the verb precedes a negative adverb (*più, mai, ancora*) which optionally co-occurs with the negative clitic *non* (Belletti 1994: 21):

(101)   Gianni non parla (più/mai/ancora)
            *Gianni non più/mai/ancora parla

(Belletti 1994: 20)

If we assume that these adverbials and negative elements are located between T (or perhaps some other inflectional head such as Agr) and v*P, we can conclude that the verb moves to T in these languages:

(102) [$_{CP}$ C [$_{TP}$ Subj V-v*-T [$_{v*P}$ t_{V-v*} [$_{VP}$ t_V Obj]]]]

Note that if there is an auxiliary verb in the position of T, the verb stays in v* in French and Italian. Thus, the VP adverbs follow the auxiliary verb and precede the verb:

(103) a. Jean a   toujours complètement perdu la   tête   pour elle
       Jean has always   completely   lost   his mind for   her
                                     (French: Cinque 1999: 7)

    b. Gianni ha   sempre completamente perso la   testa per lei
       Gianni   has always   completely   lost   his mind for her
                                       (Italian: Cinque 1999: 7)

The basic phrase structure in (98) indicates that the auxiliary verb is in T and the verb is in v*. The data in (103) also indicate that the object stays within VP. If the object were moved to Spec-v*P (a possible A-position), it would precede the lexical verb in v*. Thus, I assume that the object stays in situ, at least overtly, in French and Italian. Then, the basic phrase structure of a transitive sentence in these languages is as follows:

(104) [$_{CP}$ C [$_{TP}$ Subj *Aux*-T [$_{v*P}$ V-v* [$_{VP}$ t_V Obj]]]]

See Ogawa (2001: 261) for further discussion of object position in relation to adverb placement in French and Italian.

    Spell-Out applying to the sister of v* in (104) gives a phonological phrase containing only the object, and Spell-Out applying to the sister of C gives the phrase containing V on v* or T, with the subject included in the domain of the next Spell-Out. This results in the phrasing of (97b), repeated here, where the subject, verb, and object are phrased separately:

(105) (S)$_\varphi$ (V)$_\varphi$ (O)$_\varphi$

This approach yields a straightforward account of basic phonological phrasing in English, French, and Italian. I will return to phrasing variation induced by branchingness, in section 3.4.3. In the next section, I consider Ewe, which also exhibits the basic phrasing in (105).

3.4.2.2   Ewe

Let us consider the positions of the verb and object in Ewe. The basic word order in Ewe is SVO, as shown in (106a), but Collins (1993) and others observe that the object moves to the left of the verb in progressive constructions, resulting in an SOV order, as in (106b-d) (see also Aboh 2004):

(106) a. me   *fo*   Kofi
         I   hit   Kofi

                              (Kpele dialect: Collins 1993: 40)

      b. me   le   Kofi   *fo*
         I   am   Kofi   hitting

                              (Kpele dialect: Collins 1993: 40)

      c. me   le   Kofi   *fo*   gbe
         I   am   Kofi   hitting prt

                              (Kpele dialect: Collins 1993: 40)

      d. me   le   Kofi   *fo*   m
         I   am   Kofi   hitting prt

                              (Aŋlɔ dialect: Collins 1993: 40)

Collins (1993) argues that in (106b) the object *Kofi* moves over the verb *fo* 'hitting' to the Spec of AGRoP, where the Case feature of the object is checked. The following data suggest that this is A-movement since only DP may undergo this word order alternation; CP, which does not require Case, stays in situ:

(107) a. Kofi   le   nya   gblɔ
         Kofi   is   word   saying
         'Kofi is saying something.'
      b. Kofi   le   gbɔgblɔ be   Yao dzo
         Kofi   is   saying   that Yao left
         'Kofi is saying that Yao left.'

                              (Collins 1993: 42)

Similarly, a locative PP, which does not require Case, may not undergo movement, as the following contrast shows:

(108) a. afi   wo   le   gege   ɖe   xɔ-me
         mouse   PL   are   falling   LOC   room-in
         'Some mice are falling into the room.'
      b. *afi   wo   le   ɖe   xɔ-me   gege
         mouse   PL   are   LOC   room-in   falling

                              (Collins 1993: 42)

In the phrase structure I adopt here, the Case feature of the object DP is checked by v*. Then, the SOV order results from the movement of the object DP to the Spec of v*P over the verb on v*:

(109) $[_{CP}$ C $[_{TP}$ Subj T $[_{v*P}$ Obj V-v* $[_{VP}$ t_V t_{Obj}]]]]

Then, the object DP should stay in situ in the SVO order:

(110) [$_{CP}$ C [$_{TP}$ Subj T [$_{v*P}$ V-v* [$_{VP}$ t_V Obj]]]]

This structure is parallel to that of an English transitive construction and yields the following basic phonological phrasing in Ewe:

(111) (S)$_\varphi$ (V)$_\varphi$ (O)$_\varphi$

This is exactly what we have observed in Ewe (see section 3.3.1).

It is expected in the SOV order that the shifted object in Spec-v*P and V on v* will be phonologically phrased together: Spell-Out applied to the sister of v* is vacuous, and Spell-Out applied to the sister of C gives a phonological phrase containing Obj and V, while excluding Subj. This prediction is borne out. The relevant phonological rule is M Raising, which raises M to R (extra-high) if M is between Hs (see section 3.3.1). Clements (1978: 46) considers the following frame sentence:

(112) mē ___ ʃlē-gé
      I   buying-PRT
      'I'm going to buy ___ .'

(Clements 1978: 46)

The tones in (112) are underlying tones. If an object ending in an H is inserted in '___,' the M tone on the verb is raised:

(113) mē kpé ʃlē-gé → mè kpé̋ ʃlé̆-gé
      I   stone buy-PRT
      'I'm going to buy a stone.'

(Clements 1978: 48)

The following example makes the same point:

(114) a. ākɔ̄dú
          'banana'
     b. m' ākɔ̄dŭ ʃlĕ-gé
          I   banana buy-PRT
          'I'm going to buy a banana.'

(Clements 1978: 48)

So, in the SOV order, the object and verb are phrased together, verifying the prediction that the object in Spec of v*P is phrased together with the verb on v*.

In this section, I have shown that the linearization procedure *Assembly Process*, which applies to the domains of Spell-Out, allows the null hypothesis regarding phonological phrasing in (12), repeated in (115), to account for the basic phonological phrasing in English, Ewe, Italian, and French in a straightforward manner.

(115) Null hypothesis
A phonological string that is mapped to the phonological component corresponds to a phonological phrase.

This also gives a clear account of phrasing in the Ewe SOV order. The phrasing difference in VO and OV orders in Ewe results from the difference in object position. This approach suggests that the phrase structure required for analysis of phonological phrasing is more elaborate than that assumed in the standard theories of the 1980s and 1990s, when most of the studies of sentential phonology were based on more or less simplistic syntactic analyses.

In the next section, I will argue that the object position directly accounts for the basic phrasing in Chichewa, Kinyambo, and Kimatuumbi, in which V and O are always phrased together, in line with the analysis of the Ewe OV word order.

3.4.2.3   *Chichewa, Kinyambo, and Kimatuumbi*

Consider the basic phonological phrasing in (97a)-type languages, repeated here:

(116) $(S)_\varphi$ $(V\quad O)_\varphi$ [Kimatuumbi, Kinyambo, Chichewa]

All three are Bantu languages. For verb position in Bantu, some assume that the verb moves to T, as in French and Italian (Seidl 2001; Pak 2008; Ura 2000); others argue that it moves between T and v* (Julien 2002; Buell 2005). I assume that the verb moves to T (for clarity), although even if it does not reach T and stays between T and v* my analysis of phonological phrasing is unchanged, because both positions are within the same domain transferred to the phonological component, i.e., within the domain of Spell-Out applying to the sister of C. A more important point is whether the object stays in situ or moves out of the VP. Below, I argue that the object in Chichewa, Kinyambo, and Kimatuumbi moves to Spec-v*P.

Chichewa, perhaps the most widely studied Bantu language of the three, exhibits the following word order variation in transitive constructions when the verb bears the object marker.

(117) a. SVO: Njûchi   zi-ná-wá-lum-a   alenje
               bees   SM-PST-OM-bite- INDIC   hunters
       b. VOS: Zináwáluma alenje njûchi
       c. OVS: Alenje zináwáluma njûchi
       d. VSO: Zináwáluma njûchi alenje
       e. SOV: Njûchi alenje zináwáluma
       f. OSV: Alenje njûchi zináwáluma

(Bresnan and Mchombo 1987: 747)

Bresnan and Mchombo (1987: 745) argue that the subject marker is ambiguously used as grammatical agreement or as an anaphoric pronoun, while the object marker is unambiguously used as an incorporated pronoun that is anaphorically linked to the topic NPs. If the subject marker is used as grammatical agreement, then the subject NP must be in a position local to the verb. If the subject marker is used as an anaphoric pronoun, it is anaphorically linked to a topic, like the object marker (Bresnan and Mchombo 1987: 755). Thus, the free word order in (117) is accounted for by assuming that the topic subject and object are freely generated under S in the following structure, which Bresnan and Mchombo adopted in their work at the time:

(120)

```
            S
          /   \
       NP       VP
```

If the verb does not bear the object marker, the object NP is not interpreted as a topic and must occur in a position local to the verb or in a position immediately after the verb:

(121) a. SVO: Njûchi zi-ná-lúm-a   alenje
             bees   SM-PST-OM-bite-INDIC   hunters
                  'The bees bit the hunter.'
      b. VOS: Zinálúma alenje njûchi
      c. OVS: *Alenje zinálúma njûchi
      d. VSO: *Zinálúma njûchi alenje
      e. SOV: *Njûchi alenje zináluma
      f. OSV: *Alenje njûchi zináluma
                              (Bresnan and Mchombo 1987: 744–745)

The lack of the object marker prevents topicalization of the object and forces the object to stay in its canonical position. In sum, the following hold:

(122) Chichewa:
      a. The subject marker is used ambiguously as grammatical agreement or as an anaphoric pronoun.
      b. The object marker is an incorporated pronoun, used unambiguously as an anaphoric pronoun.
      c. The object marker is anaphorically linked to a topic NP/DP.

To offer a unified account of these properties, I assume the following:

(123) v* has an EPP feature in Chichewa.

Here, the EPP feature requires an overt lexical item in its local domain and can be checked by (I) the object pronoun, which shows up as an object marker within the verbal morphology (that it, the object marker is head-adjoined to V-v*) or by (II) the full DP, which occupies the Spec-v*P (see Ura 2000; Henderson 2006 for a similar proposal that the full DP agreeing with v* occupies Spec-v*P in Bantu). Then, on the assumption that the verb moves up to T, the verb "picks up" the object pronoun on its way to T via v* in the case of (I) (here, the trace or copy of Subj is omitted):[20]

(124) i. [$_{CP}$ C [$_{TP}$ Subj   T [$_{v*P}$ v* [$_{VP}$ V Obj]]]]
      ii. [$_{CP}$ C [$_{TP}$ Subj   T [$_{v*P}$ Obj-V-v* [$_{VP}$ t_V t_{Obj}]]]]
      iii. [$_{CP}$ C [$_{TP}$ Subj Obj-V-v*-T [$_{v*P}$ $t_{Obj-V-v*}$ [$_{VP}$ t_V t_{Obj}]]]]

Then, the full DP that is coreferential with the object marker should be generated in an extra-clausal position. It does not stay in Spec-v*P or in the complement of V and is anaphorically related to the object marker.

In the case of (II), we will have the following structure, where the full DP object occupies the Spec-v*P:

(125) [$_{CP}$ C [$_{TP}$ Subj V-v*-T [$_{v*P}$ Obj t_{V-v*} [$_{VP}$ t_V t_{Obj}]]]]

This explains why the full DP object appears in the canonical position local to the verb on T in the absence of the object marker: it must be in Spec-v*P to check the EPP feature of v*, and the verb on T is adjacent to Spec-v*P.

Above, on the basis of the data in (69), repeated here, I argued that the verb and object are invariably phrased together in Chichewa, irrespective of whether the object is branching:

(126) a. (Mwaána)$_\varphi$ (anaményá   nyuúmba)$_\varphi$
          child   SM-hit   house
          'The child hit the house.'
      b. (Mwaána)$_\varphi$ (anaményá   nyumbá   ya bwiíno)$_\varphi$
          child   SM-hit   house   of good
          'The child hit the good house.'

The verb in these examples does not have an object marker. The morphological segmentation of *anamenya* is as follows (cf. Mchombo 2004):

(127) a-na-meny-a
       SM-PST-HIT-FV

Here, *a-* is a subject marker, *-na-* marks past tense, *-meny-* is a verbal root, and *-a* is a final vowel. This morphological verbal complex does not include the object marker: therefore, the sentences in (126) have the structure of (125), repeated here in (128a), which corresponds to the phonological phrasing in (128b), where V-v*-T and Obj are transferred to the phonological component together:

(128) a. [$_{CP}$ C [$_{TP}$ Subj V-v*-T   [$_{v*P}$ Obj t_{V-v*} [$_{VP}$ t_V t_{Obj}]]]]
      b.   (anaményá   nyuúmba)$_\varphi$

Thus, I conclude that the full DP object in Chichewa moves to Spec-v*P to check the EPP feature of v* when the object marker (pronominal clitic) is absent in the verbal morphology. Moreover, the object in this position, whether branching or not, is always phrased with the V on T as a result of Spell-Out applying to the sister of C.

Let us next consider Kinyambo. Recall that the data in (65), repeated here, show that the verb is phrased with the following object, since the H of the verb is deleted in the presence of another H of the following word:

(129) a. okubón
       'see'
    b. ómuntu
       'person'
    c. okubon' ómuntu
       'to see the person'

(Bickmore 1989: 139)

    d. *okubón' omuntu

Note that the verb *okubon* 'to see' contains no object marker. The underlying form of the verb is as follows:

(130) o-ku-bon-a
      PP-Inf-see-FV
      'to see'

(Bickmore 1989: 139)

Here, PP is a pre-prefix and -Inf is an infinitive marker (which is arguably a Class 15 nominal prefix), to use Bickmore's (1989: 11) terms. The rule of *Vowel Elision* deletes the final vowel -*a* in (130), according to Bickmore (1989: 139), resulting in *obubon'* in (129c). The verb in this particular example and those examined in section 3.3.4 do not have an object marker, but verbs in Kinyambo may accompany object markers. Thus, a grammar book of Runyambo (Ruge-malira 2005) includes the following examples of monotransitive constructions:

(131) a. muséja akatemá omuti   'A man cut a tree.'
    b. omukázi akareetá omugisa 'The woman brought luck.'
    c. akagutéma   'He cut it.'   (pronominalization)
    d. akaguréeta   'She brought it.'   (pronominalization)

(Rugemalira 2005: 89)

In (131a, b), the object noun phrase immediately follows the verb, and the object marker does not appear in the verbal complex. Rugemalira describes the examples in (131c, d) as involving pronominalization, where the object marker -*gu*- shows up within the verbal complex. Moreover, the same book (p. 90) states that "[t]he object prefix and the object noun phrase may not co-occur. The noun phrase may be preposed, and so belong outside the clause," and gives the following examples:

(132) a. (amajúta)   a-ka-ga-mú-n-siij-ir-a.
        oil   she-PST3-it-him-me-smear-APP-FV
        '(As for the oil) she smeared it on him for me.'
      b. (ecitabo)   a-ka-ci-mu-m-pé-er-a.
        book   she-PST3-it-him-me-give-APP-FV
        '(As for the book) she gave it to him for me.'

(Rugemalira 2005: 90)

As the intended interpretation of each example indicates, the preposed noun phrase coreferential with the object marker is construed as a topic. Furthermore, in discussing causative constructions, Rugemalira (1993a: 130) explicitly points out that the causative argument is interpreted as a topic (old information) when it is realized as an object marker or "prefix" on the verb:

(133) (akasyó) a-ka-**ka**-saz-á   omwáná isócé aha-mútwe.
      (razor)   he-PST-**it**-but+CAUS-FV   child   hair   LOC-head
      '(The razor) he cut the child's hair from the head with it.'

(adapted from Rugemalira 1993a: 130)

Although further study is needed, these descriptions indicate that the object markers in Kinyambo are similar to those in Chichewa, in that they are more like incorporated pronouns than like agreement morphemes, and they are coindexed with the topicalized element. Therefore, I assume that the DP argument that shows up without an object marker, as in (129), agrees with v*, raising to the Spec of v*P to check the EPP feature, which is consistent with the analysis of Chichewa, above. Hence, basic phonological phrasing in Kinyambo is accounted for: the full DP object in Spec-v*P, whether branching or not, is always phrased with the verb on T (see (66) for an example with a branching object).

Unlike Chichewa and Kinyambo, the Kimatuumbi data above have object markers. Consider (47b), which is repeated here, in (134):

(134) naa-ká-langjte   chóolyá.
      I-it-took   food
      'I fried food.'

(Odden 1987: 16 (11))

Here we have the object marker -*ká*-. If the object markers in Kimatuumbi were like those in Chichewa and Kinyambo, they would be incorporated pronouns, which would lead us to incorrectly predict that the full DP object *chóolyá* 'food' in (134) is in fact right-dislocated or base-generated in an extra-clausal position and that it does not remain in Spec-v*P.

Henderson (2006) argues that there are two types of object markers in Bantu: a pronominal clitic and an agreement morpheme. If it is a pronominal clitic, as in Chichewa and Kinyambo, then it itself is an argument of the verb and has a feature-checking relation with v*. Moreover, it can have an anaphoric relation with a (topicalized/dislocated) full DP generated outside the clause. If the object marker is an agreement morpheme, then it appears as a result of agreement between v* and a full DP object. A diagnostic for this distinction is the structural locality between the verb and full DP object. If the object marker is an agreement morpheme, then it can co-occur with the full DP object within the same clause, as in (135a); however, if it is a pronominal clitic, then it cannot, as in (135b):

(135) a. Ni-me-*m*-pa   Juma   vitabu vyote vitatu pale.
      SM1S-PERF-OM1-give 1Juma 8book 8all   8three 16there
      'I have given Juma all three books there.'
                                             (Swahili, Riedel 2009: 62)

     b. *A-ba-aana   ba-a-ra-*bi*-ri-ye   i-bi-ryo   ejo.
      AUG-2-child   SM2- REM- DJ-8.OM-eat-PERF AUG-8-food yesterday
      Intended: 'The children ate the food yesterday.'
                                       (Kinyarwanda, Zeller 2014: 3)

In (135a) the object marker -*m*- co-occurs with the indirect object *Juma* within a local domain and precedes the adverb *pale* 'there.' In (135b), on the other hand, the direct object *i-bi-ryo* 'food' cannot immediately follow the verb that has the object marker and precede the adverb *ejo* 'yesterday.'

It is not easy to determine whether the object marker is an agreement morpheme or a clitic pronoun in Kimatuumbi, since the syntactic analysis is limited, but Odden's work contains the following example:[21]

(136) a. nịịmpéendịlé píta.
      'I really like him.'
   b. * nịịmpendịle píta

(137) a. nịịmpendị kịtúumbilí píta.
      'I really like the monkey.'
   b. * nịịmpendịlé píta kịtúumbili.
                            (Odden 1990: 264, 1996: 241)

Odden points out that adverbs like *píta* 'very' (and *kwaálị* 'perhaps') do not trigger Shortening on the verb, as the contrast in (136) shows, indicating that they are outside the prosodic domain containing the verb. He further points out that these adverbs cannot intervene between the verb and its object, as shown by the contrast in (137). The morphological system in Kimatuumbi is highly complicated, and Odden does not give morpheme-by-morpheme glosses to these examples, but -*m*- in the verbal complex in (136) and (137) seems to be the Class 1 object marker, for -*m*- is explicitly identified as the Class 1 object marker in example (138a), below. Moreover, the verbal complex whose root is 'like' is glossed, as in (138b), indicating that *aa-* is a subject marker 'he,' *-m-* is a Class 1 object marker 'him,' and *pendi* is a verbal stem (the morphological segmentation for (138b) is given by the present author):

(138) a. naa-*m*-mwénị mụ́ụ́ndúụ.
I-him-saw   person
'I saw the person.'

(Odden 1996: 34)

b. Mamboondó   aa-m-pendi   lị   sáána.
Mamboondo   he-him-like   NEG   very
'Mamboondo really doesn't like him.'

(Odden 1987: 17, 1996: 226)

Thus, I conclude that the verbal complex in (137) has the Class 1 suffix *-m-*. The contrast in (137) is thus on par with (135a) rather than with (135b), indicating that the object marker is an agreement morpheme rather than a pronominal clitic in Kimatuumbi, unlike in Chichewa and Kinyambo. If we assume that v^* has an EPP-feature in Kimatuumbi, the only way to check it is to move the full DP object to Spec-v^*P, thereby revealing the agreement marker.[22]

Analysis of these Bantu languages, where V raises to T and the full DP object moves to the Spec-v^*P, yields the following phrase structure:

(139) $[_{CP}$ C $[_{TP}$ Subj V-v^*-T $[_{v^*P}$ Obj t_{V-v^*} $[_{VP}$ t_V t_{Obj} $]]]]$

Spell-Out applying to the sister of (trace of) v^* yields no phonological material since everything has moved out, and Spell-Out applying to the sister of C gives phrasing where V and Obj are phrased together, as in (97a) = (116).

This approach also explains why these languages do not allow optional phrasing of the verb and object. As we have seen in sections 3.3.3 and 3.3.4, the object is always phrased with the verb, whether it is branching or not. Because the object is always sent to the phonological component together with the verb, there is no room for optionality: the object and verb are, in principle, phrased together in these languages.

3.4.3   *Phrasing variations*

In the previous section, phase theory with Multiple Spell-Out gave a straightforward account for the basic phonological phrasing (84)/(97), repeated here again, which depended on object position:

(140) a. $(S)_\varphi$ $(V)_\varphi$ $(O)_\varphi$
b. $(S)_\varphi$ $(V$ $O)_\varphi$

In section 3.3, we observed further variations in phrasing that were attributable to branchingness of the subject and object, as summarized in (71)-(74), reproduced here:

(141)　　(S)$_\varphi$ (V)$_\varphi$ (O)$_\varphi$　　　　　　　　　Aŋlɔ Ewe, French
(142)　a.　(S)$_\varphi$ (V)$_\varphi$ (O)$_\varphi$　　　　　　　　　Italian
　　　　b.　(S)$_\varphi$ (V　O)$_\varphi$　　if O is non-branching.
(143)　　(S)$_\varphi$ (V　O)$_\varphi$　　　　　　　Kimatuumbi
(144)　a.　(S)$_\varphi$ (V　O)$_\varphi$　　　　　　　Kinyambo, Chichewa
　　　　b.　(S　V　O)$_\varphi$　　if S is non-branching.

When non-branching, the object may be phrased with the verb, as in (141b), in languages like Italian, and the subject may be phrased with the following verb, as in (144b), in languages like Kinyambo.

Relation-based theory accounts for (142b) by the φ-restructuring rule, which refers to "complement":

(145)　φ restructuring (Nespor and Vogel 1986: 173)
　　　　A non-branching φ which is the first complement of X on its recursive side is joined into the φ that contains X.

The reference to the complement is necessary, presumably because the languages discussed in Nespor and Vogel (1986) always phrase a subject separately from a following element (an auxiliary verb or main verb), while a non-branching object may be phrased with a verb in some languages (optionally in Italian, and obligatorily in Ewe, for instance). But as we have seen, languages like Kinyambo and Chichewa allow restructuring of subjects, as schematically shown in (144), so the restructuring rule (145) needs to be reconsidered.

Within the framework of End-based Theory, Bickmore (1990: 17) proposes that the reference to branching maximal projection accounts for the phrasing in (144):

(146)　a.　　　$]_{Xmax\text{-}b}$　　　　　　(Mende)
　　　b.　$_{Xmax\text{-}b}[$　　　　　　　(Kinyambo)
　　　　　　Xmax-b = a branching maximal projection

Both these approaches to branchingness make direct reference to syntactic notions such as complements or maximal projections. However, as Inkelas and Zec (1995: 536ff.) argue, access to syntactic information should be minimized in a restrictive theory of phonological phrasing, and the reference to complements or maximal projections should be avoided. Inkelas and Zec argue that prosodic domain formation is sensitive to prosodic binarity but not to syntactic branchingness. Prosodic binarity is considered to play a role in defining prosodic domains of various sizes. Thus, Prince and Smolensky (2004: 56) propose the following constraint on feet, following McCarthy and Prince (1986) (see also N.-J. Kim 1997; Selkirk 2011, and references cited therein):

(147) Foot Binarity (FᴛBɪɴ)
       Feet are binary at some level of analysis (μ, σ).

Given this, the following foot structure, consisting of two morae, is preferred:

(148) $(\mu\ \mu)_f$

Inkelas and Zec (1995: 544) suggest that binarity also holds at the level of phonological phrase and propose the following constraint requiring that a phonological phrase consist of two prosodic words:

(149) $(\omega\ \omega)_\varphi$

Then the restructuring of phonological phrases applies to satisfy (149) for prosodic reasons, but not for syntactic reasons, unlike (145) and (146):

(150) $(\omega)_\varphi\ (\omega)_\varphi \rightarrow (\omega\ \omega)_\varphi$

To determine how this binarity constraint works, let us consider the *Rhythm Rule* in English. Nespor and Vogel (1986) observe that for many English speakers, the Rhythm Rule is sensitive to phonological phrasing. It shifts the main stress of a word leftward in the presence of the main stress of a following word, if the stressed syllables are adjacent within a phonological phrase. If a subject and a verb phrase are both non-branching, the main stress of the subject may be shifted, as shown in (151c):

(151) a.   Ànnemaríe
       b.   Ànnemaríe   áte.
            (   )$_\varphi$ (   )$_\varphi$
       c.   Ánnemarie   áte.
            (   )$_\varphi$
                                    (Inkelas and Zec 1995: 543; Dobashi 2003: 83)

Given the null hypothesis regarding phonological phrasing, the phrasing in (151b) is defined by Spell-Out. Then, given Inkelas and Zec's prosodic approach to the branchingness, (151c) is analyzed as resulting from restructuring that applies to (151b), to satisfy (149). This approach does not need to complicate the processes of syntax-phonology mapping, and the restructuring falls within the phonological component. Moreover, since the restructuring is often optional and affected by pragmatic factors such as speech rate, restructuring is assumed to be a matter of phonology rather than of syntax-phonology mapping based on the core computational operation of Spell-Out, the application of which is not optional in principle.

   Notice, however, that if the VP is branching, the non-branching subject does not restructure:

(152) Ànnemaríe áte sandwiches.
     (   )$_\varphi$ (   )$_\varphi$

This suggests that the restructuring is constrained by directionality (cf. Dobashi 2010). Suppose that restructuring applies leftward in English:

(153) A phonological phrase X restructures to the left if X violates the binarity constraint.

                                                           (149)

Thus, in (151b) the phonological phrase (*ate*)$_\varphi$, being non-branching, restructures leftwards, resulting in (151c). By contrast, in (152), even though the subject (*Ànnemaríe*)$_\varphi$ is non-branching and violates the binarity constraint (149), it does not restructure, since it has no other phonological phrase on its left side. Similarly, a non-branching object may restructure leftwards, forming a phonological phrase with the verb as in (154a), but a branching object cannot, as in (155b):

(154) a.   John   réproduces   prints.
          (   )$_\varphi$ (   )$_\varphi$
      b.   John   reprodúces   óld prints.
          (   )$_\varphi$ (   )$_\varphi$ (   )$_\varphi$

                                                  (Dobashi 2003: 83)

Thus, I conclude that restructuring is uniformly leftward in English.

In contrast to English, restructuring in Chichewa and Kinyambo seems to be rightward:

(155) A phonological phrase X restructures to the right if X violates the binarity constraint.

                                                           (149)

In Chichewa, if the subject and verb are both non-branching, they are optionally phrased together, as in (156c-d). But if the subject is branching, then the restructuring does not apply, as in (156e):

(156) a.   mwaná   'child' [lexical form]
      b.   njovu   'elephant' [lexical form]
      c.   (Mwaána)$_\varphi$ (anagoona)$_\varphi$
            child   SM-slept
        'The child slept.'
      d.   (Mwaná anagoona)$_\varphi$
             child   SM-slept
        'The child slept.'
      e.   (Mwaná wa njoovu)$_\varphi$ (anagoona)$_\varphi$
              child of elephant   SM-slept
        'The child of an elephant slept.'
                                (Sam Mchombo, personal communication)

Furthermore, a non-branching subject seems to be able to restructure to the right even when the predicate is complex:

(157) a. Zipáatso   zikupsyá páng'ónópang'óono.
         (   )$_\varphi$ (   )$_\varphi$
         'The fruit is ripening gradually.'

(Kanerva 1990:149)

     b. Zipátso   zikupsyá páng'ónópang'óono.
         (   )$_\varphi$
         'The fruit is ripening gradually.'

(Sam Mchombo p.c.)

Kanerva (1990) observes that the subject in (157a) is phrased alone but can be easily phrased together with a following predicate, as in (157b), especially in faster speech. In contrast to the subject, the object (branching or not) is always phrased with the verb in Chichewa because of the basic phrasing, as we have seen above.

Directionality cannot be defined in syntax but is a property of the phonology. Then, in addition to the optionality of restructuring, sensitivity to the directionality suggests that the restructuring applies for purely phonological reasons, without reference to the syntax.

In sum, phase-by-phase Spell-Out creates basic phonological phrasing, and the difference in syntactic structure (i.e., object position) accounts for the difference in basic phonological phrasing (i.e., the difference between (140a) and (140b) in SVO languages, repeated below):

(158) a. (S)$_\varphi$ (V)$_\varphi$ (O)$_\varphi$
     b. (S)$_\varphi$ (V   O)$_\varphi$

Further variation, shown in (141)–(144), repeated below, is attributed to the restructuring of phonological phrases in the phonological component, which is induced by the prosodic binarity:

(159)   (S)$_\varphi$ (V)$_\varphi$ (O)$_\varphi$ Aŋlɔ Ewe, French
(160) a. (S)$_\varphi$ (V)$_\varphi$ (O)$_\varphi$ Italian
     b. (S)$_\varphi$ (V   O)$_\varphi$ if O is non-branching.
(161)   (S)$_\varphi$ (V   O)$_\varphi$ Kimatuumbi
(162) a. (S)$_\varphi$ (V   O)$_\varphi$ Kinyambo, Chichewa
     b. (S   V   O)$_\varphi$ if S is non-branching.

This approach requires the presence of phonological objects (i.e., phonological phrases) to which the prosodic operation of restructuring applies, indicating that the indirect-reference theory is plausible.

3.4.4 Further issues: Multiple Spell-Out and prosodic domains

A theoretically desirable aspect of the Multiple Spell-Out theory of phonological phrasing is that it is a null hypothesis; it does not require an independent algorithm that creates phonological phrases:

(163) Null hypothesis:
  A phonological string that is mapped to the phonological component corresponds to a phonological phrase.

In other words, phonological phrasing can be reduced to the operation Spell-Out. However, viewed from the broader perspective of the entire prosodic hierarchy, the Multiple Spell-Out theory cannot be a true null hypothesis. It is fundamentally impossible for the Multiple Spell-Out theory to account for the formation of other prosodic categories, for it merely demarcates intermediate-size prosodic domains (i.e., phonological phrases) between clause-size prosodic domains (i.e., intonational phrases) and word-size prosodic domains (i.e., prosodic words). The standard theories of prosodic domains (Relation-based Theory and End-based Theory), and especially Match Theory, are designed to account *uniformly* for all the prosodic categories in a consistent, comprehensive manner. On the other hand, the Multiple Spell-Out theory appears to have neglected (or says nothing about) prosodic categories other than phonological phrase. That is, the Multiple Spell-Out theory is not a true null hypothesis, because it requires additional mechanisms to account for intonational phrases and prosodic words. Therefore, I will reconsider the entire architecture of prosodic domains, from a different perspective, in the next section. In line with Dobashi (2013), I suggest that it is basic units of the linearization procedures that correspond to prosodic domains. Specifically, I argue that externalization requires (at least) three kinds of linearization, and that each of these three procedures defines prosodic word, phonological phrase, and intonational phrase. I further argue that these three linearization procedures account for hierarchical prosodic structure. The formation of prosodic hierarchy is thus unified in terms of linearization. Unlike Match Theory, the prosodic hierarchy does not directly reflect syntactic structure, but rather results from linearization, which is the essential property of externalization.

3.5. Linearization processes

As we have seen so far, the phase theory with Multiple Spell-Out seems to successfully account for the basic phonological phrasings and their variation, but fails to account for other prosodic categories, such as intonational phrase and prosodic word. In this section, I will attempt to shed new light on the prosodic hierarchy in terms of linearization. To grasp the relation between linearization and prosodic domain, it is helpful to consider the theory of Pak (2008). Although I do not adopt her specific mechanisms, her theory is insightful because it suggests that linear ordering – the key concept in externalization – can provide a principled account of prosodic categories of different sizes.

3.5.1   Linear strings and prosodic domains

Pak (2008) argues that two layers of prosodic domains, which differ in size, result from two different types of linearizations: head-level and phrase-level linearizations (see also Idsardi and Raimy 2013 for multiple linearization procedures). She shows that linear strings created by these linearization procedures correspond to the prosodic domains.

Below is a rough, simplified illustration of Pak's theory, with the technical details removed. She suggests that the linear order among words is defined in two steps: head-level linearization and phrase-level linearization. In the first step, linear order between overt heads is defined in terms of left-adjacency and c-command, in a pairwise fashion. Thus, in the following syntactic structure where only X, Y, and Z are overt, X is defined as being left-adjacent to Y because X c-commands Y and no other overt head intervenes between them. However, Y cannot be defined as being left-adjacent to Z in this first step of the linearization, because Y does not c-command Z.

(164)

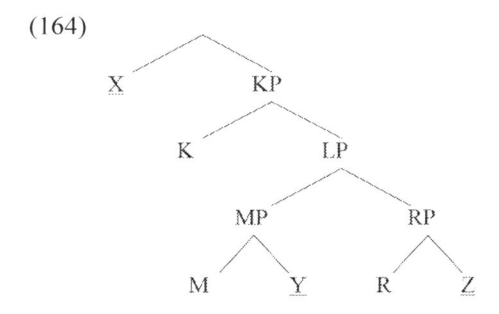

Y is defined as being left-adjacent to Z in the second step of linearization, i.e., the phrase-level linearization. Y precedes Z because of their mother nodes: MP dominating Y precedes RP dominating Z. Given this linearization procedure, Pak proposes that different phonological rules apply to different steps of linearization. That is, some rules apply to the structure created by the head-level linearization, and others apply to the structure created by the phrase-level linearization.

Under this proposed model of linearization, Pak uses two domain-specific rules to analyze prosodic domains in the Bantu language Luganda. One is the rule of *Low Tone Deletion* (LTD), which applies between two H_nL_n words, deleting L on the first word and forming an H-Plateau between the two words. The other is the rule of *High Tone Anticipation* (HTA), which spreads an H leftward onto tone-less morae.

(165) a. No LTD between the indirect object and direct object:

(Pak 2008: 29–30)

　　　　　i. bá-lìs-a　　　　　kaamukúúkùlu doodô.
　　　　　　　sm2-feed-indic　1a.dove　　　1a.greens
　　　　　　　'They're feeding greens to the dove.'
　　　　ii. → (bálísá káámúkúúkùlù) (dòòdô)

b. HTA applies throughout the double-object structure:
   i. a-lis-a   empologoma doodô.
      SM1-feed-INDIC 9.lion   1a.greens
      'S/he's feeding greens to the lion.'
   ii. → (àlís' émpólógómá dóódô)

In (165a), LTD applies between the verb and indirect object but not between the indirect object and direct object. By contrast, in (165b), which has the same syntactic structure as (165a) but differs only in that the verb and indirect object are toneless, HTA spreads the H tone of the direct object leftward to the indirect object and verb. That is, the domain of LTD is smaller than that of HTA.[23]

Pak proposes that LTD is an early rule that applies to the output of the first step of linearization (head-level linearization) and that HTA applies later to the output of the second step (phrasal linearization). She assumes the following syntactic structure for double-object constructions:

(166)

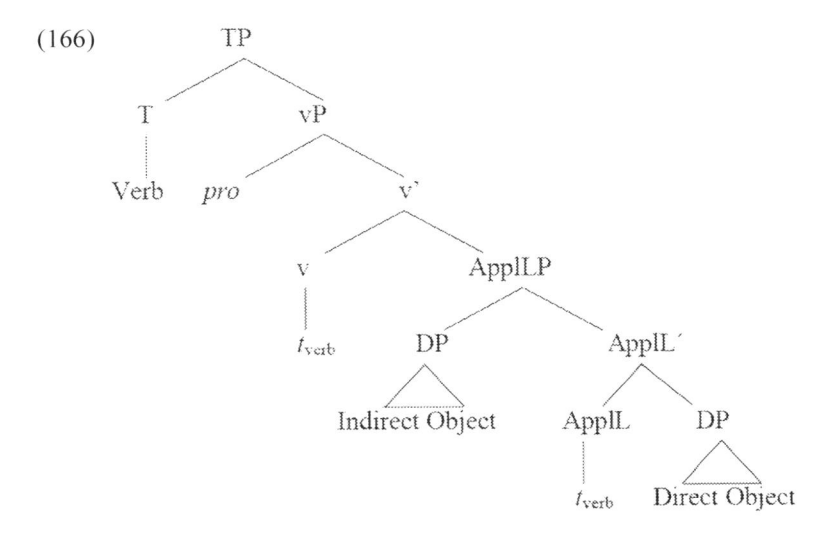

Here, ApplLP is a low applicative phrase, and the verb originates as the head of ApplLP and moves up to T through v (cf. Seidl 2001). She assumes quite naturally that both DP objects have their own internal structure. Given this structure, the first step of linearization defines the linear order among overt heads. The verb in T is defined as being left-adjacent to the indirect object, but the indirect object is embedded within DP and cannot be defined as being left-adjacent to the direct object (cf. (164) above), so the first step merely gives the string V-IO. This string serves as the domain for the "early rule" LTD. The next step is the phrasal linearization, which defines the string of V-IO as being left-adjacent to the direct object. At this point, we have the string V-IO-DO, to which the late rule HTA applies.

Note in passing that this is a direct-reference approach, as we do not construct any prosodic domain. Moreover, there is no need to stipulate the prosodic hierarchy in this approach, according to Pak (2008: 43). The apparent hierarchy is derived from the linearization procedures. I will, however, continue to maintain an indirect-reference approach, for at least two reasons. Empirically, we need to posit phonological phrases that undergo purely phonological restructuring rules, as we have seen in section 3.4.3. Theoretically, linear ordering should be part of the phonological component, which is completely independent of narrow syntax/C-I devoid of linearity, and linearly ordered strings must be independent phonological objects (as opposed to syntactic objects), which are placed in the phonological component (see Bonet et al. 2018 for more arguments for indirect-reference approaches).

3.5.2   Unifying prosodic word and phonological phrase in terms of linearization

While putting aside the issue of direct/indirect reference, it is important to notice that Pak's theory implies that linearization is closely tied to formation of prosodic domains. That is, a string defined by a particular linearization procedure, say head-level linearization, corresponds to a prosodic domain, and another string demar-cated by another linearization (i.e., phase-level linearization) serves as another type of prosodic domain. With this in mind, recall that Dobashi's (2003) theory of phonological phrasing, reviewed in section 3.4.1, is also tied to a linearization procedure, called the Assembly Process. This process defines the linear order between two Spell-Out domains, which correspond to phonological phrases. That is, in this theory a domain of Spell-Out serves as an elementary unit or "prime" for the linearization (Assembly Process), and the prime acts as a phonological phrase. This indicates that it is not a string (as in Pak's theory) but rather a prime for lin-earization that corresponds to a prosodic domain. Generalization of this idea sug-gests the following hypothesis:

(167) A prime for linearization is a prosodic domain.

Now let us reconsider the linearization processes handled by Spell-Out, in line with the approach discussed in section 3.4. Notice that Spell-Out needs to define at least two kinds of linear order – linear order among the terminal elements of syntactic structure and linear order between the units of Spell-Out – which I refer to as Lin(W) and Lin(S-O), respectively.[24] Then, given (167), the following will hold:

(168) a. A prime for Lin(W) is a prosodic word.
       b. A prime for Lin(S-O) is a phonological phrase.

This gives a uniform account of the two types of prosodic categories in terms of linearization. Consider the derivation of "John read the book" on this approach:

(169) $[_{CP}$ C $[_{TP}$ John T $[_{v*P} t_{John}$ read-v* $[_{VP} t_{read}$ the book $]]]]$

Here, C and v* are strong phases, t indicates a copy, the object DP *the book* stays in situ, *saw* moves to adjoin to v*, and the subject DP *John*, base-generated in Spec-v*, moves to Spec-T. In the bottom-up derivation, Spell-Out first applies to the complement of v* and defines a linear order among the three terminal elements, t_{saw}, *the*, and *book*, as shown in (170a) below. This linearization is Lin(W). Given (168a), these three terminal elements are potentially prosodic words, since they are primes for Lin(W). However, t_{saw} cannot be a prosodic word, as it lacks phonological features. The determiner *the*, a function word, also cannot be an independent prosodic word (Selkirk 1984) and will thus be part of a prosodic word containing a lexical element (content word). The noun *book* is a lexical element and serves as a prime for Lin(W) here, thereby qualifying as a prosodic word. Then, if we assume that functional elements are incorporated into the prosodic word containing their adjacent lexical element, *the* and *book* constitute a single prosodic word. (For specific mechanisms of prosodic word formation, see Nespor and Vogel (1986) and Selkirk (1996), among others.) In addition to Lin(W), Lin(S-O) also applies at this stage of derivation, vacuously in this case, as in (170b). In the system of Dobashi (2003) reviewed in section 3.4, the copy of *saw* (t_{saw}), being the initial element in the linear string in (170a), will be available to the next Spell-Out. So, *the book* as a whole is the only prime for Lin(S-O) and forms a phonological phrase. As a result of these linearization procedures, the prosodic structure shown in (170c) is obtained in the phonological component Φ:

(170) a. Lin(W): t_{read} < the < book
     b. Lin(S-O): the book
     c. Transferred to Φ: ((the book)$_\omega$)$_\varphi$

As the derivation reaches the CP phase, Spell-Out applies to the complement of C, and Lin(W) and Lin(S-O) apply:

(171) a. Lin(W): John < T < t_{John} < read-v* < t_{read}
     b. Lin(S-O): read < the book
     c. Transferred to Φ: ((read)$_\omega$)$_\varphi$ ((the book)$_\omega$)$_\varphi$

As in (171a), Lin(W) defines the linear order among all terminal elements in this domain of Spell-Out, including t_{saw}, which has been left available for this linearization. The initial element in this linear string, *John*, is not transferred to the phonological component at this stage, and so the verb *read*, which is the only element that has phonological features in this transferred domain, serves as a prime for Lin(S-O). This Lin(S-O) defines *read* as preceding *the book* in (171b) because of the Assembly Process: t_{read} precedes *the* in (170a) and follows *read-v** in (171a), whereby *read-v** precedes *the book*. Since *read* is a prime for Lin(S-O) as well as for Lin(W), it is interpreted as a prosodic word and as a phonological phrase in the phonological component, as in (171c).

Spell-Out applying to the root of the sentence gives rise to Lin(W) and Lin(S-O), as follows:

(172) a. Lin(W): C < John
    b. Lin(S-O): John < read
    c. Transferred to Φ: ((John)$_\omega$)$_\varphi$ ((read)$_\omega$)$_\varphi$ ((the book)$_\omega$)$_\varphi$

Lin(W) defines *John* as being preceded by C. That is, *John* is a prime for Lin(W) and forms a prosodic word in the phonological component. Lin(S-O) defines *John*, which is now a prime for Lin(S-O), as preceding *read*, by virtue of the Assembly Process, and forms a phonological phrase. As a result, the prosodic phrasing shown in (172c) is obtained.

I have shown that the two types of linearization, Lin(W) and Lin(S-O), are involved in Spell-Out, and the primes for these linearization procedures correspond to the two kinds of prosodic categories – prosodic word and phonological phrase. If this approach is correct, then a unit of Spell-Out is a phonological phrase not because it demarcates a domain in the phonological component, as stated in the form of the supposed "null hypothesis" (163), but because it is a prime for Lin(S-O). This approach unifies the two prosodic categories in terms of linearization. This is not possible with the "null hypothesis," which is now considered to be derivable from (167). This seems to be a welcome result, since it presents a new means of unifying yet another prosodic category, i.e., intonational phrase, in terms of linearization, as we will see in the next section.

3.5.3   *Further unification: intonational phrase*

Investigating topicalization and word order in Italian and other languages, Lambrecht (1994) argues that there are two factors that determine word order: the grammatical/syntactic factor and the pragmatic/information-structure factor. In our terms, the former corresponds to Lin(W) and Lin(S-O), but what is the latter? Since pragmatics is independent of syntax, let us call it Lin(¬S), which stands for linearization based on non-syntactic factors. Although the exact mechanism of Lin(¬S) is beyond the scope of the present study, I assume that Lin(¬S) is not part of phase-by-phase Spell-Out, unlike Lin(W) and Lin(S-O), and that it applies without reference to the internal structure of syntactic objects.[25]

Linearization in terms of information structure results in free word order in many languages, and, importantly, these freely ordered elements constitute intonational phrases. As described in section 3.4.1, in Chichewa (and other Bantu languages such as KiYaka (Kidima 1990, 1991)), the word order is free when the subject and object are construed as topics, as observed by Bresnan and Mchombo (1987: 744–745). Note that "free" here means that the word order is permissible with respect to grammaticality; pragmatic interpretation varies in relation to the specific order:

(173) a. SVO: Njûchi   zi-ná-wá-lum-a   alenje
           bees   SM-PST-OM-bite-INDIC   hunters
           'The bees bit the hunters.'
      b. VOS: Zináwáluma alenje njûchi
      c. OVS: Alenje zináwáluma njûchi
      d. VSO: Zináwáluma njûchi alenje
      e. SOV: Njûchi alenje zináwáluma
      f. OSV: Alenje njûchi zináwáluma

(Bresnan and Mchombo 1987: 744–745)

As pointed out by Kanerva (1990: 147), topics, as well as vocatives, parentheticals, nonrestrictive relative clauses, etc., regularly form their own intonational phrases in this language.

Similarly, in Italian, a topic phrase usually shows comma intonation, thus constituting an intonational phrase, as observed by Frascarelli (2000), among others:

(174) a. A Carlo, sul tavolo,   quel libro, non glielo   lascio.
         to Carlo on-the table that book   not to.him-it leave-1SG
         'I won't leave that book on the table for Carlo.'
      b. Sul tavolo, quel libro, a Carlo, non glielo lascio.
      c. Quel libro, sul tavolo, a Carlo, non glielo lascio.
         etc.

(Frascarelli 2000: 160)

(175) a. Non   glielo   lascio,   a Carlo, sul tavolo,   quel libro.
         not   to.him-it leave-1SG   to Carlo on-the table that book
      b. Non glielo lascio, sul tavolo, quel libro, a Carlo.
      c. Non glielo lascio, a Carlo, quel libro, sul tavolo.
         etc.

(Frascarelli 2000: 160)

Here, the three topicalized elements, *a Carlo*, *sul tavolo*, and *quel libro*, can be arranged in any order in the left and right peripheries, as in (174) and (175), respectively. Since this free word order results from topicalization (but not from, say, A-movement to a Case position), we can assume that linearization of topicalized phrases is non-syntactic in the sense that it applies on the basis of information structure.[26] Given these considerations, I hypothesize the following:

(176) A prime for Lin($\neg$S) is an intonational phrase.

Let us now consider if (176) holds in cases of non-syntactic linearization other than topicalization. Zubizarreta (1998: 148ff.) argues that the Heavy NP Shift

(HNPS) in English is prosodically motivated.[27] Although several syntactic approaches to HNPS have been suggested (Guéron 1980; Rochemont and Culicover 1990; Kayne 1994; Takano 1998), they do not consider prosodic factors that condition HNPS and seem not to accommodate the fact that the DP is shifted for prosodic reasons (see Shiobara 2010: 137ff. for further discussion). Let us briefly review Zubizarreta's prosodic analysis of HNPS. Consider the following examples, where parentheses indicate intonational phrases (marked with ɩ) and diacritics mark nuclear stress:

(177) a. (Max pút)ɩ (all the boxes of home fúrnishings)ɩ (in his cár)ɩ.
     b. (Max put in his cár)ɩ (all the boxes of home fúrnishings)ɩ.

(Zubizarreta 1998: 148, 149)

She argues that a "heavy" constituent can be preceded and followed by an intonational phrase boundary, as in (177a),[28] but such intonational phrasing is unbalanced and sounds awkward. A more natural intonational parsing, however, can be obtained by placing the heavy constituent on the right side of the PP *in his car*, as in (177b), which consists of two intonational phrases. So, technical details aside, the word order in (177b) results from non-syntactic, prosodically motivated, linearization, i.e., Lin(¬S). Then, (176) accounts for the fact that the shifted DP and the rest of the sentence are intonational phrases, because they are primes for Lin(¬S).

Another case that may conform to (176) is multiple pre-nominal modification. Sproat and Shih (1991) observe that the unmarked word order among adjectives modifying a noun is QUALITY > COLOR > PROVENANCE, and the sentence is pronounced suitably without comma intonation in this order, as in (178a), while the order becomes free with comma intonation, which indicates an intonational phrase, as in (178b):

(178) a. She loves all those wonderful orange Oriental ivories.
     b. She loves all those Oriental, orange, wonderful ivories.

(Sproat and Shih 1991: 578)

Sproat and Shih suggest that the adjectives in (178b) modify the head noun in parallel, as schematically shown in (179):

(179)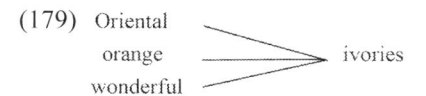

Adapting this idea for the present framework, we can say that *wonderful* asymmetrically c-commands *orange*, which in turn asymmetrically c-commands *Oriental* in (178a), and that these three adjectives are linearized by Lin(W), on the basis of these syntactic relations, pronounced without comma intonation. By contrast, in (178b), all the adjectives are equally related to the head noun,[29] as they are unable to establish an asymmetric syntactic relation with one another. That is, they cannot be ordered based on syntactic relations among them. Then, technical details aside, they are linearized non-syntactically, thus constituting intonational phrases, given (176).

A final case to consider here is the matrix clause, an intonational phrase in the neutral, broad-focus, context in English (Downing 1970: 28; Emonds 1976: 44; Nespor and Vogel 1986: 188).

(180) (You realize (that) the books have already arrived)$_\iota$.

(adapted from Emonds 1976: 44)

Notice that root sentences are linearized with respect to other root sentences in the discourse (sometimes vacuously, when there is no other matrix clause around it). In this sense, it is linearized on the basis of extra-sentential, non-syntactic factors. That is, the intonational phrasing of the matrix clause can also be considered to fall within (176). The matrix clause as a whole corresponds to an intonational phrase.[30]

So far, we have seen that non-syntactic linearization results in the formation of intonational phrases. We have suggested that the following three kinds of linearizations correspond to their own type of prosodic domain:

(181) a. A prime for Lin(W) is a prosodic word.
 b. A prime for Lin(S-O) is a phonological phrase.
 c. A prime for Lin(¬S) is an intonational phrase.

Importantly, all these follow from (167), repeated here:

(182) A prime for linearization is a prosodic domain.

Note that intonational phrases properly contain phonological phrases, which in turn properly contain prosodic words, as in (183a). That is, intonational phrases do not contain part of a phonological phrase in the way that a phonological phrase spans across two intonational phrases, as in (183b):

(183) a. [(ω ω)$_\varphi$]$_\iota$ [(ω ω)$_\varphi$ (ω ω)$_\varphi$]$_\iota$
 b. *[(ω ω)$_\varphi$ (ω]$_\iota$ [ω)$_\varphi$ (ω ω)$_\varphi$]$_\iota$

This follows from the way linearization applies: Lin(¬S) applies to a sequence of phonological phrases, without breaking up the phonological phrases. Likewise, phonological phrases properly contain prosodic words, since Lin(S-O) arranges domains of Spell-Out but not prosodic words. Then, it follows from (182) that there are three layers in the prosodic hierarchy – the higher ones properly contain the lower ones:

(184) (   )$_\iota$ (   )$_\iota$ IntP ← Lin(¬S)
 (   )$_\varphi$ (   )$_\varphi$ (   )$_\varphi$ PhP ← Lin(S-O)
 (   )$_\omega$ (   )$_\omega$ (   )$_\omega$ (   )$_\omega$ (   )$_\omega$ (   )$_\omega$ PrW ← Lin(W)

Unlike the (supposed) null hypothesis regarding phonological phrasing in (163), this approach offers a principled account of *why* a domain of Spell-Out is a prosodic domain: namely, because it is a prime for linearization. Moreover, this linearization-based approach yields a principled, uniform account of *how* three layers of prosodic categories are formed and hierarchically structured in terms of linearization procedures, which are the essential and distinctive properties of the phonological component.

Interestingly, Ito and Mester (2012, 2013) conclude on empirical grounds that there are only three universal prosodic categories: the prosodic word, phonological phrase, and intonational phrase. They argue that other prosodic categories, if they exist, are recursive manifestations of these categories. Moreover, they argue that the three universal categories are derived by Match Theory, which relates word, phrase, and clause to prosodic words, phonological phrases, and intonational phrase, respectively (Selkirk 2009, 2011, see Chapter 2). This effect of Match Theory is further reducible to the three types of linearization, each of which is independently necessitated by the processes of externalization. I will leave open whether and how the theoretical ideas explored here can be harmonized with Match Theory.

3.6. Conclusion

In this chapter, I first reviewed Dobashi (2003), an example of the theoretical investigations of phonological phrasing that have been spurred by the development of syntactic conceptions such as phases and Multiple Spell-Out within the framework of the Minimalist Program from the mid-1990s to the 2000s. These approaches seem to have largely prevailed in recent work on the syntax-phonology interface. However, especially since the rise of Selkirk's (2009, 2011) Match Theory, it increasingly appears (to me, at least) that they are too narrowly focused, as they account for only one layer of the prosodic hierarchy.

The theory of phonological phrasing proposed in Dobashi (2003) is in fact a theory of linearization, which takes a domain of Spell-Out as a prime for linearization. This prime is in turn interpreted as a phonological phrase in the phonological component. Generalizing this idea to other kinds of linearization, I have suggested that a prime for the linearization of syntactic terminals Lin(W) and that for the non-syntactic linearization Lin($\neg$S) be additionally interpreted as prosodic domains – the former being the prosodic word and the latter the intonational phrase (Dobashi 2013). The Multiple Spell-Out theory of phonological phrasing is then subsumed under the more general theory of linearization. It turns out that the result of this linearization-based theory conforms to Ito and Mester's (2012, 2013) empirical thesis: namely, that there are only three prosodic categories universally.

Note that the phase-by-phase Multiple Spell-Out theory adopted in this chapter assumes that phases are invariably CP and v*P. However, some syntactic studies of phases have argued that phases should be contextually defined rather than fixed (see Bošković 2014, and papers cited therein). Moreover, Chomsky (2015) argues that phase-hood can be inherited and that the domain of Spell-Out varies accordingly. Thus, if the phase-hood of v* is inherited by V, then Spell-Out applies to the sister of V but not to that of v*. These new theoretical positions on phases would all undermine the premise of the "null hypothesis" of phonological phrasing. Furthermore, recent reconsiderations of the architecture of grammar, which are based on the strict internalist perspective of language (Chomsky 2016, 2017a), have started to show that the traditional Y-model is open to question. That is, language is a generative procedure that yields hierarchically structured expressions at C-I, and the computation to SM is merely secondary, implying that the operation Spell-Out itself has no place in narrow syntax. Although phase-by-phase Multiple Spell-Out has been important in understanding the prosodic properties of language for the last two decades, a fresher perspective on the architecture of syntax-phonology connection may be required.

In the next two chapters, I will attempt to update the typology and mechanism of syntax-phonology mapping. In Chapter 4, I will carefully review the notion of externalization and propose a new interpretive theory of phonological phrasing within the framework of the Labeling Algorithm (Chomsky 2013, 2015), thus dispensing with the operation Spell-Out. I will also review some new empirical findings on basic phonological phrasing. Specifically, I will reconsider the typology of phonological phrasing in (159)–(162), which was based on previous studies, especially those done in the 1970s through the 1990s. Some more-recent studies have found that subjects may in fact be phrased with a following element in some languages. I will show that these and other new findings can also be accommodated in the proposed interpretive theory of phonological phrasing. In Chapter 5, I will consider intonational phrases again and attempt to identify what can be considered as a prime for non-syntactic linearization Lin($^{-}$S), based on the notion of Workspace explored by Chomsky (2017b) and Chomsky et al. (2017). These new approaches to phonological and intonational phrasing are, of course, unified in terms of linearization, as indicated by the ideas advanced in this chapter.

Notes

1 Chomsky (2000: 108) proposes the following version of PIC:

(i) The domain of H is not accessible to operations outside HP; only H and its edges are accessible to such operations.

This formulation implies that Spell-Out applies to the complement of H when HP is complete in (6). On the other hand, Spell-Out applies when the next-higher phase is complete under (7). Since the timing of Spell-Out does not affect phonological phrasing, I will leave this issue open. See Chomsky (2001, 2008) and Citko (2014) for further discussion.

2 See Tokizaki (2005, 2008) for an alternative minimalist theory of syntax-phonology mapping that does not resort to labels and projections.

3 See also Frascarelli (2000) and Ghini (1993). In northern Italian, *Stress Retraction* (Nespor and Vogel 1986: 174) or *Rhythm Rule* (Frascarelli 2000: 20) is sensitive to phonological phrasing.

4 Although Nespor and Vogel argue that syntactic branchingness affects restructuring, I will argue that what matters is prosodic branchingness. I will return to this point later.

5 There are some lexical exceptions to Shortening; see Odden (1996: 223).

6 Note that the domain of Shortening is different from that of Phrasal Tone Insertion in some environments. The domain of Shortening is properly contained in the domain of Phrasal Tone Insertion. However, since the presence of an inserted phrasal tone always corresponds to the right edge of the domain of Shortening, I use Phrasal Tone Insertion as a diagnostic of phonological phrasing here. As seen in Chapter 2, Truckenbrodt (1995, 1999) proposes that the difference in phrasing is accounted for in terms of recursive phonological phrases. Elaborating on Kaisse (1985), Seidl 2001 proposes that the difference is attributable to restructuring of phonological phrases and that Shortening applies before the restructuring applies, and Phrasal Tone Insertion applies after that.

7 According to Odden (1987: 35, footnote 3), "Shortening applies only in the stem; surface long vowels in prefixes are not shortened (*viz. naa-*)."

8 Note that the final vowel *-ée* of the verb is long; however, this is due to another independent phonological rule, *Lengthening*. See Odden (1987).

9 Odden (1996: 223) uses (54b) to show that *nchéengowé* 'her husband' undergoes Shortening because of the presence of *Malííya* 'Mary.'

10 The inalienable possessive-suffix *-we* added to *nchéengo* 'husband' does not trigger Shortening of *nchéengo*.

(i) a. nchéengo   'husband'
    b. nchéengowe 'her husband'

(Odden 1996: 222)

Here, irrespective of whether *-we* is added, the noun retains its long vowel. Therefore, *-ee-* is shortened in (54b) because of the possessor.

11 Kinyambo is also known as Runyambo (Rugemalira 1993a, 1993b, 2005).

12 Bickmore (1989: 139) notes that in this example High Deletion (or Beat Deletion in his (1989) terms) is "optional (but preferred), as one syllable intervenes between the clashing stresses." I assume this is because of the nature of the phonological rule, not the phonological phrasing.

13 The H on the prefix in *omukama* results from application of High Insertion. It is not deleted by High Deletion. See Bickmore (1989).

14 The following example also shows that the (syntactically) branching object is phonologically phrased with the verb:

(i) Mbonir' [émbw' [[érire   múno]$_{VP}$]$_S$]$_{NP}$ Kénya]$_{NP}$
    (   )$_\varphi$ (   )$_\varphi$
    I-saw   dog   REL-ate well   Kenya
    'I saw the dog who, while in Kenya, ate well.'

(Bickmore 1990: 16)

Here, the object is modified by the relative clause, and the verb does not have an H tone; thus, there is no phonological phrase boundary between the verb and object. According to (65a), the verb 'see' has an H tone in isolation. However, since I do not find the specific underlying representation of the verb form used in (i) in Bickmore (1989, 1990), I include this example in an endnote.

15 For the purpose of illustration, I assume here and below that Spell-Out applies to the complement of the phase α upon completion of α. See footnote 1.

16 Thanks to Chris Collins for suggesting this term to me.

17 The standard theories (Relation-based Theory and the right-XP edge-setting of End-based Theory) also predict that C is phrased with Subj. See also Fuß (2007), for prosodic phrasing of C and Subj in German.

18 See Seidl (2001) for cross-linguistic variation within Bantu languages, and see Samuels (2009, 2011) and Samuels and Narita (2013) for further elaboration of the typology and

for the hybrid approach incorporating Uriagereka's (1999) Multiple Spell-Out Theory and Chomsky's phase theory.

19 I will discuss feature inheritance and its effect on the position and phonological phrasing of the object DP in English within the more recent theory of syntax, in Chapter 4.

20 Henderson (2006: Ch.4) argues that object marker in Chichewa is in fact an agreement morpheme rather than a pronominal clitic, contra Bresnan and Mchombo (1987) and Mchombo (2004). See also Zeller (2014) and Riedel (2009). I do not address this point here, for our main concern is case (II), where the object marker is absent as in (69) (= (126) below), to which we will return shortly.

21 It is not clear why the suffixial element -*le* on the verb is missing in (137a).

22 Collins (2004) suggests that agreement always gives rise to movement in Bantu.

23 It remains to be seen if this phrasing can be recast in terms of recursive phrasing, or if the recursive phrasing can be recast in Pak's model.

24 I do not distinguish head-level linearization and phrase-level linearization, unlike Pak (2008). I assume that these two procedures are parts of Lin(W).

25 For example, Pereltsvaig (2004) argues that the position of topic is determined linearly, independently of syntactic structure, in Italian and Russian.

26 Frascarelli (2000) argues that a topic is base-generated and "extraneous" to feature-checking operations and therefore corresponds to an intonational phrase. This seems consistent with Nespor and Vogel's (1986: 189) formulation of Intonational Phrase, which states that an Intonational Phrase is "not structurally attached to the sentence tree." See (32) in Chapter 2.

27 Zubizarreta (1998) proposes the operation of *p-movement* (prosodically motivated movement), which is not triggered by feature-checking of formal features but applies in the syntactic component. See also Takano (2014) for prosodically motivated postposing in Japanese, which applies in the phonological component. I will leave open the technical details of movement (or linearization) triggered by prosodic factors.

28 Shiobara (2010) argues that a constituent is heavy if it has extra prosodic prominence, or if it has a larger number of prosodic words than the string that is crossed by the shifted DP. In the following examples, the question sentence A situates the answer sentences B1 and B2 in the broad focus context, so that there is no particular emphatic stress in the sentences (see also Hawkins 1994; Wasow 1997, 2002):

(i) A: What happened yesterday?
  B1: Jack received (from Betty)$_\omega$ [$_{DP}$ (the report)$_\omega$ (on Jim)$_\omega$]
  B2: #Jack received (from Betty)$_\omega$ [$_{DP}$ (the report on him)$_\omega$]
  (Shiobara 2010: 85–86)

In (iB1), the PP *from Betty*, containing just one prosodic word, is crossed by the DP *the report on Jim* containing two prosodic words, and the sentence is acceptable, if not perfect, especially when it is compared with (iB2). The shifted DP in (iB2) contains only one prosodic word (*him* being a weak pronoun that cannot serve as a prosodic word), and the sentence sounds degraded. This contrast indicates that the shifted DP must contain a larger number of prosodic words than the crossed string. See also Ross (1967/1986), Rochemont and Culicover (1990).

29 I will not pursue the technical details of these constructions, but perhaps we could restate (179) as follows, using set-theoretical notation:

(i) {{Oriental, ivories}, {orange, ivories}, {wonderful, ivories}}

Here, only one of the copies of *ivories* is pronounced (presumably for economy reasons, cf. Collins (2017)), and the adjectives are linearized non-syntactically as syntactic linearization fails.

30 We will discuss intonational phrases further in Chapter 5.

4 Minimal search and phonological phrasing

4.1. Introduction

In this chapter, I first review the status of externalization in the context of a strict internalist perspective on language (Chomsky 2016, 2017a) and then propose an interpretive theory of prosodic domains that does not have recourse to the operation Spell-Out. In the syntactic framework incorporating the labeling algorithm (Chomsky 2013, 2015), I point out that an interpretive asymmetry exists between syntax and phonology, in that syntactically inert, unlabelable elements like a root R are phonologically interpretable. Given this, I suggest that a syntactic object SO is interpreted as a phonological phrase if such an unlabelable element is detectable with minimal search within the SO. I show that this approach accounts for (i) the cross-linguistic difference in the complementizer-trace effect, (ii) possible locations of intonational phrase boundaries in ECM and simple transitive constructions in English, (iii) the cross-linguistic difference in phonological phrasing of applicative constructions in Bantu languages, (iv) the effects of case suffixes on prosodic domains in Japanese, (v) the effects of conjunctions on prosody, and (vi) the distribution of weak pronouns in English, all of which cannot be adequately accounted for by Multiple Spell-Out approaches to phonological phrasing that have been largely central to the study of the syntax-phonology interface in the last decade or two.

This chapter is organized as follows. In section 4.2, I will review the architecture of grammar, in line with the conception of externalization crystalized by Chomsky (2005, *et seqq.*), who argues that language is nothing more than a generative procedure that produces an infinite array of hierarchically structured expressions mapped to the conceptual-intentional interface, in which the processes of externalization are ancillary operations. I argue, on conceptual grounds, that Spell-Out is no longer formulable within this particular model of grammar and thus discard the Multiple Spell-Out theory of phonological phrasing. In section 4.3, I briefly review the labeling algorithm (Chomsky 2013, 2015), which provides the syntactic framework for the present study. In section 4.4, I propose a theory of phonological phrasing that is based on the interpretation of SOs. In section 4.5, I discuss some empirical consequences of this theory, which are mentioned above. In section 4.6, I propose a new procedure of linearization that does not resort to Spell-Out. Given this proposed ordering procedure, I reconsider the prosodic word and phonological phrase in terms of linearization, in line with Dobashi (2013), as reviewed in Chapter 3. Section 4.7 concludes this chapter.

4.2.   What is externalization?

In the extended standard theory (EST) model of generative grammar, the architecture of grammar was assumed to be equipped with D-structure, S-Structure, LF, and PF, taking the following form (Chomsky and Lasnik 1977; Chomsky 1981, 1986a. See also Chomsky 2005: 10, 2008: 137):

(1)   EST-model (Y-model)

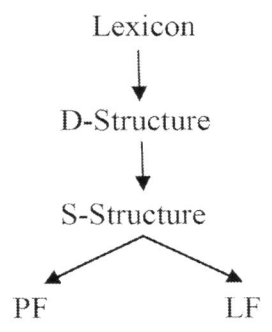

Since this architecture looks like an (inverted) Y, it is often called a Y-model. This model was basically carried over to the early framework of the minimalist program, which dispensed with D- and S-structures, as in (2) (Chomsky 1995). In this model, a derivation starts with Numeration and splits into LF and PF when Spell-Out applies at some point of the computation (see Irurtzun 2009 for further discussion).

(2)   Early minimalism (Y-model):

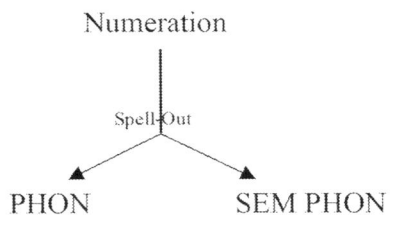

Then, as discussed in Chapter 3, the so-called Multiple Spell-Out theory was proposed by Epstein et al. (1998) and Uriagereka (1999). It was later incorporated into a phase theory by Chomsky (2000, 2001). Specifically, Chomsky (2000: 131ff.) argues that Spell-Out applies phase-by-phase, concomitantly with feature-checking, thus reducing the distinction between overt and covert operations and eliminating principles and conditions with "look-ahead" properties such as Procrastinate (see Epstein and Seely 2002 for further discussions on feature-checking and Spell-Out; see Chomsky 1995 for Procrastinate). Then, Chomsky (2004) further unifies syntactic, phonological, and semantic cycles by generalizing Spell-Out (i.e., mapping to the phonological component) to the operation TRANSFER (i.e., mapping to the phonological and semantic components). Thus, he assumes that the language L generates a pair <PHON, SEM> and that PHON and SEM are interpreted by the sensorimotor (SM) and conceptual-intentional (C-I) systems, respectively. L has three components: (i) narrow syntax (NS) that maps a lexical array LA to a derivation D-NS, (ii) the phonological component Φ that maps D-NS to PHON, which is accessed by SM, and (iii) the semantic component Σ that maps D-NS to SEM, which is interpreted by C-I. Hauser et al. (2002) call component (i) the faculty of language in the narrow sense (FLN), and the system comprising components (i), (ii), and (iii) the faculty of language in the broad sense (FLB).

In this architecture of grammar, the derivation starts with LA, and the computation of all the three components proceed cyclically in parallel. The cyclic units are called phases. At each phase of a derivation, TRANSFER applies to the derivation, mapping D-NS to Φ and Σ. In particular, the mapping to Φ is called Spell-Out. Schematically, it takes the following form, which I will call the Multiple Y-model:

(3)   Multiple Y-model:

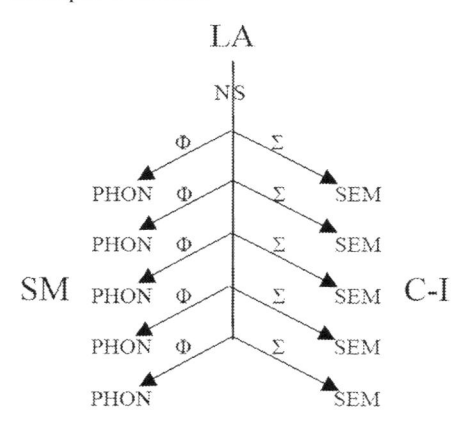

Notice that this architecture of grammar is symmetrical, in that computation of these three components proceeds in parallel, with NS centered between Φ and Σ.

The Multiple Y-model has been widely adopted, often without much discussion, in minimalist studies of syntax and its interaction with the interface components. However, Chomsky (2005, *et seqq.*) has started to reconsider this view, making explicit the notion of *externalization*. Thus, Chomsky (2016) examines the following example:

(4)   Can eagles that fly swim?

Here, *can* is semantically understood with *swim* rather than *fly*. This is in a sense surprising because *can* is closer to *fly* than to *swim* if we measure the distance in terms of the empirically observable linear order that holds among the words in (4). Chomsky (2016: 10) points out that, "[l]anguage makes use of a property of minimal structural distance, never using the much simpler operation of minimal linear distance," and emphasizes that semantic interpretation and syntactic rule application are invariably dependent on structure. Then, linear order turns out to be external to language, and thus the processes of externalization that assigns a particular mode of expression (speech, sign, touch, etc.) are also external to language since they depend on linear order. Thus, Chomsky (2016: 4) at first defines the Basic Property of language as follows: "each language provides an unbounded array of hierarchically structured expressions that receive interpretations at two interfaces, sensorimotor for externalization and conceptual-intentional for mental processes." This formulation of the Basic Property seems to presuppose the Multiple Y-model in (3), which symmetrically connects NS with Φ and Σ. However, considering the structure-dependence of linguistic rules and interpretations, as well as the traditional internalist concepts of language (a la René Descartes, Wilhelm von Humboldt, Charles Darwin, Otto Jespersen, and others) and his own concept of I-language (Chomsky 1986a), Chomsky (2016: 13) restates the Basic Property as follows: "the Basic Property is generation of an unbounded array of hierarchically structured expressions mapping to the conceptual-intentional interface, providing a kind of 'language of thought' – and quite possibly the only such LOT." That is, the mapping to Φ is not part of the processes that generate LOT (see Chomsky 2005: 4, 2008: 136ff, for earlier discussions on this issue; see Fodor 1975 for LOT). Then, the architecture of grammar would look like (5), which does not include the phonological component:

(5)   Language: Lexicon

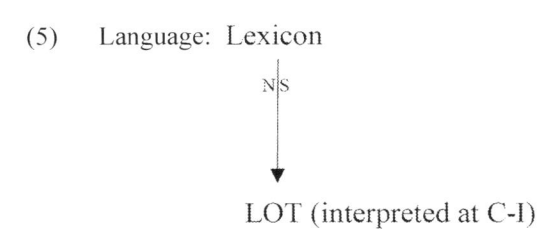

LOT (interpreted at C-I)

If this is correct, then I-language is I-shaped but not Y-shaped. I would therefore call it the I-model. The distinction between FLN and FLB thus no longer exists: language is something that roughly corresponds to FLN and the (perhaps trivial) mapping to C-I.

   Given these considerations, Chomsky (2017a: 201r) concludes that "there is a fundamental asymmetry between the two interfaces." A generative procedure produces an infinite array of structured expressions at C-I, while the ancillary operations of externalization map the structured expressions to SM, linearly ordering them so that SM can interpret them. Chomsky (2014: 7) states this asymmetry as follows:

(6)   Language is optimized relative to the C-I interface alone, with externalization a secondary phenomenon.

Thus, language generates not a pair <PHON, SEM> but a singleton SEM.

Therefore, externalization is not part of language. That is, Φ is not a linguistic component. If this is the case, language will not "care about" Φ or SM. Then, it is unlikely that language performs any operation for Φ, as there is no reason to adopt Spell-Out as a linguistic operation that affects the computational system of language.

Furthermore, quite independently of these considerations, Chomsky et al. (2017: 14) suggest eliminating Spell-Out from the architecture of grammar. They point out that if a syntactic object containing a phase P undergoes Internal Merge, the complement of P, which is supposed to have been spelled-out in its original position, is actually pronounced in the derived position (Obata 2010). Consider the following example, where α and β are phases, and t_α is a copy of α:

(7) $[_\alpha$ The verdict $[_\beta$ that Tom Jones is guilty]] seems to have been reached t_α by the jury.

Here, β is not pronounced in the position of t_α, where it could have been spelled-out but is actually pronounced in the matrix subject position (I will return to this issue in section 4.6). Therefore, they conclude that Spell-Out does not exist in a literal sense. Note that even though β is not spelled-out or pronounced in its original position, the domain of β should be syntactically inaccessible because of the Phase-Impenetrability Condition. Chomsky et al. (2017) then reformulate Transfer as follows:

(8)   Transfer renders β inaccessible to subsequent manipulation.

Despite its name, Transfer does not literally send syntactic objects to external components; it is a property of syntactic derivation derived from a third-factor principle of efficient computation, which allows the computational system to forget the "transferred" domain. This conforms to the I-model (5), where there is no such Spell-Out operation.

Linguistic operations are generally motivated by or associated with a third-factor principle of efficient computation. Thus, Merge is a minimal operation affecting two objects; Agree is a minimal search operation holding between a probe and goal; Labeling Algorithm is also a minimal search operation allowing syntactic objects to be interpreted at the interfaces (or perhaps just at C-I); and Transfer in the form of (8) helps reduce the computational burden. But how about Spell-Out? Given (8), Spell-Out (Transfer to Φ) is no longer necessary for the reduction of computational burden: it cannot be motivated as an independent operation associated with minimal computation.

Therefore, I conclude that Spell-Out has no place in the architecture of grammar. Note that, even before the I-model crystallized, as seen above, Epstein et al. (1998: 140; 157ff.) had suggested formulating Spell-Out not as a rule that maps a syntactic phrase marker to phonology, but as a cyclic interpretive procedure applying to each step of a syntactic derivation, given their strictly derivational model of syntax, which totally dispenses with the distinction between overt and covert operations. Moreover, Boeckx (2003/2007) has suggested that Spell-Out be eliminated from the grammar, for still other reasons. Spell-Out, in its original form, is formulated as a stripping operation (Chomsky 1995: 229). It "strips away" phonological features from the syntactic object already formed in the derivation. Boeckx (2007: 419) points out that Spell-Out is inconsistent with the Inclusiveness Condition (Chomsky 1995: 225), a fundamental conditions of narrow syntax. The Inclusiveness Condition requires that narrow syntax only rearrange lexical items and that nothing be added or deleted. Spell-Out physically deletes phonological features from narrow syntax and should thus not be an operation of narrow syntax. He further points out that multiple application of Spell-Out could be problematic since the phonological component would have to look at a full representation, not at each spelled-out partial piece of structure, to determine, for example, intonation contour, such as falling intonation in declarative sentences or rising intonation in interrogative sentences. Since Multiple Spell-Out chunks a sentence into several pieces, additional recombinatory processes would be required (cf. Chomsky 2004: 107ff). If Spell-Out does not chunk a sentence, we can eliminate such a redundant recombination procedure. Given these and other considerations, Boeckx (2007: 419) proposes that Spell-Out be eliminated and that interfaces be "invasive," that is, "external systems look into narrow syntax and pick and choose what they want."

Note that the term "invasive" might be slightly misleading, because nothing physically "invades" the syntax, which remains unaffected. Therefore, I will use the term "interpretive." An "interpretive" procedure is a series of processes in the phonological component (i.e., externalization) that generates phonological objects by referring to the computational system of language. The phonological objects so generated are eventually interpreted by the SM system.

I do not have much to say here about the semantic side of the interface, but given the formulation of Transfer in (8), the mapping to Σ would not apply in a multiple manner either, unlike the Multiple Y-model in (3). Citing a personal communication with Norbert Hornstein, Boeckx (2003/2007: 418) points out that, for example, the semantic component needs to look at the full representation of a sentence for pronominal binding, indicating that the Multiple Y-model would require redundant recombinatory processes, as in the case of intonation contour.

In what follows, I will adopt the I-model and interpretive approach to the phonology side of the interface and assume that phonological interpretations apply cyclically, in parallel with a phase-by-phase syntactic derivation. Furthermore, contra Boeckx (2003/2007), I will argue that it is necessary for externalization to have "recombinatory" processes. These are not processes that restore the syntactic structure. Rather, they are processes of linearization that allow the SM system to "use" language in its own mode. Thus, the phonological component interprets hierarchically structured expressions as linearly ordered strings, which are then converted into hierarchically structured phonological objects (see section 3.5). These processes are therefore not additional redundant mechanisms – they make it possible for the SM system to interpret syntactic objects as phonological objects.

Hence, dispensing with Spell-Out, I assume the following architecture of grammar, where the processes of externalization look into language (i.e., narrow syntax) without affecting it and generate PHON on the basis of linguistic information available to them:

(9)   Lexicon

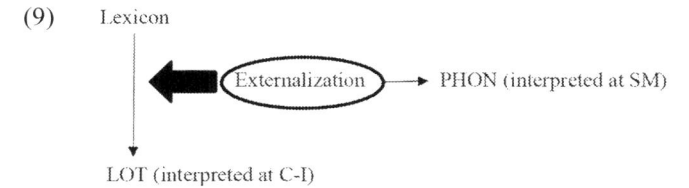

LOT (interpreted at C-I)

Given this model, processes of externalization can look into LOT as well (see Chomsky 2014: ft.9), unlike the (Multiple) Y-model, in which syntax mediates phonology and semantics. I will return to this issue in Chapter 5.

How do we demarcate phonological phrases without Spell-Out? Let us now critically reconsider the null hypothesis regarding phonological phrasing (Dobashi 2003), which I reviewed in Chapter 3 and restate here:

(10)   A domain of Spell-Out is a phonological phrase.

The following are prevailing assumptions in the phase-theoretic investigation of syntax (Chomsky 2000, *et seqq.*):

(11)   a. CP and v*P are phases
       b. Spell-Out applies phase-by-phase.
       c. Spell-Out applies to the complement of a phase head.

For the bottom-up derivation of the structure in (12a), Spell-Out first applies to VP, which is the complement of v*P phase, and then to TP, which is the complement of phase head C. Finally, Spell-Out applies to the root of the structure, resulting in three domains of Spell-Out, as in (12b):

(12)   a. Syntax: [$_{CP}$ **C** [$_{TP}$ Subj T [$_{vP}$ YP V-**v*** [$_{VP}$ t_V Obj]]]]
       b. Spell-Out: (C) (Subj T   YP V-v*) (t_V Obj)

Given the null hypothesis (10), we would predict that the Spell-Out domains (12b) correspond to phonological phrases. But, as we discussed at length in Chapter 3, the following are basic phonological phrasings in SVO languages:

(13)   a. (C Subj)$_\varphi$ (T V-v*)$_\varphi$ (Obj)$_\varphi$
           Aŋlɔ Ewe (M-tone raising: Clements 1978)
           Colloquial French (Liaison: Nespor and Vogel 1986; Selkirk 1984)
           English (Iambic Reversal: Hayes 1989; Nespor and Vogel 1986)
           Italian (Raddoppiamento Sintattico, Stress Retraction: Nespor and Vogel 1986)
           Germanic (Complementizer Agreement: Fuß 2007), *etc.*

b. (C Subj)$_\varphi$ (T V-v* Obj)$_\varphi$
Chichewa (Tone Retraction, etc.: Bresnan and Kanerva 1989; Kanerva 1990)
Chi-mwi:ni (Vowel Shortening: Kisseberth and Abasheikh 1974)
Kimatuumbi (Vowel Shortening: Odden 1996)
Kinyambo (High Deletion: Bickmore 1990), *etc.*

These differ from (12b), especially in the phrasing of the subject. Given (10) and (12b), Subj would be expected to be phrased with T and V but is actually phrased with C, as shown in (13a, b). That is, there is a discrepancy between the domains of Spell-Out and phonological phrases. I therefore proposed a theory that systematically readjusts domains of Spell-Out to phonological phrases. Thus, for the syntactic structure (14a), Spell-Out domains are created as in (14b), and these domains are readjusted to phonological phrases as in (14c).

(14)   a. Syntax: [$_{CP}$ **C** [$_{TP}$ Subj   T [$_{vP}$ YP V-v* [$_{VP}$ t_V Obj]]]]
       b. Spell-Out: (C) (Subj   T   YP V-v*) (t_V Obj)
       c. Phonology:(C   Subj)$_\varphi$ (T   YP V-v* t_V)$_\varphi$ (Obj)$_\varphi$

Crucially, this analysis was theoretically feasible because we had Spell-Out. Now that Spell-Out is not formulable, I conclude that the discrepancy was merely an indication that phase-by-phase Spell-Out is irrelevant to prosodic domains.

Furthermore, recent studies suggest that the domain of Transfer/Spell-Out varies according to the inheritance of phase-hood (Chomsky 2015), as we will discuss in sections 4.5.2 and 4.5.4. Phase-by-phase Spell-Out approaches to phonological phrasing would be totally undermined by the phase-hood inheritance, since they presuppose that the domain of Spell-Out is invariably the complement of a phase head.

Then, the theory of phonological phrasing should be formulated so that it does not depend on Spell-Out. One such current theory is Match Theory (Selkirk 2009, 2011; Elfner 2012, among many others). As mentioned in Selkirk and Lee (2015: fn.7), Match Theory defines prosodic structure "in one fell swoop" on a complete syntactic representation, departing from cyclic approaches to the syntax-phonology interface. As I pointed out in Chapters 2 and 3, a problem with Match Theory is that it does not explain *why* maximal projections are relevant to phonological phrasing. Below, I will propose a derivational alternative to Match Theory that seeks to define a phonological phrase in terms of the third-factor principle of minimal search, without recourse to cyclic Spell-Out.

4.3. Labeling algorithm

The basic idea to be explored here is to attribute phonological phrasing to phonological interpretation of syntactic objects SOs. To implement this idea, I adopt the general framework of the Labeling Algorithm, developed by Chomsky (2013, 1015), because it specifies how SOs are interpreted at the interfaces, as stated in (15).

(15) *Labeling Algorithm*

(Chomsky 2013: 43):

"We assume, then, that there is a fixed labeling algorithm LA that licenses SOs so that they can be interpreted at the interfaces, operating at the phase level along with other operations."

Chomsky argues that LA is a minimal search operation and discusses the following three cases of labeling:

(16) a. H is the label in {H, XP}
      b. The label of YP is the label of K in (i):
          (i) XP . . . {$_K$ XP, YP}
      c. The most prominent feature shared by XP and YP is the label of K in (ii):
          (ii) {$_K$ XP, YP}

Here, H is a simple lexical item, and XP and YP are phrases that have an internal structure constructed by Merge. In (16a), H is detected with minimal search because it is the only lexical item immediately contained within {H, XP} and serves as the label in {H, XP}. In (16b-i), the syntactic object K has XP-YP structure, and minimal search cannot detect a label, unlike (16a). But in (16b-i), XP has undergone Internal Merge (or movement); not all members of the chain of XP are in K, and YP is the only full SO in K. Therefore, the YP provides the label of K. In (16c-ii), we have the XP-YP structure again, but if, for example, XP is a subject DP and YP is a finite TP (or T-bar in the traditional notation), then phi-features are shared by XP and YP and therefore serve as the label of K, depicted as <φ, φ>, which indicates that this is an SO with a subject-predicate relation.

In this way, the syntactic objects in (16a-c) can be interpreted at the interfaces. Note that (15) states that SOs are interpreted at the interface-*s* (plural), which implies that SOs need to be interpreted at both interfaces. But given the asymmetric formulation of grammatical architecture (6), repeated here in (17), I assume that labels are needed only at the C-I interface, not at the SM.

(17) Language is optimized relative to the C-I interface alone, with externalization a secondary phenomenon.

(Chomsky 2014: 7)

Note that the first Merge in a derivation creates an SO of the form {H, H}, which does not fall within the three cases in (16), and minimal search cannot determine its label because both Hs are equally detectable. However, such an SO generally takes the form {*f*, R}, where R is a root and *f* is a functional element that provides R with a category. Thus, if *f* is v and R is *play*, then {v, play} is interpreted as a verb *play*; if *f* is n and R is *play*, then {n, play} is interpreted as a noun *play* (Borer 2005a, 2005b, 2013; Marantz 1997). Chomsky then suggests that R does not qualify as a label (Chomsky 2013: 47, 2015: 8), and $\{f, R\}$ is unambiguously labeled f:

(18)   In $\{f, R\}$, only f is visible to the Labeling Algorithm.

In addition, on the basis of the observation that T is similar to R, Chomsky (2015: 9) argues that not only R but also T is too weak to serve as a label:[1]

(19)   a. R is too weak to serve as a label.
       b. T is too weak to serve as a label.

Given these assumptions, let us consider the derivation of a simple transitive construction:

(20)   *The man can hit the thief.*
       a. $\{n, R_{thief}\}$
                                                                        $\rightarrow$ n
       b. $\{the, \{n, R_{thief}\}\}$
                                                                        $\rightarrow$ *the*
       c. $\{_\alpha R_{hit}, \{the, \{n, R_{thief}\}\}\}$
                                                                        $\rightarrow \alpha = ??$
       d. $\{_\beta v^*, \{_\alpha t_{Rhit}, \{the, \{n, R_{thief}\}\}\}\}$
                                                                        $\rightarrow \alpha = <\varphi,\varphi>$
       e. $\{_\beta R_{hit}\text{-}v^*, \{_\alpha t_{Rhit}, \{the, \{n, R_{thief}\}\}\}\}$
                                                                        $\rightarrow \beta = R\text{-}v^*$
       f. $\{_\gamma \{the, man\}, \{_\beta R_{hit}\text{-}v^*, \{_\alpha t_{Rhit}, \{the, \{n, R_{thief}\}\}\}\}\}$
                                                                        $\rightarrow \beta = ??$
       g. $\{_\delta T_{can}, \{_\gamma \{the, man\}, \{_\beta R_{hit}\text{-}v^*, \{_\alpha t_{Rhit}, \{the, \{n, R_{thief}\}\}\}\}\}\}$
                                                                        $\rightarrow \delta = ??$
       h. $\{_\varepsilon \{the, man\}, \{_\delta T_{can}, \{_\gamma t_{the\text{-}man}, \{_\beta R_{hit}\text{-}v^*, \{_\alpha t_{Rhit}, \{the, \{n, R_{thief}\}\}\}\}\}\}\}$
                                                                        $\rightarrow \gamma = R\text{-}v^*$
                                                                        $\delta = ??$
       i. $\{_\zeta C, \{_\varepsilon \{the, man\}, \{_\delta T_{can}, \{_\gamma t_{the\text{-}man}, \{_\beta R_{hit}\text{-}v^*, \{_\alpha t_{Rhit}, \{the, \{n, R_{thief}\}\}\}\}\}\}\}\}$
                                                                        $\rightarrow \varepsilon = C,$
                                                                        $\delta = <\varphi,\varphi>$

In (20a), n and a root R of *thief* undergoes External Merge EM. Here, n is the label since R is too weak to serve as a label, and n is a functional element and detectable with minimal search. In (20b), *the* undergoes EM with $\{n, R_{thief}\}$, and it is the label of the resulting SO since it is the only functional element that can be detected with minimal search. In (20c), R_{hit} undergoes EM. At this point, R is too weak and therefore cannot be the label of α, so α remains unlabeled. In (20d), v^* is externally merged with α. At this stage of derivation, the phi-features of v^* are inherited by R_{hit} (see Chomsky 2008 for feature inheritance); they are shared with $\{the, \{n, R_{thief}\}\}$, and α is labeled $<\varphi,\varphi>$.[2] In (20e), R_{hit} raises to v^*, forming an amalgam.

Following Chomsky (2015: 12), I assume that the amalgam can be a label. So β is labeled R-v*. In (20f), the external argument is introduced by EM. γ cannot be labeled since it has an XP-YP structure at this point of derivation.[3] In (20g), T, which is pronounced as *can*, is externally merged with γ. Since T is too weak to serve as a label, δ is unlabeled at this stage of derivation. In (20h), {*the man*} undergoes free merge (Internal Merge IM), forming ε.[4] As a result of this IM, γ can be labeled because {*the, man*} in γ is now just part of a chain of {*the man*}, and β can provide the label of γ (see (16b)). So γ is labeled R-v*. In (20i), C undergoes EM with ε, the phi-features of C are inherited by T, and ε is labeled <φ, φ>. Although T is too weak to serve as a label, Chomsky (2015: 9–10) argues that T can label after "strengthening" by Spec-T. So, δ is labeled T, and all the SOs are labeled and can now be interpreted at the C-I interface.

   Then, what can be said about interpretation of this sentence at the SM interface? Recall from Chapter 3 that a widely attested basic phonological phrasing in SVO languages is the following, which also conforms to the prediction by Nespor and Vogel's (1986) Relation-based Theory:

(21)   (C Subj)$_\varphi$ (T V)$_\varphi$ (Obj)$_\varphi$

In the present interpretive approach to the interface, the phonological component should be able to identify these three phonological phrases by looking into the syntax. With this in mind, consider the final stage of the derivation of a simple transitive construction, repeated here in (22):

(22)   {$_\zeta$ C, {$_\varepsilon$ {the, man}, {$_\delta$ T$_{can}$, {$_\gamma$ $t_{the\text{-}man}$, {$_\beta$ R$_{hit}$-v*, {$_\alpha$ t_{Rhit}, {the, {n, R$_{thief}$}}}}}}}}}

Comparing (21) and (22), we notice that phonological phrase boundaries correspond to α and δ. We further note that α and δ immediately contain unlabelable elements R (the copy of R$_{hit}$) and T, respectively. That is, the copy of R$_{hit}$ and T are detectable with minimal search within α and δ, respectively. Given this, I will explore the idea that SOs are interpreted as phonological phrases in the phonological component if unlabelable elements can be detected with minimal search within the SOs. In what follows, I will argue on conceptual and empirical grounds that this idea yields a better understanding of phonological phrasing than do Multiple Spell-Out approaches. Phonological phrasing is recast as the phonological interpretation of SOs, which is guided by a third-factor principle of minimal search.

4.4.   Phonological phrasing and the processes of externalization

As discussed in the previous section, *f* is the label in {*f*, R}, where *f* is a functional element and R is a root (see (18)). This indicates that *f* is active while R is inert in syntactic computation. Thus, *f* drives the computation not only by serving as a label but also by inducing agreement, licensing Case, and providing a landing site of movement, among other functions, while R is more or less dependent on what *f* does. By contrast, previous work indicates that function words are invisible, while content words are visible, in the computation of post-syntactic phonology (Chomsky and Halle 1968: 366; Selkirk 1984: 337; Truckenbrodt 1999: 226). Thus, Selkirk (1984: 337) proposes the following condition (here "rules" refer to phonological rules):

(23)   *The Principle of the Categorial Invisibility of Function Words*
        "Rules making crucial appeal to the syntactic category of the constituents to which they apply are blind to the presence of function word constituents."

In the same vein, Truckenbrodt (1999) proposes the following condition:

(24)   *Lexical Category Condition LCC*
        Constraints relating syntactic and prosodic categories apply to lexical syntactic elements and their projections, but not to functional elements and their projections, or to empty syntactic elements and their projections.

Then, we have the following asymmetric situation:

(25)   a. In $\{f, R\}$, only f is visible to the syntax.
        b. In $\{f, R\}$, only R is visible to the post-syntactic phonology.

We can generalize this asymmetry in the following manner:

(26)   *Syntax-Phonology Asymmetry (SPA):*
        Syntactically inert elements are visible in the processes of externalization Φ.

I assume that the syntactic inertness here conforms to labelability. Thus, *f* is not syntactically inert, i.e., syntactically active, since it can serve as a label and therefore is invisible in the processes of externalization.[5] R, being unlabelable, is syntactically inert and therefore visible to the processes of externalization. Likewise, unlabelable weak T is visible to the processes of externalization. Note that R and weak T would be able to label SOs after they inherit phi-features from the phase heads. I assume that the labelability relevant here is the intrinsic property of lexical items. So, even though R and weak T can label SOs after the feature inheritance, they are visible to the phonology because they are originally unlabelable.

I will leave open what explains SPA in (26), but such asymmetries seem to be observed generally. For example, Nasukawa and Backley (2015) point out that head-dependent relations are reversed in syntax and phonology. Thus, in the VP "drink coffee," *drink* is a head in syntax (i.e., a structural head), while *coffee* is a head in phonology (i.e., an informational head) in that it receives prominence. Similarly, in the DP "the garden," *the* is a syntactic head, but *garden* carries more semantic information and phonological prominence. So, these observable asymmetries could be relevant to SPA.

Another asymmetric situation is displacement. Thus, a phrase is often not pronounced where it is interpreted:

(27) a. John was hit t_{John}.
      b. What did you read t_{what}?

In (27a), *John* is interpreted in the complement of *hit* but is pronounced in Spec-T. In (27b), the operator-variable chain (what, t_{what}) is involved in the semantic interpretation, but *what* is lexically interpreted in the complement of *read* while pronounced in Spec-C. In these cases, the asymmetry seems to hold between phonology and semantics. In the grammatical architecture of the I-model, semantics (C-I/LOT) is inseparable from syntax, and it is no surprise that the asymmetry holds between phonology, on the one hand, and semantics, on the other. These cases might reflect SPA or whatever explains it.

Now given SPA (26), let us again consider the derivation of a simple transitive sentence and the phonological interpretation of SOs. The final stage of the derivation is repeated schematically here in (28), with irrelevant parts omitted:

(28) $\{_\zeta$ C, $\{_\varepsilon$ {the, man}, $\{_\delta$ T_{can}, $\{_\gamma$ $t_{the\text{-}man}$, $\{_\beta$ R_{hit}-v^*, $\{_\alpha$ t_{Rhit}, {the, thief}$\}\}\}\}\}\}$

Suppose that an SO is interpreted as a phonological phrase if it is identifiable in the phonological component Φ. How are SOs identified in Φ? We do not want to stipulate, as in End-based Theory or Match Theory, that some particular level of "projection" of SOs, such as XPs, be identified in Φ. We would like to explain which SOs are interpreted in Φ on principled grounds. A plausible answer is that a third-factor principle of minimal search comes into play in the syntax-phonology interface. I propose that Φ identify SOs with minimal search in a manner similar to that of the labeling procedure. Specifically, Φ interprets an SO as a phonological phrase if it detects a phonologically visible element with minimal search within the SO. Under SPA in (26), weak T and R are visible to the phonology. Note that a copy of R is visible to the phonology since it is syntactically inert; likewise, T is visible to the phonology even if it lacks phonetic content since it is syntactically inert. Note also that R that has raised to v^* forms an amalgam, which is labelable (see Chomsky 2015). Since the amalgam behaves as if it is a single lexical item, I assume that the R on v^* is invisible to the phonology.

Then, in (28), α and δ are identifiable in Φ: they have syntactically inert unlabelable elements (a copy of R and T, respectively) that are detectable with minimal search.[6] This is on par with (16a), where H is detected with minimal search in {H, XP}. Let us then formulate the phonological interpretation of SOs as follows:

(29) An SO is interpreted as a phonological phrase if an unlabelable element is detectable with minimal search within the SO.

Thus, SO = {U, XP}, where U is an unlabelable element, is interpreted as a phonological phrase. This phonological identification of SOs is not "labeling" for Φ/SM. Thus, an SO that contains R detectable with minimal search is not labeled R for Φ/SM. Φ/SM does not need to know whether it is weak T or R since the postlexical phonology is generally not category-specific (see Scheer 2011: 337 and references cited therein; cf. Smith 2011b). It simply needs to know whether an SO has a detectable unlabelable element.

Assuming that phonological interpretation proceeds along syntactic cycles, I propose the following implementation of phonological cycles based on phases:

(30)   An SO receives a phonological interpretation when its containing phase is complete.

Note that the phonological interpretation may not apply as soon as a syntactically inert element is introduced into the structure. If it did, it could not account for the effects of Internal Merge. Thus, T cannot be interpreted as soon as it is introduced into syntax, because if it were, the external argument in Spec-v* would be phonologically interpreted there, before it moves to Spec-T. Thus, phonological interpretation must wait until the phase completes.

Given (29) and (30), let us consider in more detail the derivation of a simple transitive sentence:

(31)   a. NS: [$_\alpha$ R   Obj]
          Φ:
       b. NS: [$_\gamma$ Subj [$_\beta$ R-v*   [$_\alpha$ t_R Obj]]]
          Φ: (Obj)$_\varphi$
       c. NS: [$_\zeta$ C [$_\varepsilon$ Subj [$_\delta$ T [$_\gamma$ t_{Subj} [$_\beta$ R-v*   [$_\alpha$ t_R Obj]]]]]]
          Φ: (T   R-v*   —   )$_\varphi$
       d. Φ: (T R-v)$_\varphi$ (Obj)$_\varphi$
       e. NS: [$_\zeta$ C [$_\varepsilon$ Subj [$_\delta$ T [$_\gamma$ t_{Subj} [$_\beta$ R-v*   [$_\alpha$ t_R Obj]]]]]]

Here, NS = narrow syntax and Φ = phonological component. The SO α in (31a) has an unlabelable R that is detectable with minimal search but does not yet receive a phonological interpretation at this point, under (30). If α were interpreted at this stage of derivation, the verbal root R, which will undergo Internal Merge later, would be interpreted here, and R and Obj would be in the same phonological phrase, contrary to fact. In (31b), the v*P phase is complete with R raised to v* and with Subj externally merged. This is the stage where the phonological interpretation applies under (30): α is interpreted as a phonological phrase since the copy of R is detectable with minimal search within α. As mentioned above, I assume that the copy of R is visible for the detection of SOs by Φ. Then, as in (31b), the phonological phrase containing only Obj is obtained. The derivation then proceeds to the root of the sentence, as in (31c). At this point, the CP phase is complete, and the SO δ is interpreted as a phonological phrase, since unlabelable T can be detected with minimal search within δ. At this point, α, which contains

Obj, has already been interpreted at the v*P phase, so it does not receive another phonological interpretation at the CP phase.[7] Therefore, a phonological phrase corresponding to δ does not include Obj, as in (31c). This phonological phrase and the one in (30b) are then put in order, as in (31d).[8] The root clause ζ then needs to be interpreted somehow. I assume that the root clause "CP" is in fact selected by a phonetically null lexical item, which roughly corresponds to an implicit performative element in the sense of Ross (1970) (see also Chomsky 2004: fn.17). Since this element has lexical meaning, I assume that it is unlabelable R, which I designate here as $R_\emptyset$. For parallelism with other lexical elements, I further assume that $R_\emptyset$ is part of an abstract phase headed by F, so that the entire clause corresponds to a phase. Then, when this F-phase is complete, the phonological interpretation applies, and the SO η is interpreted as a phonological phrase, which contains C and Subj:

(32)   NS: [F [$_\eta$ $R_\emptyset$ [$_\zeta$ C [$_\varepsilon$ Subj [$_\delta$ T [$_\gamma$ t_{Subj} [$_\beta$R-v* [$_\alpha$ t_R Obj]]]]]]]]]

   Φ: (C   Subj   —   —   —   )$_\varphi$

The materials within δ (T, R-v*, and Obj) are not included in the phonological phrase here since they have already been interpreted in the previous phases. Finally, the following phonological phrasing is obtained:[9]

(33)   (C Subj)$_\varphi$ (T R-v*)$_\varphi$ (Obj)$_\varphi$

This is identical to the attested phrasing of (13a) = (21).[10] Notice that, just like the Multiple Spell-Out approaches, the proposed cyclic phonological interpretation of syntactic objects accounts for the mismatch between syntactic and prosodic constituents: (33) has a flat prosodic organization unlike the corresponding syntactic structure. I will return to the discussion of the mismatch in connection with linearization procedures in section 4.6.

   In the next section, I will argue that this proposed approach to phonological phrasing has much wider empirical consequences than the Multiple Spell-Out approaches.

4.5.   Consequences

In this section, I will show some empirical consequences of the proposed theory of phonological phrasing. However, the term *phonological phrase* should be approached with caution. I have used this term to refer to a domain demarcated in the processes of syntax-phonology mapping. Thus, it refers to a domain of Spell-Out in the Multiple Spell-Out theory of phonological phrasing (Dobashi 2003; see Chapter 3) and to a domain identified by the phonological component through minimal search for an unlabelable element in the present approach. But *phonological phrase* is also often defined solely in terms of phonological phenomena, with no reference to syntax (e.g., Jun 1998). For example, we can say that a domain within which Raddoppiamento Sintattico applies is a phonological phrase;

likewise, a domain whose right edge is the locus of Penultimate Lengthening is a phonological phrase.

To avoid this circularity, I use the term phonological phrase to refer to the domain identified by the phonological component through minimal search for an unlabelable element. That is, the phonological component creates phonological phrases by making reference to syntax and decides how to use them in accordance with the phonology of the language in question. Thus, in the present approach, a phonological phrase is used as a domain of Raddoppiamento Sintattico in Italian and as a domain of Penultimate Lengthening in Chichewa. Moreover, the usage of phonological phrases may even vary in the same language. Thus, in Japanese, it is used as a domain of accentuation and initial rise (called *Minor Phrase* or *Accentual Phrase*) if it contains a word with a lexical accent, but not when it contains an unaccented word: in this latter case, a larger domain is posited to account for accentuation and initial rise. I will return to this issue in section 4.5.5.1, where I discuss phonological phrasing in Japanese (see Ito and Mester 2012, 2013; Ishihara 2015 and works cited therein).

Therefore, the term phonological phrase should be considered a "nickname," to borrow Selkirk and Lee's (2015: 4) term, and is used here to refer to a domain defined through the phonological interpretation of syntactic objects. Note, finally, that this is merely a terminological clarification for the purposes of theoretical exposition and is of course not intended to deny identification and description of prosodic domains based on phonological/phonetic phenomena.

4.5.1 Cross-linguistic basic phrasing patterns

In Chapter 3, we reviewed cross-linguistic patterns of phonological phasing in SVO languages, as observed by Dobashi (2003):

(34) $(S)_\varphi$ $(V)_\varphi$ $(O)_\varphi$ Aŋlɔ Ewe, French
(35)   a. $(S)_\varphi$ $(V)_\varphi$ $(O)_\varphi$ Italian, English
         b. $(S)_\varphi$ (V $O)_\varphi$ if O is non-branching.
(36) $(S)_\varphi$ (V $O)_\varphi$ Kimatuumbi
(37)   a. $(S)_\varphi$ (V $O)_\varphi$ Kinyambo, Chichewa
         b. (S   V $O)_\varphi$ if S is non-branching.

In this section, I will show that the proposed approach can readily carry over Dobashi's (2003) account of the patterns in (34)–(37).

Consider the phrasing of subjects. As we see in (34)–(37), subjects are generally phrased separately from a following verb, which is exactly the phrasing the present theory predicts. For the syntactic derivation in (38a), the phrasing in (38b) is predicted:

(38)   a. [F [$_\eta$ R$_\varnothing$ [$_\zeta$ C [$_\varepsilon$ Subj [$_\delta$ T [$_\gamma$ t_{Subj} [$_\beta$ R-v* [$_\alpha$ t_R Obj]]]]]]]]]
         b.. (C   Subj)$_\varphi$ (T   R-v)$_\varphi$ (Obj)$_\varphi$

Here, the unlabelable weak T is detected with minimal search within the syntactic object δ, and δ is identified as a phonological phrase. This indicates that we always have a phonological phrase boundary between the subject in Spec-T and T. However, what happens if T is labelable? I give a detailed discussion of this issue in the next section.

As shown in (37), subjects are phrased with a following element when they are prosodically non-branching (i.e., consist of just one prosodic word) in languages like Kinyambo. As we have reviewed in Chapter 3, this phrasing is not a result of syntax-phonology mapping but comes from the restructuring of phonological phrases that applies in the phonological component for purely phonological reasons, to attain the binary structure of prosodic domains. This restructuring analysis can be transferred intact to the present approach since it is not affected by the way basic phonological phrases are formed. Therefore, we can account for the cross-linguistic patterns of phrasing of subjects, in line with Dobashi (2003).

Let us consider objects. They show three patterns: they are not phrased with a preceding verb, as in (34); they are optionally phrased with a preceding verb, as in (35); or they are always phrased with a preceding verb, as in (36). Analysis of optional phrasing of objects is analogous to that of subjects: restructuring applies for prosodic reasons in the phonological component. Thus, the basic phrasing (35a) is restructured as (35b) when objects are non-branching. Then, the following two patterns of basic phonological phrasing are attributed to the syntax-phonology mapping:

(39)   a. $(S)_\varphi$ $(V)_\varphi$ $(O)_\varphi$ [Aŋlɔ Ewe, English, Italian, French]
       b. $(S)_\varphi$ $(V$ $O)_\varphi$ [Kimatuumbi, Kinyambo, Chichewa]

Let us first consider (39a)-type languages. As I discussed in Chapter 3, objects stay in situ in these languages. Verbs (Rs) raise to v^* in Aŋlɔ Ewe and English, as in (40a), while they move further up to T in Italian and French (in the absence of overt auxiliaries) as in (41a):

(40)   a. [F [$_\eta$ R$_\varnothing$ [$_\zeta$ C [$_\varepsilon$ Subj   [$_\delta$ T [$_\gamma$ t_{Subj} [$_\beta$ R-v^* [$_\alpha$ t_R Obj]]]]]]]]
       b. (Subj)$_\varphi$ (T   R-v^*)$_\varphi$ (Obj)$_\varphi$

(41)   a. [F [$_\eta$ R$_\varnothing$ [$_\zeta$ C [$_\varepsilon$ Subj   [$_\delta$ R-v^*-T [$_\gamma$ t_{Subj} [$_\beta$ t_{R-v^*} [$_\alpha$ t_R Obj]]]]]]]]
       b. (Subj)$_\varphi$ (R-v^*- T   )$_\varphi$ (Obj)$_\varphi$

In the present approach, first, the copy of R (t_R) is found with minimal search within α, and α is identified as a phonological phrase, which contains the object, as in (40b) and (41b). Then, T is detected with minimal search within δ, and δ corresponds to a phonological phrase, which contains R, whether it is on v^*, as in (40), or on T, as in (41). Therefore, objects are not phrased with the verb (R) on v^*. Note that I have adopted the assumption that while the R cannot label SOs, the amalgam R-v^* can, following Chomsky (2015: 12). Then, how about the amalgam R-v^*-T in (41)? I assume that the (un)labelability of T is carried over to R-v^*-T, as the labelability of v^* is carried over to R-v^*. Thus, given that weak T is unlabelable, R-v*-T is also unlabelable; therefore, δ is identified as a phonological phrase since it immediately contains R-v*-T, which is detectable with minimal search within δ.

Let us next consider (39b)-type languages, which are all Bantu. As we have discussed in Chapter 3, objects move up to Spec-v*, and verbal roots R move to T via v* in these languages, as in (42a). Here I assume, for expository purposes, that objects move to the outer Spec of v* in these languages, but they might also move to the inner Spec, below the copy of the subject. Since the unpronounced copy of the subject does not affect phonological phrasing, I leave this question open:

(42)   a. [F [$_\eta$ R$_\o$ [$_\zeta$ C [$_\varepsilon$ Subj   [$_\delta$ R-v*-T [$_\gamma$ Obj t_{Subj} [$_\beta$ R-v* [$_\alpha$ t_R t_{Obj}]]]]]]]]
       b. (Subj)$_\varphi$ (R-v*-T   Obj   )$_\varphi$ Ø

At the v*P phase, the copy of R (t_R) is detected with minimal search within α, but no phonological phrase is formed corresponding to α since there is no overt item in α, indicated by Ø. At the CP phase, T is detected with minimal search within δ, and δ is identified as a phonological phrase, which contains the verb (R-v*-T) and object. Then, the verb and object are included in a single phonological phrase. Therefore, the phrasing in (39b) follows.

I have shown that the basic ideas of Dobashi's (2003) account of cross-linguistic patterns of phonological phrasing can readily be assumed by the present approach. Note, however, that more recent work on phonological phrasing suggests that the cross-linguistic tendency of subjects to be phrased separately correlates with the topic-hood of subjects in some languages (Downing and Mtenje (2011), among others, which we will review later). In the next section, I will discuss this issue in relation to cross-linguistic variations in the labelability of T, and reconsider the basic phrasing of subjects within the present theory of phonological phrasing.

4.5.2 T

So far in this chapter we have assumed that T is too weak to serve as a label, following Chomsky (2015: 8ff.). A weak T enables the phonological component to identify the SO immediately containing T, and the subject is thereby excluded from the phonological phrase containing T and R-v*:

(43)   Syntax: [F [R$_\o$ [C [Subj [$_\alpha$ T [t_{Subj} [R-v* [t_R . . .
       Phonology: (C Subj)$_\varphi$ (T   R-v*)$_\varphi$ . . .

Here, the SO α has an unlabelable T that can be detected with minimal search, which explains the strong cross-linguistic tendency to place a prosodic boundary between Subj and T, as we saw in the previous section.

However, Chomsky (2015: 9) argues that T is in fact labelable in languages like Italian, which are rich in subject agreement. This "strong T" could be problematic for the present approach, since the SO immediately containing strong T cannot be identified as a phonological phrase. As we have seen in Chapter 3, subjects are generally not phrased with the following T or V – not only in English, which has a weak T, but also in Italian and Bantu languages that are rich in subject agreement.

To address this issue, I will first review Chomsky's (2015) argument that English T is unlabelable while Italian T is labelable. He argues that this distinction is necessary in order to account for the difference in the EPP effect (Spec-T must be filled) between English and Italian, and that it also accounts for the parametric difference in ECP (complementizer-trace effects), unifying EPP and ECP in terms of the labeling algorithm. Then, I will highlight some problems with his analysis of ECP, and argue that the complementizer-trace effects should be accounted for in terms of prosody, in line with Sato and Dobashi (2016). I will show that the difference between English and Italian can be reduced to the difference in phonological phrasing, which can in turn be reduced to the labelability of T. We will then return to phonological phenomena in Italian and Bantu. On the basis of observations made by Downing and Mtenje (2011) and others, we will see that subjects are actually phonologically phrased with a following T/V when they are not interpreted as a topic, and conclude that labelable strong T in Italian and Bantu languages yields a principled account of the basic phonological phrasing, as well as the lack of complementizer-trace effects in these languages.

4.5.2.1 Labelable T

As we have seen in section 4.3, R is universally weak and cannot serve as a label. Thus, the Labeling Algorithm can determine the label of $\{H, H\}$, which is of the form $\{f, R\}$, where f is a functional element that determines the category of $\{f, R\}$. Chomsky (2015: 9) argues that T is similar to R, as it is too weak to serve as a label in English, and shows that unlabelable T accounts for EPP in English:

(44)   [C [$_\alpha$ SPEC-TP]]

If the subject is in the SPEC position, α is labeled $<\varphi, \varphi>$; if it moves up further, unlabelable T remains alone and labeling fails.

Chomsky (2015: 9) further argues that T can serve as a label in null-subject languages like Italian since T is rich in agreement. This difference in labelability of T gives a principled account of the well-known correlation between the so-called subject *pro*-drop and the lack of the complementizer-trace (COMP-*t*) effect (Perlmutter 1968; Rizzi 1982). Italian-type languages with strong T freely allow null subjects in tensed clauses and do not show the COMP-*t* effect, as in the (a)-examples below, while in English-type languages with weak T, subjects must be present in tensed clauses and the COMP-*t* effect is seen, as in the (b)-examples:

(45)   a.   *e* verrà
        b.   *e will come

(46)   a.   Chi$_i$ credi che e_i verrà?
        b.   *Who$_i$ do you think that e_i will come?

(Rizzi 1982: 117)

This correlation has been attributed to the properties of verbal inflection since Rizzi (1982) (cf. Taraldsen 1978; see also Pesetsky 2017 for a comprehensive review), and Chomsky (2015) recasts this analysis in terms of the labeling algorithm. If we assume that T is labelable in Italian, it can label the SO α in (47) without a subject in Spec-T:

(47) $[_\alpha$ T [Subj [R-v*. . . . $\alpha = $ T

That is, the subject does not need to be in Spec-T in Italian. In contrast, as we have seen above, weak T in English cannot label α, and the subject must therefore undergo Internal Merge with α, constructing β as in (48), and β is labeled $<\varphi, \varphi>$. As a result, T can label α after "strengthening" by Spec-T:

(48) $[_\beta$ Subj $[_\alpha$ T [t_{Subj} [R-v*. . . . $\alpha = $ T, $\beta = <\varphi, \varphi>$

This difference in the strength of T explains why subjects do not have to be in Spec-T in Italian-type languages while they must be there in English-type languages (the EPP effects).

Now, suppose that the subject is a *wh*-phrase that undergoes long-distance movement:

(49)   [who do you think C $[_\beta$ t_{who} $[_\alpha$ T [t_{who} [R-v*, ...
        "Who do you think that read the book?"

Suppose that T is weak. In English, *who*, which originates in Spec-v*, raises to Spec-T, as we have just seen above. Subsequent movement of *who* to the matrix clause will be problematic for labeling reasons: the complement of C would be transferred after *who* has raised out of Spec-T. In this domain of transfer, t_{who} in Spec-T is merely part of the whole chain and can no longer label β $<\varphi,\varphi>$. As a result, English displays the COMP-*t* effect. By contrast, in Italian-type languages T is strong and labels α; (49) is thus a legitimate structure. Note that *who* does not have to go through Spec-T in Italian, as we have seen in (47) above, and β does not have to be constructed. Therefore, there is no labeling problem, and Italian does not induce the COMP-*t* effect.

Now suppose that C is deleted in English (marked by Ø), as Chomsky suggests:

(50)   [who do you think Ø $[_\beta$ t_{who} $[_\alpha$ T [t_{who} [R-v*. . . .
        "Who do you think read the book?"

He argues that T inherits phase-hood of C before C deletes. Then in (50), T is a phase head, and Transfer applies to the complement of T. The copy of *who* in Spec-T is now in the same phase as the raised *who*. On the assumption that memory is phase level (Chomsky 2015: 11), the information that β is labeled $<\varphi,\varphi>$ is retained when labels are interpreted at C-I. Therefore, C-deletion saves the derivation.

So far, we have reviewed Chomsky's (2015) approach to the unification of EPP and ECP (the COMP-*t* effect) in terms of labeling. The C-deletion approach, however, is not without problems. First, it seems to violate the No Tampering Condition (NTC), which is usually formulated as a condition on Merge: Merge (X, Y) leaves X, Y unchanged (Chomsky 2005, 2008). It seems that C-deletion is not subsumed under Merge, but the basic concept behind NTC is a third-factor principle of minimal computation. The deletion or modification of part of the syntactic objects already formed would be computationally inefficient. Moreover, as Nakanishi (2016) observes, C-deletion also seems to have an empirical problem. As is widely assumed in the literature, long-distance *wh*-movement goes though intermediate Spec-C positions. (51a) shows that the reflexive pronoun *himself* requires a local antecedent. The grammaticality of (51b) entails that at some stage of derivation *himself* can be locally bound by *John*. It is standard to assume that *which pictures of himself* stops by the embedded Spec-C, where *himself* can be locally bound by *John*.

(51)   a. *Mary told John$_i$ that she would buy these pictures of himself$_i$.
       b. [Which pictures of himself$_i$]$_j$ did Mary tell John$_i$ that she would buy t_j ?
                                                        (Nakanishi 2016: 54)

If C is deleted and removed from the structure in the absence of an overt complementizer, then we predict that the deleted C cannot provide an intermediate landing site for the long-distance *wh*-movement, where the reflexive can be bound in the course of derivation. With this in mind, consider the following contrast:

(52)   a. *Mary told John$_i$ (that) these pictures of himself$_i$ surprised Bill.
       b. ? [Which pictures of himself$_i$]$_j$ did Mary tell John$_i$ t_j surprised Bill?
                                                        (Nakanishi 2016: 54)

(52a) shows that the reflexive *himself* within the embedded subject DP cannot be coreferential with the indirect object *John*. By contrast, in (52), where the complementizer *that* is not overtly expressed, the embedded subject DP containing *himself* is *wh*-moved to the matrix clause, and the reflexive can be coreferential with *John*. This indicates that the *wh*-phrase stops by the embedded Spec-C and licenses the reflexive, as in (51b). That is, even though covert, the complementizer C should not be deleted or removed from the structure and should provide an intermediate landing site for the *wh*-phrase where *himself* can be licensed.

Therefore, I conclude that the C-deletion approach needs to be reconsidered. However, any alternative approach must provide a unified account of the parametric difference in ECP and EPP in terms of the strength of T. Below, I outline such an alternative approach.

4.5.2.2   *A prosodic analysis of* that-*trace effects*

As we have seen, the correlation between *pro*-drop and the COMP-*t* effect has been attributed to the inflectional properties in the field of syntax. That is, the COMP-*t* effect has been considered a syntactic phenomenon. But prosodic approaches to the COMP-*t* effect have also been pursued in the literature. One reason for this is that the COMP-*t* effect shows systematic exceptions, which seem to resist straight-forward syntactic analysis. In this section, I review Sato and Dobashi's (2016) prosodic approach to the *that*-trace effect in English. Although this approach can-not alone account for the correlation between *pro*-drop and the COMP-*t* effect in terms of agreement, I will show that, when combined with the proposed theory of phonological phrasing, the prosodic approach can capture the correlation between the *pro*-drop and COMP-*t* effect in terms of the strength of T.

Sato and Dobashi (2016) adopt the mechanism of phonological-phrase forma-tion proposed by Dobashi (2003), which we reviewed in Chapter 3. They suggest that the following condition accounts for the COMP-*t* effect in English.

(53)   Function words cannot form a prosodic phrase on their own.

This condition is derived from the Invisibility of Function Words (Selkirk 1984) or Lexical Category Condition (Truckenbrodt 1999), which we discussed in sec-tion 4.4. Because function words are invisible in the processes of phonological-phrase formation, a phonological phrase cannot consist solely of function words (cf. Zwicky 1982; Saito 2019):

(54) $*(\ f\ )_\varphi$, where f is a function word.

This entails that a complementizer may not constitute a phonological phrase on its own, since it is a function word:

(55) $*(\ COMP\ )_\varphi$

Given this, consider the following subject-object asymmetry concerning the COMP-*t* effect:

(56)   a.   What$_i$ do you think (that) John read t_i ?
          b.   Who$_i$ do you think (*that) t_i read the book?

For (56a), the following phonological phrasing is defined (irrelevant parts omitted):

(57)   What do you (think)$_\varphi$ (that John)$_\varphi$ (read)$_\varphi$

Here the complementizer *that* is phrased with the content word *John*, avoiding a violation of (55). On the other hand, for sentence (56b), the following phonological phrasing is defined. Note that here and below I include the phonetically empty trace *t* in phonological phrases, for the purpose of illustration:

(58)   Who do you (think)$_\varphi$ (that t)$_\varphi$ (left)$_\varphi$

Here, the complementizer *that*, if overt, constitutes a phonological phrase on its own, violating (55). In contrast, no phonological phrase is created if the complementizer is covert, thus avoiding a violation of (55).

This prosodic approach to the COMP-*t* effect yields a straightforward account of some exceptional cases. One well-known exception is the so-called adverb effect (Bresnan 1977; Culicover 1993). The COMP-*t* effect is ameliorated in the presence of an adverbial element between *that* and the subject trace:

(59) a. Robin met the man who$_i$ Leslie said that *(for all intents and purposed) t_i was the mayor of the city.
 b. This is the tree Op$_i$ that I said that *(just yesterday) t_i had resisted my shovel.
 c. I asked what$_i$ Leslie said that *(in her opinion) t_i had made Robin give a book to Lee.

(Culicover 1993: 557ff.)

The relevant part of these sentences has the following configuration:

(60) . . . said that ADV *t* was/had . . .

Given the mechanism of phonological phrase formation adopted here, the following phonological phrasing is obtained:

(61) . . . (said)$_\varphi$ (that ADV *t*)$_\varphi$ (left)$_\varphi$

Here, the phonological phrase containing *that* does not violate (55), since it contains a lexical adverbial element that is visible to the phonological component.

In addition to the adverb effect, Sato and Dobashi (2016) discuss amelioration by parenthetical expressions, resumptive pronouns, focus, and auxiliary reduction, among other effects (see also Ackema 2011; Drury 1999; Kandybowicz 2006, 2009; Sobin 2000, 2002, among others). All these cases support the claim that the COMP-*t* effect is sensitive to phonological phrasing of *that*. Among these cases, let us consider focus here. Focus affects phonological phrasing (Kanerva 1990 for Chichewa, Frascarelli 2000 for Italian, Nagahara 1994 for Japanese, among many others). Kenesei and Vogel (1995) illustrate the effect of focus on phonological phrasing in English. The Rhythm Rule applies within a phonological phrase in English (Hayes 1989). If the primary stresses of two words ω_1 and ω_2 are adjacent within a phonological phrase, as in $(\omega_1\ \omega_2)_\varphi$, then the rule eliminates this stress clash by "shifting" the stress of ω_1 leftward, as illustrated in (62):

(62) a. thirtéen wómen   →   thírteen wómen
 b. Japanése dish   →   Jápanese dísh

This rule applies within a phonological phrase. Thus, in (63) the (non-branching) object *budgets* is phrased with the preceding verb *okay*, and the stress of the verb is shifted leftward to eliminate the clashing effect.

(63)   Our committee's task is to okáy búdgets for research projects.
$\rightarrow$ . . . ókay búdgets . . .

(Kenesei and Vogel 1995: 19)

When a phonological phrase boundary is present between two words, the Rhythm Rule does not apply, even if the primary stresses are adjacent:

(64)   a. It's hard to outcláss Délaware's football team.
       b. The racketéer ácted innocent, but he really wasn't.

(Kenesei and Vogel 1995: 19)

In (64a), the branching object *Delaware's football team* is not phrased with the verb *outclass*, and the stress of *outclass* therefore does not shift leftward. Likewise, in (64b) the subject and the verb are not phrased together, and the stress of *racketeer* does not shift. However, as Kenesei and Vogel (1995) observe, if *Delaware's* and *acted* receive a focal stress, the Rhythm Rule applies:

(65)   a. It's hard to óutclass DÉLAWARE'S football team.
       b. The rácketeer ÁCTED innocent, but he really wasn't.

(Kenesei and Vogel 1995: 22)

This indicates that focus restructures the phonological phrasing so that the two words in question are included in a single phonological phrase. Kenesei and Vogel (1995: 28) formulate such focus restructuring for English as follows:

(66)   Left Focus Restructuring Rule (LFR): English
       If some word in a sentence bears focus, place a phonological phrase boundary at its right edge, and join the word to the phonological phrase on its left.

Given this, *outclass* and *Delaware's* in (65a) and *racketeer* and *acted* in (65b) belong to a single phonological phrase, and the Rhythm Rule applies across word boundaries between the two words:

(67)   a. It's hard (to óutclass DÉLAWARE'S)$_\varphi$ football team.
       b. (The rácketeer ÁCTED)$_\varphi$ innocent, but he really wasn't.

(Kenesei and Vogel 1995: 22)

Then, it is predicted that the COMP-*t* effect is also affected by focus if it is a prosodic phenomenon. That is, if the phonological phrase containing *that* is restructured by focus so that it results in a phrase containing *that* and a lexical element, then the *that*-trace effect will be mitigated. Drury (1999) and Kandybo-wicz (2006) indeed observe that the *that*-trace effect is ameliorated when a contrastive focal stress is placed on the subordinate verb, which immediately follows the complementizer:

(68)   (?) Who$_i$ do you think that t_i WROTE Barriers (as opposed to say, *edited* it)?
       (Kandybowicz 2006: 222)

Given LFR (66), the focused verb *WROTE* in (68) affects phonological phrasing so that it is phrased with the complementizer *that*:

(69)   Who do you (think)$_\varphi$ (that t_i)$_\varphi$ (wrote Barriers)$_\varphi$
       → (think)$_\varphi$ (that t_i WROTE)$_\varphi$ (Barriers)$_\varphi$

Here, LFR places a phonological phrase boundary on the right side of the focused verb *WROTE* and joins *WROTE* into the phonological phrase containing *that* on its left side. As a result, we obtain a legitimate phonological phrase containing not only *that* (a function word) but also *WROTE* (a content word), satisfying (55). Placing focus on any other phrase in the sentence does not alter the phrasing of the complementizer and hence does not mitigate the *that*-trace effect

(70)   a. *Who$_i$ do you THINK that t_i wrote Barriers (as opposed to say, know)?
            → THINK (that t_i)$_\varphi$ (wrote Barriers)$_\varphi$
       b. ?? Who$_i$ did you say that t_i wrote BARRIERS yesterday?
            → say (that t_i)$_\varphi$ (wrote BARRIERS)$_\varphi$ (yesterday)$_\varphi$
            (Kandybowicz 2006: 222, 223)

In (70a), LFR requires a phonological phrase on the right of *THINK*, which does not affect the phrasing of *that*. In (70b) LFR places a boundary on the right of *BARRIERS*, and *wrote* is phrased with BARRIERS, without affecting the phrasing of *that*. Therefore, the acceptability of these sentences does not change. These examples indicate that the *that*-trace effect is in fact a prosodic phenomenon.

So far, we have briefly sketched Sato and Dobashi's (2016) prosodic account of the COMP-*t* effect. Although this approach is attractive in that it accounts for exceptional cases, such as the adverb effect and focus effects, without any ad hoc stipulation, it seems impossible to incorporate the well-established cross-linguistic correlation among EPP, ECP (the COMP-*t* effect), and the strength of agreement. The root of this problem may lie in the assumption that the richness of agreement is irrelevant to the formation of prosodic domains. To my knowledge, no theory of phonological phrasing refers to agreement. Thus, the Multiple Spell-Out theory of phonological phrasing refers only to the domains of phases, Relation-based Theory refers to syntactic relations defined in the tree, and End-based Theory and Match Theory refer to the edges of syntactic structure. If we can integrate two (apparently) heterogeneous factors, i.e., agreement and prosodic domains, we may be able to develop a theory that captures the correlation among EPP, ECP, agreement, and the prosodic aspects of the COMP-*t* effect. In the next section, I will show that the present theory of phonological phrasing offers such an account, in terms of the labelability of T.

4.5.2.3 Agreement and complementizer-trace effect

Let us first consider English. We have assumed that T is weak in English and that the weak T is visible to the phonological component since it is "inert" in syntax, in accordance with the principle of Syntax-Phonology Asymmetry, repeated below:

(71) *Syntax-Phonology Asymmetry (SPA):* = (26)
    Syntactically inert elements are visible in the processes of externalization Φ.

We have defined phonological phrases as follows:

(72) An SO is interpreted as a phonological phrase if an unlabelable element is detectable with minimal search within the SO. = (29)

Given the foregoing, let us consider the following contrast:

(73) a. What$_i$ do you think that John bought t_i ?
    b. *Who$_i$ do you think that t_i bought the apple?

The derivation of (73a) is illustrated below:

(74) a. what do you think-v* $[_\gamma t_{Rthink}$ $[$ C_{that} $[$ John $[_\beta$ T $[$ t_{John} $[$ R_{bought}-v* $[_\alpha$ $t_{Rbought}$ t_{what}]]]]]]
    b. what do you think   (that   John)$_\varphi$ (bought)$_\varphi$ Ø

Let us skip the first v*P phrase and consider the subordinate CP phase. Here, weak T is detected with minimal search within β, and β is interpreted as a phonological phrase containing *bought*. At the matrix v*P phase level, γ is interpreted as a phonological phrase since it contains a copy of the raised R$_{think}$ (t_{Rthink}), which is detectable with minimal search within γ. Since *bought* was already interpreted phonologically in the previous stage, we obtain a phonological phrase corresponding to γ, which contains *that* and *John*. As a result, we have the phonological phrasing shown in (74b) above. Here, the phonological phrase containing *that* also contains a content word *John*, satisfying the constraint in (55).

By contrast, the sentence (73b), which involves a typical violation of the COMP-*t* effect, results in a violation of (55). Let us consider the derivation:

(75) a. who do you think-v* $[_\gamma t_{Rthink}$ $[$ C_{that} $[$ t_{who} $[_\beta$ T $[$ t_{who} $[$ R $_{bought}$-v* $[_\alpha$ $t_{Rbought}$
        the apple]]]]]]]
    b. who do you think   (that   )$_\varphi$ (bought)$_\varphi$
        (the apple)$_\varphi$

Let us skip the subordinate v*P phrase and consider the subordinate CP phase. Here, weak T is detected with minimal search within β, and β is interpreted as a phonological phrase containing *bought*. At the matrix v*P phase, the copy of R_{think} is detected with minimal search within γ, and γ is interpreted as a phonological phrase containing only *that*. This is an offending phonological phrase, violating (55). If C is covert, no phonological phrase is formed for the domain of γ; hence, no violation of (55) occurs. Thus, Sato and Dobashi's (2016) prosodic analysis of the COMP-*t* effect can be transferred to the present theory of phonological phrasing.

Now, let us consider the lack of COMP-*t* effects in Italian-type languages, in which T is labelable, as we have seen in section 5.2.1.[11] Let us consider the derivation of the following sentence in Italian, which involves a typical COMP-*t* configuration:

(76) Chi pensi che t_{chi} ha incontrato i linguisti?
      Who you.think C has met the linguists
      'Who do you think (that) has met the linguists?'

$$\text{(Pesetsky 2017: 997)}$$

Note that the trace or copy of *chi* 'who' is indicated between *che* and *ha* in (76), but as discussed by Rizzi (1982`) and Brandi and Cordin (1989), long-distance *wh*-movement of an embedded subject would have to be analyzed as originating in the postverbal subject position (see also Pesetsky 2017). As we will discuss shortly, however, our prosodic analysis of the COMP-*t* effect in Italian-type languages does not depend on the base position of subject.

(77) illustrates the derivation of (76):

(77) a. Chi pensi $[_δ t_{RV}$ $[_{CP}$ che $[_γ (t_{chi})[_β T_{ha}$ $[t_{chi}$ $[$ $R_{incontrato}$-v* $[_α t_R$ i linguisti]]]]]]]
      b. Chi pensi (che   ha   incontrato $)_φ$ (i linguisti $)_φ$

Skipping the embedded v*P phase, let us consider the embedded CP phase. Here, T_{ha} is strong and labelable in Italian, so β is not interpreted as a phonological phrase, which is not the case in English. Note that if *chi* 'who' moves into Spec-T and leaves a copy there, we will have a COMP-*t* configuration. In this case, γ is not interpreted as a phonological phrase either, since it does not contain an unlabelable element. If *chi* 'who' does not move into Spec-T_{ha}, then the SO γ is not created. So, regardless of whether the copy of the extracted *wh*-subject is in Spec-T, no phonological phrase is formed at the embedded CP phase level. As the derivation goes on, the matrix v*P phase is reached, the phonological component detects the copy of R with minimal search within δ, and δ is interpreted as a phonological phrase, which contains *che* 'that', *ha* 'has', and *incontrato* 'met', as in (77b). Here, the complementizer *che* does not form a phonological phrase alone but is phrased with the auxiliary verb *ha* and, crucially, with the lexical verb *incontrato*, observing the prosodic constraint on complementizers (55). Therefore, the lack of the COMP-*t* effect in Italian can be accounted for in terms of agreement and prosody:

labelable T forces the complementizer to be phonologically phrased with a following lexical verb.

The phonological phrasing in (77b) suggests that there are phonological phenomena that apply between the complementizer and a following element that occupies T or v when the subject is dropped in strong-T languages, since T does not create a phonological phrase boundary. One such example is found in D'Alessandro and Scheer (2015). They observe that in the eastern upper-southern Italian dialect Abruzzese, spoken in Arielli (Chieti), Abruzzo, *Raddoppiamento Fonosintattico* (RF) applies across word boundaries within a phonological phrase. RF is gemination of the initial consonant of a word, triggered by a lexically defined set of words, including the complementizer *chə* 'that.' In the following example, the subject is dropped in the subordinate clause, and the initial consonant of the verb *ve* 'come' is lengthened in the presence of *chə*:

(78)   Jè mmeje   chə   vve.
       is   better   that come.3sG
       'It's better that he/she comes.'

(D'Alessandro and Scheer 2015: 614)

This shows that there is no phonological phrase boundary between the complementizer and the verb on T. That is, the strong T in the subordinate clause does not contribute to the creation of a phonological phrase, and the complementizer and verb are phrased together, just like in (77b). See Bonet et al. (2018) for further discussion of RF and phonological phrasing. I will further discuss strong T and phonological phrasing in the next section.

To summarize section 4.5.2, the present approach (i) maintains Chomsky's account of EPP/*pro*-drop: weak T requires Spec-T while strong T does not, for labeling reasons; (ii) accounts for the ECP (COMP-*t*) effects in terms of prosody, without recourse to C-deletion; (iii) is consistent with the empirical consequences of Sato and Dobashi's (2016) prosodic analysis of COMP-*t* effects in English, accounting for several "exceptional" data on principled grounds; and (iv) can reduce cross-linguistic variations in COMP-*t* effects to the richness of agreement of T, which in turn correlates with *pro*-drop. Thus, the proposed analysis combines the advantages of the syntactic and prosodic approaches.

A remaining issue is that our approach predicts that overt subjects in Spec-T are, in general, phrased with a following verb in *pro*-drop languages, contrary to the attested strong tendency we observed in Chapter 3 and reviewed in section 4.5.1. In the next section, we examine this point.

4.5.3   *Subject and topic*

As discussed in Chapter 3, extensive research on phonological phrasing indicates that subjects are generally phrased separately from a following element such as an auxiliary verb or lexical verb in SVO languages. Thus, in Italian, *Raddoppiamento Sintattico* (RS) lengthens the initial consonant of ω_2 if ω_1 ends with a vowel that bears the main stress of the word within the phonological phrase (ω_1 ω_2)$_\varphi$ but does not apply between a subject and a following element, indicating that a phonological phrase boundary is present there (Nespor and Vogel 1986):

(78) a. Papá   mangia
          daddy   eat.3SG
          (Papá)$_\varphi$ (mangia)$_\varphi$
          'Daddy is eating.'
      b. La cecitá   puó   essere guarita
          the blindness can.3SG be   cure.PP
          (La ceritá)$_\varphi$ (puo essere guarita)$_\varphi$
          'Blindness can be cured.'

(Ghini 1993: 43ff.)

Whether the subject is followed by a lexical verb, as in (78a), or by an auxiliary verb, as in (78b), a phonological phrase boundary is placed on the right side of the subject. However, as discussed in section 4.5.2, the proposed approach to phonological phrasing predicts that subjects are phrased with a following element in Italian since T is strong and labelable in this language:

(79) a. Attested: (Subj)$_\varphi$ (T V-v*)$_\varphi$
      b. Predicted: (Subj T V-v*)$_\varphi$

In what follows, I attempt to show that preverbal subjects in Italian are in fact topicalized when they are phrased separately from following material and that, in some cases, subjects are phrased with a following element in Italian (Section 4.5.3.1). Moreover, on the basis of more recent analysis of prosodic phrasing in Zulu and Chichewa by Cheng and Downing (2009, 2016), Downing and Mtenje (2011), among others, I discuss correlations among strength of T, topic-hood of subjects, and prosodic phrasing (Section 4.5.3.2).

4.5.3.1 Italian

First, consider the syntactic position of overt preverbal subjects in Italian. Alexiadou and Anagnostopoulou (1998: 504ff.) argue that the scopal properties of a quantifier in its pre-movement position are reserved when it moves to an A-position but not to an A´-position (Riemsdijk and Williams 1981; Cinque 1982; Haik 1984; May 1985). Drawing on this diagnostic of the A/A´ status, Frascarelli (2007) shows that preverbal subjects in Italian can be in an A´-position and interpreted as a topic. Consider (80):

(80) Qualche studente ha   archiviato ogni libro della   biblioteca.
      some   student have.3SG filed   every book of-the library
      'Some   student filed every book in the library.' (ambiguous)

(Frascarelli 2007: 715)

This sentence is ambiguous. The subject QP may either have either a specific or distributional interpretation. In the specific (wide scope) interpretation, the subject quantifies over events, and the sentence is interpreted as follows: 'some specific students have filed every book at different times.' In the distributional (narrow scope) interpretation, the sentence means 'each book was filed by different students,' indicating that preverbal subjects can be in an A-position and preserve the original scopal properties. However, if the subject QP serves as an antecedent for a *pro*-dropped subject, it can only take a wide scope, receiving a specific reading, as shown in (81a). This is paralleled with the clitic-left dislocated (CLLD) object, which receives a specific interpretation, as in (81b):

(81) a. [qualche studente]$_k$ ha   archiviato ogni libro della biblioteca e
          some   student   have.3SG filed   every book of-the library   and
          pro$_k$ è   stato   premiato.
                 be.3 SG been   prized
          'Some (specific) student filed every book in the library and got a prize.'
      b. [qualche studente]$_k$ lo$_k$ ha   interrogato ogni   professore.
          some   student   him have.3SG interviewed every professor
          'Some (specific) student was examined by every professor.'

(Frascarelli 2007: 715)

Frascarelli then concludes that preverbal subjects in Italian can be base-generated as a topic in the left-peripheral domain and that they provide a referential value to *pro*, just like CLLD objects.

Let us then suppose that the subject DPs, when topicalized, are in Spec-TOP (topic), in line with Rizzi's (1997) theory of left periphery (see also Nakamura 1994 for Topic Phrases):

(82)   [DP$_i$ [TOP [*pro*$_i$ [T [t_{pro} [R$_V$-v* [t_{Rv} . . . . .

Here, I assume, following Frascarelli, that *pro* occupies Spec-T and that it is bound by the DP base-generated in Spec-TOP.

Now let us consider the phonology. As Frascarelli (2000: 23) argues, topicalized elements correspond to prosodic domains (intonational phrases) in Italian. *Intervocalic Spirantization* (IS) is a lenis phenomenon, which is sensitive to intonational phrase boundaries in Italian. IS changes the affricates /tʃ/ and /dʒ/ into the corresponding fricatives [ʃ] and [ʒ], respectively, between [-consonantal] segments within an intonational phrase (Frascarelli 2000: 21). Thus, in (83), where the entire sentence corresponds to a single intonational phrase, the underlying affricates, sandwiched between vowels, are realized as the corresponding fricatives:

(83)   (gli ami[ʃ]i di [ʒ]ianni andranno al   mare [ʒ]iovedì mattina)$_1$
         the friends of Gianni go-FUT-3PL to-the seaside Thursday morning
         'Gianni's friends will go to the seaside on Thursday morning.'

(Frascarelli 2000: 21)

The following example shows that a topicalized DP is an independent intonational phrase in Italian:

(84)   (gli amici   di Sara)ₜ ([dʒ]iani è   partito   senza   neanche
       the friends of Sara   Gianni   be-3sɢ leave-pp without even   salutarli)ₜ
       to say good-bye-to.them

(Frascarelli 2000: 47)

'Gianni left without saying good-bye to Sara's friends.'

Here, the DP *gli amici di Sara* 'the friends of Sara' is topicalized, forming a single intonational phrase. Thus, there is an intonational phrase break between *Sara* and *Gianni*, and the initial consonant of *Gianni* therefore does not undergo IS, as there is no [-consonantal] segment preceding it within the intonational phrase.

To reconcile creation of intonational phrases with application of topicalization in our proposed approach, let us consider the phonological interpretation of TOP, whose Spec is occupied by a base-generated topic, as in (82) above. Frascarelli (2000: Ch. 4) argues that a topic is base-generated outside of the structure where the core computation is carried out, without entering into any feature-checking relation, and it is interpreted at the C-I and SM interfaces "by virtue of its exclusion from checking operations" (p. 194). The phonological component distinguishes a topic and the rest of the structure, which are then mapped to different independent intonational phrases. In our labeling terms, TOP is similar to R in that it does not contribute to the core-computational processes of agreement/feature-checking and labeling. Therefore, I hypothesize the following:

(85)   TOP is too weak to serve as a label.

Given SPA (26), TOP is syntactically inert and therefore visible to the phonological component, and a syntactic object immediately containing TOP is interpreted as a prosodic domain as a result of minimal search for TOP. Note that we have assumed that syntactic objects immediately containing an unlabelable element (R, weak T) are interpreted as phonological phrases rather than as intonational phrases. In general, an intonational phrase boundary corresponds to a phonological phrase boundary (but not vice versa), as is clear from the traditional formulation of prosodic hierarchy:

(86)   ({ . . . }_φ{ . . . }_φ{ . . . }_φ)ₜ ({ . . . }_φ{ . . . }_φ)ₜ ({ . . . }_φ{ . . . }_φ{ . . . }_φ)ₜ

Then, creating an intonational phrase in terms of TOP does not, at a minimum, contradict the assumption that syntactic objects immediately containing an unlabelable element correspond to certain prosodic domains. As I have discussed at the start of section 4.5, "phonological phrase" refers to the prosodic domain identified by the phonological component through minimal search for an unlabelable element; how such a domain is used depends on the phonology. I will put aside the question of why TOP corresponds to a higher prosodic boundary in the hierarchy.[12]

Given these considerations, let us consider the subject topicalization in a simple transitive construction in Italian. For the syntactic derivation in (87a), we have the prosodic phrasing in (87b):

(87) a. $[_F [_\gamma R_\emptyset [C [DP_i [_\beta TOP [pro_i [T [t_{Subj} [R_V\text{-}v^* [_\alpha t_{Rv} \cdots$
      b.   (   )$_\pi$ (   )$_\pi$ (   )$_\pi$

Here, I abstract away the distinction between intonational and phonological phrases and hence mark the prosodic domains π. I assume that "CP" is above "TOPP." In the bottom-up derivation, first at v*P phase, α is interpreted as a prosodic domain since it immediately contains the copy of R, which is detectable with minimal search within α. Then, at the CP phase, the phonological component fails to detect T, since it is strong, but instead detects TOP with minimal search within β, which is interpreted as a prosodic domain. Lastly, the performative element $R_\emptyset$ is detected by the phonological component, and γ is interpreted as a prosodic domain, which contains the topicalized (base-generated) DP coreferential with *pro*. Hence, this DP "subject" is not phrased with following material such as T or R on v*, and the attested phrasing in (79a), repeated here in (88a), is accounted for.

(88) a. Attested: (Subj)$_\varphi$ (T V-v*)$_\varphi$
      b. Predicted: (Subj T V-v*)$_\varphi$

What about the prediction in (88b)? As the ambiguity in (80) suggests, the preverbal subject can be in an A-position, which is presumably Spec-T. That is, the subject will stay in Spec-T if it is not interpreted as a topic in Italian. Then, it is predicted that the non-topic subject is phonologically phrased with the following T and V-v*, as in (88b), since the strong T does not create a prosodic boundary. Numerous studies of phonological phrasing in Italian, including the influential work by Nespor and Vogel (1986), have observed that subjects are invariably not phrased with T or V in this language, as we have seen in Chapter 3. However, in an earlier study of RS, Napoli and Nespor (1979: 830ff.) state that "we find that RS is possible between the last word of the subject and the first word of the predicate whenever the subject is sentence-initial – regardless of whether the subject is a single word, several words, or a complex NP." They offer the following examples, where " • " indicates the application of RS:

(89) a. La città • cadde.
          'The city fell.'
      b. L'ultimo re • morì.
          'The last king died.'
      c. La religione che pratica • perde fedeli.
          'The religion he practices is losing adherents.'

The context in which these sentences are uttered is not clear from Napoli and Nespor's (1979) discussion, but preverbal subjects, whether branching or not, can in fact be phrased with a following element in Italian. That is, the prediction (88b) does not seem to be entirely incorrect, but rather merits further consideration.

4.5.3.2   Zulu and Chichewa

Interestingly, more recent work on prosody in Bantu languages by Cheng and Downing (2009, 2016), Downing (2011, 2013), and Downing and Mtenje (2011) shows a strong correlation between topic-hood and the prosodic status of subjects. They point out that if subjects are phrased separately from a following element, they are interpreted as a topic. Consider the following examples from Zulu (see also Downing and Mtenje 2011: 1975):

(90)   a. ú-Síph' ú-phekél'   ú-Thánd' in-kû:khu).
          1-Sipho sm1-cook.for 1-Thandi 9-chicken
          'Sipho cooked chicken for Thandi.'
       b. ín-kosíka:zi) í-théngel'   ábá-fán' ízím-ba:tho).
          9-woman   sm9-buy.for 2-boy   10-clothes
          'The   woman is buying clothes for the boys.'

(Cheng and Downing 2009: 209)

Following Cheng and Downing's (2009) notation, I mark the end of phonological phrases by round brackets ")". In this language, a penultimate vowel is lengthened at the end of a phonological phrase. Thus, in (90a), the penult vowel of the sentence-final word is lengthened. However, lengthening does not apply to the subject *ú-Síph'*, indicating that it is phrased with the following verb. In contrast, the subject *ín-kosíka:zi* in (90b) is followed by a phonological phrase boundary, and the penultimate vowel is lengthened. Cheng and Downing (2009) and Downing and Mtenje (2011: 1975) point out that this difference is due to the topic-hood of the subject. The subject is topicalized in (90b) but not in (90a).[13]

Similarly, in Chichewa, the subject is not interpreted as a topic when it is phonologically phrased with the verb, as discussed by Cheng and Downing (2016) (cf. Bresnan and Mchombo 1987; Kanerva 1990,). One relevant phonological rule is penultimate lengthening, just like in Zulu. Thus, the subject *m-fúumu* 'the chief' is not phrased with the following verbal element and is interpreted as a topic in (91a), while the subject *ma-kóló* 'the parents' is phrased with the following element and is not interpreted as a topic (91b):

(91)   a. (M-fúumu)$_\varphi$ (i-na-pátsá   mwaná zó-óváala)$_\varphi$
          9-chief   sm9-TAM-give 1.child 10.clothes
          'The chief gave the child clothes.'
       b. (Ma-kóló a-na-pátsíra   mwaná ndalámá zá   mú-longo wáake)$_\varphi$
          6-parent sm6-TAM-give 1.child 10.money 10.of 1-sister   1.her
          'The parents gave the child money for her sister.'

(Cheng and Downing 2016: 160)

Downing and Mtenje (2011: 1970, 1975) further show that embedded subjects, which are unlikely to be topicalized, are never followed by a phonological phrase break in Chichewa:

(92) a. (A-ná-kwíyá   ndí [m-phunzitsi a-méné a-lendó
        SM2-TAM-get angry with 1-teacher   1-REL   2-visitor
        á-ná-mu-gulílá   zóóváala].)
        SM2-TAM-OM1-buy for 10.clothes
        'They got angry with [the teacher for whom the visitors bought clothes].'
  b. (m-waná wá súkúlú a-ná-lémba   [káláta i-méné m-phunzitsi
        1-child 1.of 9.school SM1- PST2-write 9.letter 9-REL   1-teacher
        á-ná-weléenga])   (kwá á-nyúuzi).
        SM1-PST2-read   for   2-newspaper
        'A student wrote [the letter which the teacher read] for the newspaper.'

Here square brackets "[. . .]" indicate DPs modified by a relative clause, and round brackets indicate phonological phrases. The subjects within the relative clause, *a-lendó* 'visitor' in (92a) and *m-phunzitsi* 'teacher' in (92b), are not followed by a phonological phrase break. Note that the matrix subject in (92b) *m-waná wá súkúlú* 'child of school' is not followed by a phonological phrase boundary either, even though it is branching. This indicates that even branching subjects are phrased with a following verb if they are not interpreted as a topic.

Note that Bantu verbal morphology generally shows class agreement, suggesting that T is strong and labelable. In addition, Zulu and Chichewa share with Italian some properties that indicate that T is strong in these languages. First, they allow topicalization to the pre-subject position, like Italian (see (84) above). Cheng and Downing observe that contrastive and non-contrastive topics can be fronted to the pre-subject position in Zulu:

(93) a. Pre-subject contrastive locative topic (underlined) in Zulu:
      Context: Did the chief build houses inside our village or outside our village?
      Answer: <u>é-sí-godi-ni</u>   se:thu) ín-duna y-akhé: izí:n-dlu),
              LOC-7-village-LOC 7.our   9-chief SM9-build 10-house
              hháyí nga-phá:ndle).
              not   LOC-outside
              'The chief built houses inside our village, not outside our village.'
                                      (Cheng and Downing 2009: 228)

  b. Pre-subject non-contrastive topic (underlined) in Zulu:
      Context: 'What did the lawyer do with the papers?'
      Answer: ámá-phe:ph') úm-mél'   ú-wá-sayín-í:le).
              6-paper   1-lawyer SM1-OM6-sign-TAM
             'The lawyer signed the papers.'
                                        (Cheng and Downing 2009: 228)

Here, the fronted topics are followed by a phonological phrase boundary. Likewise, in Chichewa, topics can be fronted to the pre-subject position:

(94)   Pre-subject topic in Chichewa:
       a-leenje) zi-ná-wáluuma)   njúuchi)
       2-hunter sm10-tam-om2-bite 10.bees
       'The hunters, they bit them, the bees [did].'

> (Kanerva 1990: 102; glosses are provided by
> Downing and Mtenje 2011: 1967)

Here the topicalized DP *a-leenje* 'the hunter' is followed by a phonological phrase boundary.

Second, Zulu and Chichewa allow *pro*-drop, like Italian:

(95)   *Pro*-drop in Zulu
       bá-ník'   ú-Síph' í-bhayiséki:li) namhlâ:nje).
       3PL-gave 1-Sipho 5-bicycle   today
       'They gave Sipho a bicycle today.'

> (Cheng and Downing 2009: 219)

(96)   *Pro*-drop in Chichewa
       a-na-góná   m-nyumbá yá   Mávúuto.
       they-TAM-sleep in-9.house 9.of Mavuto
       'Theyslept in Mavuto's house.'

> (Kanerva 1990: 98; Glosses are provided by
> Downing and Mtenje 2011: 1967)

Third, like Italian, Chichewa does not exhibit the COMP-*t* effect. In English, topicalization induces the COMP-*t* effect, as shown in (97) below. However, in Chichewa, topicalization does not induce the COMP-*t* effect, as in (98):

(97)   Mary we think (*that) __ met Sue.

> (Pesetsky 2017: 994; Bresnan 1977)

(98)   Mkángó uwu, alenje a-ku-gáníza kutí ú-ma-fúná   ku-gúmúla
       lion3   this hunters sm-pres-think that sm3-hab-want inf-pull.down
       nyumbá   yá mfûmu.
       house   of chief
       'This lion, the hunters think that it wants to pull down the chief's house.'

> (Bresnan and Mchombo 1987: 756)

In (98), the embedded subject *Mkángó uwu* 'this lion' is topicalized, the embedded clause begins with *kutí* 'that,' and the sentence is grammatical.[14] Likewise in Zulu, topicalization of a subject does not induce the COMP-*t* effect:

(99)   Abafana incwadi uThemba   u-cabang-a   ukuthi ba-ya-yi-fund-a
       boy2   book9   Themba1a sp1a-think-Fv that   sp2-foc-oc9-read-FV
       'The boys, the book, Themba thinks that they are reading (it).'

> (Zeller 2004: 9)

Here, the subject, as well as the object, of the embedded clause is topicalized to the matrix clause and does not exhibit the COMP-*t* effect (see also Sabel and Zeller 2006). Note that Zeller (2004) argues that the topicalized constituent is base-generated in the matrix clause and co-indexed with *pro* in the embedded clause: that is, a trace is not left by topicalization. The point here, however, is that the complementizer *ukuthi* does not need to be immediately followed by an overt subject, unlike English.

Given these similarities to Italian, I conclude that T is strong and labelable in Chichewa and Zulu. Then, we can account for the phrasing of subjects in these languages in exactly the same way as Italian. T is labelable and hence cannot be detected by the phonological component in forming phonological phrases. There-fore, the (non-topic) subject in Spec-T is phrased with a following verb. If subjects occupy Spec-TOP, they are interpreted as a topic and phrased separately from a following element since TOP is unlabelable and locates a prosodic boundary on the right side of the topicalized subjects.

We should note, as observed by Cheng and Downing (2009), that Zulu allows a post-subject topic in addition to the preverbal topic that we have seen above. Consider the following examples:

(100) Post-overt subject topic (underlined) in Zulu:
   a. Context: What did the visitors buy for their families?
      Answer: Ízí-vakásh' <u>ímí-ndeni yâ:zo</u>) zí-yí-thengelé: ízín-gu:bo).
         8-visitor   4-family 4.their sm8-om4-buy.for 10-clothes
         'The visitors bought clothing for their families.'
   b. Context: What did the woman buy at the market?
      Answer: Ín-kósikaz' <u>e-máke:th'</u>) í-théng'   ímí-fi:no).
         9-woman   LOC-market sm9-buy   4-vegetable
         'The woman bought greens at the market.'
   c. Context: Who did the woman buy the greens from?
      Answer: Ín-kósíka:zi) <u>ímí-fín'</u>   í-yí-thengé: kú-m-li:mi.)
         9-woman   4-vegetable sm9-om4-buy   LOC-1-farmer
   'The   woman bought the greens from a farmer.'
                                      (Cheng and Downing 2009: 227)

Cheng and Downing (2009: 226) show that the post-subject topic is prosodically phrased with the subject in 18 out of 36 examples, as in (100a, b) above. However, occasionally (7 out of 36), the subject is not phrased with the topic, and the topic is not followed by a prosodic boundary, as in (100c). Since the (100a, b)-type of phrasing seems most frequent, I take it to be (arguably) unmarked phrasing for post-subject topics in Zulu.

Following Julien (2002) and Buell (2005), Cheng and Downing assume that the verb in Zulu moves to a position between T (their I) and v. They posit a functional head X between T and v, which hosts the raised verb (labels below are just for expository purposes; vP-internal subject is omitted):[15]

(101) $[_{TP}$ Subj T $[_{XP}$ V-v-X $[_{vP}$ $t_{V\text{-}v}$ $[_{VP}$ t_V . . .

For post-subject topics, they (p. 233) posit a topic phrase between TP and vP. Specifically, let us assume that the topic phrase (TOPP) is placed between TP and XP. Furthermore, I assume that the object moves to Spec-v, as discussed in Chapter 3. Then, the entire clause has the following structure:

(102)   [F [$_\gamma$ R$_o$ [$_{CP}$ C [$_{TP}$ Subj [$_\beta$ T [$_{TOPP}$ *Topic* [$_\alpha$ TOP [$_{XP}$ V-v-X [$_{vP}$ Obj $t_{V\text{-}v}$ [$_{VP}$ t_V t_{Obj} . . .

Here, the topicalized phrase is indicated by *Topic* and occupies Spec-TOP. On the basis of these syntactic assumptions, let us determine what prosodic phrasing the present theory predicts. Consider (103), where (103a) = (102). On the assumption that TOP is too weak to serve as a label, the syntactic object α that immediately contains TOP is interpreted as a phonological phrase, which contains V and Obj. The syntactic object β, which immediately contains labelable T, is not identified by the phonological component. The syntactic object γ, immediately containing the performative element R$_o$, is identified as a phonological phrase. Then, the phonological phrasing in (103b) is obtained for the syntactic derivation (103a):

(103)   a.   [F [$_\gamma$ R$_o$ [$_{CP}$ C [$_{TP}$ Subj [$_\beta$ T [$_{TOPP}$ *Topic* [$_\alpha$ TOP [$_{XP}$ V-v-X [$_{vP}$ Obj $t_{V\text{-}v}$ [$_{VP}$ t_V t_{Obj} . . .
      b.   (Subj   *Topic*)$_\varphi$ (V   Obj)$_\varphi$ Ø

Here, the subject in Spec-T is phrased with the topicalized constituent in Spec-TOP. This result seems to be borne out by the phrasing in (100a, b), which I take to be unmarked for post-subject topics. That is, strong T not only forces Subj to be phrased with a following verb, as we have seen in SVO constructions, but also with a following topic in post-subject topic constructions.

The occasional phrasing in (100c) would hence result from the (string-vacuous) topicalization of the subject, since it is given information in this context. Thus, the subject is topicalized to Spec-TOP above TP, and a prosodic boundary is placed on its right side. But why is the post-subject topic phrased with the following elements? Perhaps prosodic weight or speech rate would affect the phrasing. Recall that I argued in 3.4.3 that the phrasing of subjects and objects may vary with their prosodic branchingness in some languages. Thus, in Chichewa, it was argued that non-branching subjects can be optionally phrased with a following verb, while branching subjects are always phrased on their own (see (156) and (157) in Chapter 3). Then, in (100a, b), the subject and topic are phrased together, forming a licit branching phonological phrase, while in (100c), the post-subject topic forms a non-branching phonological phrase on its own, because of the presence of unlabelable TOP. It is then restructured leftward, forming a phonological phrase with the following materials. But another question then arises: why is the topicalized subject phrased on its own, thus resisting restructuring? A more general question is whether and/or how branchingness interacts with topic-hood in the formation of prosodic domains. I will leave these issues for future research.

These questions aside, phonological phrasing is obviously affected by the strength or richness of agreement of T: non-topic subjects are phrased with a following element, because of the labelable T, and this following element can be a verb (in SVO configurations) or a topic (in post-subject topic constructions).

So far, I have argued that the labelability of strong/weak T accounts for the parametric differences between Italian/Bantu-type and English-type languages with regard to the COMP-*t* effect and phonological phrasing of subjects. Note that, as discussed in Chapter 3, the extensive literature on phonological phrasing in the 1980s and 1990s has consistently reported that subjects are phrased separately from following material. I therefore suggested the typology of basic phonological phrasing (39), reproduced here:

(104) a. $(S)_\varphi (V)_\varphi (O)_\varphi$ [Aŋlɔ Ewe, English, Italian, French]
       b. $(S)_\varphi (V \quad O)_\varphi$ [Kimatuumbi, Kinyambo, Chichewa]

The standard theories, such as Nespor and Vogel (1986) and Selkirk (1986), as well as the phase-based theory of Dobashi (2003), are thus all designed to phrase subjects on their own. But more recent studies have started to show that subjects can be phrased with a following element, as we have just seen in Chichewa and Zulu, and perhaps also in Italian (see (89); see also (78)). In addition, Shaked (2007: fn. 6, fn. 13, Appendix 3) observes that preverbal subjects are not followed by a phonological phrase boundary in Hebrew, which displays rich subject agreement, allows *pro*-drop (Ritter 1988), and lacks the COMP-*t* effect (Borer 1984; Shlonsky 1988).[16] By contrast, in Brazilian Portuguese, which shows impoverished subject agreement and disallows *pro*-drop (Fortuny 2008: 133), subjects are regularly phrased separately from a following verb in "the new information reading of sentences as a whole," as observed by Sandalo and Truckenbrodt (2002), who carefully controlled the information structure in eliciting the data (see their footnote 1). Note, however, that Brazilian Portuguese does not have the Comp-*t* effect. As discussed by Barbosa et al. (2005), Brazilian Portuguese is gradually losing post-verbal subjects, which indicates that T is still in the process of becoming unlabelable. I will leave this issue open here, but it is clear that there is a correlation between poverty of agreement and phonological phrasing.

The present approach yields the new prediction that phonological phrasing is correlated with the strength/richness of agreement, which, I believe, will be worth pursuing in future research.[17]

4.5.4   *Unlabelable R*

In the previous section, I examined several prosodic phenomena related to the CP phase.

In this section, I will consider the derivation of v*P in some detail. In section 4.5.4.1, I argue that the object occupies different positions in ECM and simple transitive constructions in English and that this difference accounts for prosodic differences between these constructions. In section 4.5.4.2, I attempt to account for the cross-linguistic difference in phonological phrasing of Bantu applicative constructions in terms of structural variations.

4.5.4.1   *Simple transitive and ECM constructions*

In the analysis of simple transitive constructions in English, I have assumed that the object stays in situ:

(105) a. $[_C$ C $[_{<\varphi, \varphi>}$ Subj $[_\gamma$ T $[_\beta$ t_{Subj} $[_{v*}$ R-v* $[_\alpha$ t_R Obj$]]]]]]$
     b. (C   Subj$)_\varphi$ (T   R-v$)_\varphi$ (Obj$)_\varphi$

In the syntactic structure (105a), α has an unlabelable element (a copy of R) and is interpreted as a phonological phrase, which contains only Obj, as in (105b). So, if Obj moves out of α, we will have different phonological phrasing in which Obj is phrased with the verb R.

Chomsky (2013, 2015) argues that the accusative DP (i.e., the ECM subject) undergoes Internal Merge in ECM constructions (cf. Postal 1974; Lasnik and Saito 1991):

(106) John believes Mary to be honest.

If *Mary* remains in Spec-TP, as in (107), we will have XP-YP structure, *Mary* being XP and *to be honest* being YP. Note that the label TP here is just for expository purposes:

(107) . . . [believe $[_{TP}$ Mary [to be honest]]]

Here, no features are shared by *Mary* and the embedded non-finite T, so the TP cannot be labeled. Then, given the labeling algorithm (16b), repeated here in (108) along with other subcases, *Mary* has to undergo Internal Merge.

(108) Chomsky (2013, 2015):
     a. H is the label in {H, XP}
     b. The label of YP is the label of K in (i):
         (i) $\underline{XP}$ . . . $\{_K \underline{XP}, YP\}$
     c. The most prominent feature shared by XP and YP is the label of K in (ii):
         (ii) $\{_K$ XP, YP$\}$

Chomsky (2015) suggests that ECM subjects move to Spec-R, as shown in (109). First, R and TP are merged as in (109a). In (109b) *Mary* undergoes Internal Merge to Spec of R, resolving the XP-YP structure. In (109c), v* is externally merged, its phi-features are inherited by $R_{believe}$, the phi-features are shared by *Mary* and R, and β is labeled $<\varphi, \varphi>$. In (109d), $R_{believe}$ raises to v*, restoring the correct word order *believe-Mary*.

(109) a. $[_\alpha$ $R_{believe}$ $[_{TP}$ *Mary* $[_{T'}$ to be honest$]]]$
       b. $[_\beta$ Mary $[_\alpha$ $R_{believe}$ $[_{TP}$ t_{Mary} $[_{T'}$ to be honest$]]]]$
       c. $[_\gamma$ v* $[_{<\varphi,\varphi>}$ Mary $[_\alpha$ $R_{believe}$ $[_{TP}$ t_{Mary} $[_{T'}$ to be honest$]]]]]$
       d. $[_\gamma$ $R_{believe}$-v* $[_{<\varphi,\varphi>}$ Mary $[_\alpha$ $t_{Rbelieve}$ $[_{TP}$ t_{Mary} $[_{T'}$ to be honest$]]]]]$

Here, α is identified as a phonological phrase because it immediately contains the copy of $R_{believe}$. Note that this R is now involved in labeling. One might wonder if R can no longer be detected by the phonological component since it is labelable at this stage of derivation. As I have discussed in section 4.3, I assume that the labelability relevant here is the intrinsic property of lexical items: it is the inherited features that make labeling possible here, but R itself is not intrinsically unlabelable (i.e., syntactically inert). This intrinsic syntactic inertness of R is detected by the phonological component. Note also that the amalgam $R_{believe}$-v* is labelable and that γ is thus not interpreted as a phonological phrase. The syntactic object β, now labeled <φ, φ>, is also not interpreted as a phonological phrase, because it does not contain an unlabelable element that is detectable with minimal search. Then, we predict that *Mary* is phonologically phrased with *believe*:

(110) (*believe Mary*)$_\varphi$ (*to be honest*)$_\varphi$

As we saw in Chapter 3, the object DP is generally not phrased with the verb in simple transitive sentences in English (as in (105); see also (13a)), but here the accusative DP is predicted to be phrased with the verb, given the syntactic analysis of ECM constructions in (109). To test this prediction, let us consider intonational properties of verb phrases in English. In a study of the location of the intonational phrase boundary (henceforth, IP boundary) in various constructions in English, Taglicht (1998) takes IP boundaries to be marked by final lengthening and/or deliberate insertion of a pause (p. 183). Given the prosodic structure, IP boundaries always coincide with phonological phrase boundaries (but not vice versa; see the discussion around (86)), so I take possible IP boundaries to reflect the phonological interpretation of syntactic objects.

Let us first consider (111). Taglicht observes that an IP boundary can be placed between the verb and object in a simple transitive sentence:

(111) a.   He never completed % the list of references %
      b. * He never completed the % list of references %
(Taglicht 1998: 183)

Here % marks an IP boundary. (111a) is acceptable if we have an IP boundary between the verb *completed* and the object *the list of references*. But if, for example, we have an IP boundary between *the* and *list*, the sentence sounds awkward. This suggests that the distribution of IP boundaries is grammatically restricted.

Now let us consider ECM constructions:

(112) a.   We consider Mary % to be an expert %
      b. * We consider % Mary to be an expert %
      c.   She has proved the letter % to be a forgery %
      d. * She has proved % the letter to be a forgery %
(Taglicht 1998: 193)

As (112a) shows, we may have an IP boundary between the ECM subject *Mary* and the predicate *to be honest*, but we may not have an IP boundary between the matrix verb *consider* and the ECM subject *Mary*, as in (112b). The contrast between (112c) and (112d) makes the same point.[18] These observations conform to the prediction in (110), where a prosodic boundary is placed between the ECM predicate and its subject.

Moreover, a similar observation is made about the double object constructions and dative constructions, as shown in (113) and (114):

(113) a.   Give your friend % a book %

(Taglicht 1998: 187)

b. * Give % your friend a book %

(114) a.   Return the book % to John %

(Taglicht 1998: 187)

b. * Return % the book to John %

As in (113a), an IP boundary may be placed between the two objects, but (113b) shows that an IP boundary may not intervene between the verb and indirect object. Similarly, in a dative construction (114), we may have an IP boundary between the direct object and PP but not between the verb and direct object. Although I do not offer a detailed analysis of these constructions, it can be inferred that the indirect object *your friend* in (113) and the direct object *the book* in (114) move to Spec-R just like the ECM subject and that an IP boundary cannot be placed between these DPs and the verbs, which are phonologically phrased together.

Then, does the object DP move to Spec-R in simple transitive constructions like (115), in parallel with the ECM subject?

(115) John saw Mary.

Suppose that *Mary* moves to Spec-R, just like in ECM constructions:

(116) a. $[_\alpha$ R$_{saw}$ *Mary* $]$
      b. $[_\beta$ Mary $[_\alpha$ R$_{saw}$ t_{Mary} $]]$
      c. $[$ v* $[_{<\varphi,\varphi>}$ Mary $[_\alpha$ R$_{saw}$ t_{Mary} $]]]$
      d. $[$ R$_{saw}$-v* $[_{<\varphi,\varphi>}$ Mary $[_\alpha$ t_{Rsaw} t_{Mary} $]]]$

The derivation starts with (116a), and *Mary* moves to Spec-R, as in (116b). Then, v* is externally merged, as in (116c), the phi-features of v* are inherited by R, and β is labeled $<\varphi, \varphi>$. In (116d), R$_{saw}$ moves to v*, restoring the correct word order V-Obj. Here, the syntactic object α immediately contains the copy of unlabelable R, but no phonological phrase corresponding to α is formed since R and *Mary* have moved out of α. The syntactic object β, now labeled $<\varphi, \varphi>$, is not interpreted as a phonological phrase either, since it does not contain an unlabelable element that is detectable with minimal search. Then, it would be incorrectly predicted that *saw* and *Mary* are phonologically phrased together. As we discussed in Chapter 3, the basic phonological phrasing of the verb and object in English is (117a), not (117b):

(117) a. (V)$_\varphi$ (DP)$_\varphi$
      b. (V   DP)$_\varphi$

Moreover, as we have seen, an IP boundary can be inserted between the verb and accusative DP in simple transitive constructions (111), unlike in ECM constructions (112). So, these prosodic facts support the assumption that the object DP in simple transitive constructions stays in situ, as in (118):

(118) a. [v* [$_\alpha$ R$_{saw}$ Mary]]
      b. [*saw*- v* [$_{<\varphi,\varphi>}$ t_{saw} Mary]]

Here, R can be detected with minimal search within α, and α is interpreted as a phonological phrase that contains just *Mary*. Notice that in (118a), *Mary* is not involved in XP-YP structure, unlike the ECM subject remaining in Spec-TP in (109a), reproduced here:

(119) [$_\beta$ R$_{believe}$ [$_{TP}$ *Mary* [$_T$ to be honest]]]

In this case, *Mary* is forced to move out of TP for labeling reasons. In contrast, the object DP *Mary* in the transitive construction in (118) does not have to undergo Internal Merge for labeling. Therefore, I conclude that accusative DPs raise to Spec-R in ECM constructions but do not in simple transitive constructions.

This conclusion accords with the analysis of floating quantifiers, in which a quantifier is stranded when the associated DP moves leftwards (Sportiche 1988; cf. Maling 1976). Consider the following contrast:

(120) a. I expect the men$_i$ all t_i to leave at noon.
      b. *I saw the men all.

(Bowers 1993: 618, 620)

In the present analysis of v*P, *the men* raises from Spec-T to Spec-R, stranding *all* in (120a), while *the men* stays in the complement of R. Therefore, *all* cannot be stranded (see Bowers 1993, 2001 for a similar analysis; see also Lasnik 1999). Furthermore, the assumption that the accusative DP does not move in simple transitive constructions complies with the so-called anti-locality constraint that bans movement within the same "maximal projection," which is independently motivated by Abels (2003) and Grohmann (2003/2007), among others. Thus, the movement of *Mary* in the simple transitive construction (116) is prohibited since it is from the complement to the specifier of the same lexical item R, while the movement of *Mary* in the ECM construction (109) observes the anti-locality constraint, crossing the "TP" boundary.

Note that the prosodic difference between the transitive and ECM constructions would be unexpected in the standard theories (End-based theory and Relation-based theory), since they predict that a verb-object sequence is always phrased in the same way. Thus, the alignment of the right edge of XPs with that of a phonological phrase will give the phrasing in (121), where DP is always phrased with V, while Relation-based Theory yields the phrasing in (122), where DP is always phrased alone:

(121)   *Prediction by Align-R,XP:*
    a. ECM: (V DP)$_\varphi$ (to V . . .)$_\varphi$
    b. Transitive: (V DP)$_\varphi$

(122)   *Prediction by Relation-based Theory:*
    a. ECM: (V)$_\varphi$ (DP)$_\varphi$ (to V . . .)$_\varphi$
    b. Transitive: (V)$_\varphi$ (DP)$_\varphi$

More recent Match Theory would also predict the phrasing in (122) unless some markedness constraints are posited, since the maximal projection DP would match a phonological phrase.

So far, I have argued that an unlabelable R accounts for the location of IP boundaries in ECM and transitive constructions in English, on the assumption that ECM subjects undergo Internal Merge to Spec-R, while accusative DPs stay in situ in transitive constructions.

4.5.4.2   *Bantu applicative constructions*

In this section, I will consider an unlabelable verbal root R and its effect on phonological phrasing in applicative constructions in Bantu languages.

Bresnan and Moshi (1990) argue that Bantu languages are of two types with respect to the syntax of applicative constructions. One is the symmetric type, where either of the two internal arguments can be passivized and show object agreement. The other is the asymmetrical type, in which only the indirect object can be passivized and marks object agreement. Seidl (2001) observes that there is a correlation between these language types and prosodic domains. She points out that two internal arguments are phrased together in the symmetrical type but are phrased separately in the asymmetrical type. The following table is adapted from Seidl (2001: 89):

(123)

LANGUAGE	SYNTAX	PROSODIC DOMAIN
Kikuyu	Symmetric	(V NP NP)$_\varphi$
Kinyarwanda	Symmetric	(V NP NP)$_\varphi$
Kinande	Symmetric	(V NP NP)$_\varphi$
Runyambo/Kinyambo	Symmetric	(V NP NP)$_\varphi$
Haya	Symmetric	(V NP NP)$_\varphi$
Xhosa	Symmetric	(V NP NP)$_\varphi$
Chimwiini	Asymmetric	(V NP)$_\varphi$ (NP)$_\varphi$
Kiswahili	Asymmetric	(V NP)$_\varphi$ (NP)$_\varphi$

Elaborating on Seidl's analysis, McGinnis (2001) argues that this correlation can be accounted for by assuming that a Spell-Out domain matches a phonological phrase. McGinnis (2001: 132) argues that symmetrical languages have a high applicative phrase ApplHP between v*P and VP and that asymmetrical languages have a low applicative phrase ApplLP below VP (see also Pylkkänen 2008):[19]

(124) a. High applicative (Symmetric)
$$[_{v*P} \text{ EA }\quad v* \; [_{\text{ApplHP}} \text{ IO } [_{\text{ApplH}} \text{ DO ApplH } [_{VP} \text{ V } t_{DO}]]]]$$
  b. Low applicative (Asymmetric)
$$[_{v*P} \text{ EA } \quad [_{v} \text{ IO } \quad v* \; [_{VP} \text{ V } [_{\text{ApplLP}} \quad t_{IO} \; [_{\text{ApplL}} \text{ ApplL } \quad \text{ DO}]]]]]$$

Here, EA is an external argument and V corresponds to a root element R. Here and below, labels in the structure are only for expository purposes, as usual. In (124a), ApplH takes VP as its complement, DO base-generated in the complement of V moves to the inner Spec of ApplHP, and IO is base-generated in ApplHP. In (124b), ApplLP is the complement of V, DO is the complement of ApplL, and IO is base-generated in Spec-ApplLP and moves to Spec-v*P. Given these structures, McGinnis (2001: 111) proposes that phase-hood within v*P is defined in the following way:

(125) The sister of VP heads a phase if an argument is generated in its specifier.

Thus, ApplHP in (124a) and v*P in (124b) are phases. On the assumption that the phase head complement undergoes Spell-Out, VP is spelled-out in both constructions (Spell-Out domains are bold-faced and underscored below):

(126) a. High applicative (Symmetric)
$$[_{v*P} \text{ EA }\quad v* \; [_{\text{ApplHP}} \text{ IO } [_{\text{ApplH}} \text{ DO ApplH } \mathbf{[_{VP} \; V \; \underline{t_{DO}} \;]}]]]$$
  b. Low applicative (Asymmetric)
$$[_{v*P} \text{ EA } \quad [_{v} \text{ IO } \quad v* \quad \mathbf{[_{VP} \; V \; [_{\text{ApplLP}} \; t_{IO} \; [_{\text{ApplL}} \; \underline{\text{ApplL DO}}]}]]]]$$

Since EA, as well as V and ApplL/H, moves up to higher positions, Spell-Out gives the following phonological phrasing, where IO and DO are phrased together in symmetric languages and separately in asymmetric languages:

(127) a. High applicative (Symmetric)
     (V NP NP)$_\varphi$
  b. Low applicative (Asymmetric)
     (V NP)$_\varphi$ (NP)$_\varphi$

McGinnis argues that the definition of phases in (125) accounts not only for this asymmetry in phonological phrasing but also for other syntactic phenomena, including object agreement and locality of movement within v*P. But (125) does not seem to be without problems: namely, it is category-specific (referring only to VP) and raises the question of why CP can be a phase even when its specifier is empty.

In the present approach, the typology of phonological phrasing in (123) follows straightforwardly, with McGinnis's syntactic analysis of the verb phrase intact. Moreover, the phonological phrasing above v*P phase, which is not discussed by McGinnis (2001) or Seidl (2001), can also be accounted for. That is, we can explicitly account for why V is phrased with the following NP. Consider the high applicative (symmetric) construction:

(128) High applicative (Symmetric)
   $[_{CP}$ C $[_{TOPP}$ EA $[_{TOP'}$ TOP $[_{TP}$ t_{EA} T $[_{v*P}$ t_{EA} v* $[_{ApplHP}$ IO $[_{ApplH'}$ DO ApplH $[_{VP}$ V t_{DO}]]]]]]]]

As is the case for Chichewa and Zulu, I assume that the Bantu languages discussed here have strong T that can serve as a label and that EA (usually) occupies Spec-TOP (see section 4.5.3). Then, in (128), TOP′ and VP immediately contains the unlabelable elements, TOP and V (= R), respectively. Since VP is phonetically empty, it does not form a phonological phrase, as in (129). Then, TOP′ is interpreted as a phonological phrase, containing V, IO, and DO. Note that ApplH is labelable since it is a functional element (the structure above TOPP is omitted here to save space):

(129) High applicative (Symmetric)
   $[_{TOPP}$ EA $[_{TOP'}$ TOP $[_{TP}$ t_{EA} V-Appl-v*-T $[_{vP}$ t_{EA} t_{v*} $[_{ApplHP}$ IO $[_{ApplH'}$ DO t_{ApplH} $[_{VP}$ t_V t_{DO}]]]]]]]
   (EA $)_{\varphi}$ (V   IO   DO $)_{\varphi}$

In contrast to symmetrical languages, a prosodic boundary is created between IO and DO in asymmetrical languages. I assume that these languages also have strong T and that EA occupies Spec-TOP:

(130) Low applicative (Asymmetric)
   $[_{CP}$ C $[_{TOPP}$ EA $[_{TOP'}$ TOP $[_{TP}$ t_{EA} T $[_{vP}$ t_{EA} $[_{v'}$ IO v $[_{VP}$ V $[_{ApplLP}$ t_{IO} $[_{ApplL'}$ ApplL DO]]]]]]]]]]

Here, TOP′ and VP immediately contain unlabelable elements (i.e., TOP and the copy of V (t_V), respectively) and are interpreted as phonological phrases:

(131) Low applicative (Asymmetric)
   $[_{TOPP}$ EA $[_{TOP'}$ TOP $[_{TP}$ t_{EA} Appl-V-v-T $[_{vP}$ t_{EA} $[_{v'}$ IO t_v $[_{VP}$ t_V $[_{ApplLP}$ t_{IO} $[_{ApplL'}$ t_{ApplL} DO]]]]]]]]]
   (EA $)_{\varphi}$ (V   IO $)_{\varphi}$ (DO $)_{\varphi}$

VP corresponds to a phonological phrase containing DO and TOP′ to a phonological phrase containing V and IO.

Thus, the object asymmetries in phonological phrasing receive a straightforward account in the present approach, without recourse to the somewhat ad hoc definition of phases in (125).[20]

4.5.5 Further possible consequences

I have thus far discussed three unlabelable elements, i.e., weak T, R, and TOP, which are visible in the processes of externalization. In this section, I further speculate on two other (possible) unlabelable elements: case markers in Japanese and conjunction Conj. I also speculate on the prosodic analysis of weak pronouns in English, in line with the analysis of the COMP-*t* effect.

4.5.5.1 Case markers in Japanese

The traditional Japanese grammar posits a linguistic unit called a *bunsetsu* (literally, 'a part of a sentence'), which consists of one content word and zero or more function word(s) after it (see, e.g., Hashimoto 1934). *Bunsetsu* corresponds to a prosodic word if the word contained in it is accented (also called a phonological word/minor phrase/accentual phrase/minimal phrase, see McCawley 1968; Poser 1984; Ito and Mester 2013, 2016, among many others). Thus, in the following example, each content word with an attached function word constitutes a *bunsetsu* or a prosodic word, which is marked with φ here:[21]

(132) (Ta'ro-ga)$_\omega$ (tosyo'kan-kara)$_\varphi$ (ho'n-o)$_\varphi$ (nusu'n-da)$_\varphi$
     Taro-NOM   library-from   book-ACC   steal-PST
     'Taro stole a book from a library.'

Here and below, apostrophes show that the preceding vowels bear a pitch accent. I assume, following Fukui and Sakai (2003), that verb-tense complexes such as *nusu'n-da* in (132) result from Morphological Merger applying in the phonological component. Since they are single morphological units, they automatically correspond to prosodic words if they are accented. In what follows, I will focus on *bunsetsu* consisting of DP and a case marker and attempt to provide a principled account of why it corresponds to a prosodic domain in the present approach.

Post-nominal particles, such as *ga*, *kara*, and *o* in (132), are generally called case markers or case particles and are divided into two types. Kishimoto (2017: 448) divides them into syntactic and semantic case markers and lists the following:

(133) a. Syntactic case marker: *ga* (Nominative), *o* (Accusative), *ni* (Dative), *no* (Genitive)
       b. Semantic case marker: *de* (Instrumental, Place), *ni* (Locative), *kara* (Ablative),
                     e (Direction), *made* (Goal), *to* (Comitative/Quote).

The syntactic markers are generally attached to arguments, while semantic ones are attached to adjuncts, serving as postpositions. However, both these types demarcate *bunsetsu*, or the domain of the prosodic word.

Let us first consider semantic case markers. Suppose they take a DP as a complement, as in (134). Note that the structure here and below is arranged to reflect the head-final order in Japanese for expository purposes:

(134) $[_\alpha$ DP Case]

Since semantic case markers have their own lexical meaning, I take them to be unlabelable R, which can be detected by the phonological component. On the assumption that R requires a categorizer, (134) in fact has the following structure, in which the categorizer p (postposition) selects α (cf. Takano 1996):

(135) $[[_\alpha$ DP R] p]

If R were to move to p, like English R raising to v*, then it would be predicted incorrectly that the postposition is not phonologically phrased with the DP, since the copy of R is detected with minimal search within α. Fukui and Sakai (2003), among others, argue that V stays in situ in Japanese, unlike in English. If this is the case, it is reasonable to assume that R in general stays in situ in Japanese. Then in (135), R stays within α, is detected with minimal search within α, and α is interpreted as a prosodic domain. Thus, our approach explains how semantic case markers demarcate a prosodic domain on principled grounds.

Next, consider syntactic case markers. Suppose that they also take a DP as their complement, in line with the "KP" analysis of Japanese case markers, where a DP is headed by a functional head *K(ase)* (Fukui 1995: 107 fn.11; Narita 2014, and references cited therein).

(136) $[_\alpha$ DP K]

Here, K is the locus of a syntactic case marker. Notice that K is a functional category, which seems to lack lexical meaning, unlike semantic case markers. Then, it should be labelable and it would not be detected by the phonological component. But the prosodic facts indicate that the SO α in (136) should be interpreted as a prosodic domain. That is, if our approach to prosodic domains is on the right track, K should be more like R or weak T in English and detectable in the phonological component.

Fukui (1986/1995, *et seqq.*) argues that Japanese does not have functional categories that induce agreement, which explains fundamental differences between English and Japanese. If so, the syntactic case markers in Japanese are more like weak T in English, in that they do not induce (rich) agreement (and, in fact, do not show any agreement). Then, K is expected to be unlabelable and thus detectable with minimal search within α in (136), and α is interpreted as a prosodic domain.

Moreover, in the general framework of the labeling algorithm, Saito (2016) argues that case markers serve as an "anti-labeling" device, which makes a constituent to which they attach invisible for labeling. Thus, in (137), the case marker attached to α prevents α from labeling γ, and β provides the label of γ.

(137) $[_\gamma$ α-Case β]

Saito shows that this proposal explains why Japanese allows DP-scrambling and multiple nominative constructions. DP-scrambling is allowed because DP-Case (such as *Taro-o* 'Taro-Acc') does not label an SO, so that it can be freely merged with TP or CP, without inducing an XP-YP problem. If DP-Case is merged with XP, creating $[_\alpha$ DP-Case XP], the label of α is unambiguously the label of XP. Moreover, assuming that case valuation and phi-feature agreement can be dissociated (Bošković 2007), Saito argues that multiple nominative constructions are allowed in Japanese because two or more DPs in Spec-T can probe for T, and case is valued as Nominative, without causing an XP-YP problem:

(138) $[_\gamma$ DP-Case $[_\beta$ DP-Case $[_\alpha$ DP-Case [T<NOM> . . .

Since case marker is an anti-labeler, α, β, and γ are all labeled T.

If we assume that the case marker is a "head" K, as in (136), repeated below, it follows that K, which makes α unlabelable, is also unlabelable, given the endocentric nature of α, whose labelability is attributable to its "head," i.e., K:

(139) $[_\alpha$ DP K]

Then, the phonological component can detect the unlabelable K with minimal search within α and interprets α as a prosodic domain.

I have shown how semantic and syntactic case markers in Japanese demarcate prosodic domains, or *bunsetsu*, in the proposed theory of phonological interpretation.

Note that the DP in (135) and (139) contains NP, which is in turn analyzed as [R n], where n is a categorizer. Thus, (135) has the following structure, if we assume that R does not raise to its categorizer in Japanese:[22]

(140) $[[_\alpha$ [[Rnl n] D] R_{Case}] p]

Here, the R for the semantic case marker is marked with the subscript Case. Suppose that DP is a phase (Citko 2014; Hiraiwa 2005, among others). The syntactic object [R n] is interpreted as a prosodic domain at DP phase since it immediately contains R, as in (141a). Then, at the next-higher phase, α is interpreted as a prosodic domain since it immediately contains R_{Case} and is linearly ordered to follow (R n $)_\varphi$, as in (141b):

(141) a. (R n $)_\varphi$
      b. (R n $)_\varphi$ (D R_{Case} $)_\varphi$

Likewise, the example with a syntactic case particle (139) has the structure (142), and the corresponding phonological phrases will be as defined in (143):

(142) $[_\alpha$ [[R n] D] K]
(143) (R n $)_\varphi$ (D K $)_\varphi$

Given these phrasings, [R n] and the case markers would constitute different phonological phrases, which is not true.[23] However, syntactic and semantic case markers are kinds of enclitics, in that they are usually morphologically bound to the preceding element (see Vance 1993 for discussions on morphological status of Japanese case particles). Such encliticization seems to have the effect of modifying phonological phrasing. Thus, in the prosodic analysis of the COMP-*t* effect in English, Sato and Dobashi (2016: 4.3) show that the enclitic nature of reduced auxiliary verbs ameliorates the COMP-t effect (cf. section 5.2.2). Consider (144):

(144) (?) Who do you suppose that'll leave early?

(Kandybowicz 2006: 222)

Here, the basic phonological phrasing will be as follows:

(145) . . . (that)$_\varphi$ (-'ll leave)$_\varphi$ . . .

The phonological phrase consisting only of a function word is not allowed (see (54) and (55)); hence, (145) would be ruled out incorrectly since it contains the offending phonological phrase (that)$_\varphi$. Sato and Dobashi argue that the encliticization of the reduced auxiliary - *'ll* modifies the phonological phrasing, deleting the phonological boundary between *that* and - *'ll*:

(146) . . . (that-'ll leave)$_\varphi$ . . .

This phonological phrase contains a content word *leave* and hence satisfies the condition on phonological phrases (54)/(55).

In light of these considerations, let us suppose that the enclitic nature of case markers modifies the basic phonological phrasing:

(147) a. Semantic case particles: (R n)$_\varphi$ (D R$_{Prt}$)$_\varphi$ → (R n D R$_{Prt}$)$_\varphi$
    b. Syntactic case particles: (R n)$_\varphi$ (D K)$_\varphi$ → (R n D K)$_\varphi$

These modified phrasings serve as a prosodic domain (i.e., prosodic word) when R is accented.

As I have suggested above, the prosodic units identified in this way do not always correspond to prosodic words. They are interpreted as prosodic words when each *bunsetsu* contains an accented word. Consider the following example, with an accusative DP containing two genitive DPs, cited from Ishihara (2015: 572):

(148) Na'oya-no a'ni-no   wa'in-o
     Naoya-GEN big.brother-GEN   wine-ACC
     'Naoya's big brother's wine ACC'

As Ishihara observes, an accentual fall is observed in each accented word in (148), indicating that (149) consists of three prosodic words:

(149) (Na'oya-no) (a'ni-no) (wa'in-o)

However, unaccented words show a different pattern:

(150) Naomi-no   ane-no   wa'in-o
      Naomi-GEN big.sister-GEN wine-ACC
      'Naomi's big sister's wine ACC'

(Ishihara 2015: 572)

Here, only the accented word *wa'in* 'wine' shows an accentual fall. The other two unaccented words form a single prosodic word together with the following accented word:

(151) (Naomi-no ane-no wa'in-o)

Hence, even if an SO is identified with minimal search for an unlabelable element by the phonological component Φ, it is not automatically mapped to some specific prosodic domain. That is, how it is interpreted or "used" is a matter of Φ. Thus, it is interpreted as a prosodic word only if it contains an accented word. Since the present study is concerned with basic phonological phrasing, I will not detail how the phonological component rearranges the basic phrasing in terms of accents in Japanese. See Ito and Mester (2013) for the Match-Theory approach to these issues.[24]

Saito (2016) further argues that inflectional elements are also anti-labelers in Japanese. Like verbs, adjectives exhibit inflection in Japanese. Then, we would predict that prenominal adjectival modifiers would behave in the same way as case-marked DPs, and this is borne out:

(152) a. Na'oya-no   uma'-i   wa'in-o
         Naoya-GEN tasty-INFL wine-ACC
         'Naoya's tasty wine Acc'
      b. Naomi-no   ama-i   wa'in-o
         Naomi-GEN sweet-INFL wine-ACC
         'Naomi's big sister's wine Acc'

(152a) and (152b) have exactly the same accentual pattern as (148) and (150), respectively.

In this section, I have argued that both syntactic and semantic case markers in Japanese are unlabelable and thus detectable in the phonological component. This explains (in part) why *bunsetsu* corresponds to a prosodic domain.[25]

4.5.5.2   Conjunction

Chomsky (2013: 45ff.) points out that the "head" Conj of structured coordination does not serve as a label:

(153) $[_\gamma$ Z $[_\alpha$ Conj $[_\beta$ t_Z W]]]

Here, Z moves out of β to merge with α so that β is labeled W and γ is labeled Z, indicating that Conj does not serve as a label. Given that Conj is unlabelable, α should be interpreted as a phonological phrase. Then, it is predicted that there can be a prosodic boundary between Z in Spec-Conj and Conj:

(154) $[_\gamma$ Z $[_\alpha$ Conj $[_\beta$ t_Z W]]]

     ↑

    A prosodic boundary

Saito (2016: 151 fn.14) notes that a VP coordination in Japanese requires a pause between two conjuncts, which is marked with % below. The conjunction in this case is thus phonetically empty:

(155) Hanako-wa itumo $[_{VP}$ teeburu-o os-i] % $[_{VP}$ kabin-o   taos]-u
      Hanako-TOP always   table-ACC push   vase-ACC make.fall-PRES
      'Hanako always pushes the table and makes the vase fall.'

The relevant part of the structure is schematically shown below:

(156) $[_\beta$ VP $[_\alpha$ Conj VP]]

     ↑

    Pause

If the present theory is correct, it follows that a pause is placed at the phonological phrase boundary created as a result of minimal search for the unlabelable Conj. As discussed in sections 4.5.3.1 and 4.5.4.1, a pause is a typical cue to an intonational phrase boundary, which always coincides with a phonological phrase boundary (but not vice versa), given the prosodic hierarchy. Thus, I regard the location of a pause as reflecting the phonological interpretation of syntactic objects (see also endnote 12 for related discussion).[26]

   If this correlation between Conj and a prosodic boundary is correct, one might wonder why *and* in English does not require a pause or create a prosodic boundary:

(157) John and Bill

Notice that if there are three or more conjuncts, we can omit all instances of *and* except the last one, and a pause is placed instead:

(158) a. John and Bill and Tom
      b. John, Bill(,) and Tom
      c. John, Bill, Tom(,) and Greg etc.

This suggests that the overt *and* is actually a "pause-filler," in that it is prosodically inserted into a pause site so that the overt *and* "masks" the pause, and it sounds as if there is no prosodic boundary there. Another question is why the last or lowest *and* cannot be omitted (except in the case of stylistic asyndeton), to which I do not have an answer.

Although the discussion in this section is highly speculative, it is clear that a syntactic object that immediately contains an unlabelable Conj can correspond to a prosodic domain. See Shiobara (2019) for further elaboration of the idea that Conj corresponds to a prosodic boundary.

4.5.5.3 Weak pronouns in English

As a final speculation, let us consider object weak pronouns WP in English, which might be an interesting case to consider within the present theory of phonological phrasing. As pointed out by Richards (2004: 41), among others, a WP and its host (verb) have to be in the same phonological phrase and at the same time in the same prosodic word, unlike a full DP:

(159) ((*feed him*)$_\omega$)$_\varphi$

If we assume that prosodic word formation cannot apply across a phonological phrase boundary,[27] WP must be in the same phonological phrase containing its host R-v* at the point of phonological interpretation. Suppose that a WP is D (a functional element), which is labelable. If the object WP stayed in situ, as in (160a) below, α would be interpreted as a phonological phrase that contains just the WP as in (160b):

(160) a. [$_\gamma$ Subj [$_\beta$ R-v* [$_\alpha$ t_R WP]]]
        b.   *(WP)$_\varphi$

As we have seen in the discussion of the COMP-trace effect (section 4.5.2.2), a phonological phrase containing only functional elements is disallowed, so (160b) is an illegitimate phonological phrase. Suppose instead that WP undergoes Internal Merge (IM) to SPEC-R, like an ECM subject discussed in section 4.5.4.1:

(161) [$_\gamma$ Subj [$_\beta$ R-v* [$_{\alpha'}$ WP [$_\alpha$ t_R t_{WP}]]]]

Since the SO α' does not have a detectable unlabelable element, it is not interpreted as a phonological phrase, and no phonological phrase boundary is placed between R-v* and WP. That is, R-v* and WP are included in the same phonological phrase. Then, WP can be included in the prosodic word that contains R-v*, given that prosodic word formation applies within a phonological phrase:

(162) ((R-v* WP)$_\omega$)$_\varphi$

This would explain why an object WP and its host constitute a single prosodic word in English. Note that IM of WP violates the anti-locality constraint discussed in section 5.4.1. Suppose that the complement of R may undergo IM to Spec-R, in violation of the anti-locality constraint, unless the derivation otherwise yields an illegitimate output (cf. Chomsky 1995: 297 (76)). Thus, in a simple transitive construction, the full DP complement may not undergo IM, because the failure of IM would not yield an illegitimate output. By contrast, the WP must undergo IM because it would otherwise result in an illegitimate output as in (160b).[28]

Let us now consider if a nominative subject can be a WP. Suppose that a subject WP stays in situ within v*P:

(163) $[\text{ F } [_\zeta \quad \text{R}_\emptyset \text{ } [_\varepsilon \quad \text{C } [_\delta \quad \text{T } [_\gamma \quad \text{WP } [_\beta \text{ R-v* } [_\alpha \quad t_\text{R} \cdots]]]]]]]$

Here, the syntactic object γ has the labelable WP (D), which can be detected with minimal search, so it would be labeled D. If the label of γ were D but not R-v*, then γ could not be interpreted as a verbal predicate at C-I. In that case, the WP could not be interpreted as an external argument within γ. Therefore, (163) is excluded at C-I.[29]

Suppose that the WP undergoes IM to SPEC-T:

(164) $[\text{ F } [_\zeta \text{ R}_\emptyset \text{ } [_\varepsilon \text{ C } [_\delta \text{ WP T } [_\gamma \quad t_\text{WP} \text{ } [_\beta \text{ R-v* } [_\alpha \quad t_\text{R} \cdots]]]]]]]$

Phonological phrasing for (164) will be as follows, given that $\text{R}_\emptyset$, T, and t_R are detectable unlabelable elements within ζ, δ, and α, respectively:

(165) $(\text{C WP})_\varphi \text{ } (\text{ T } t_\text{WP} \text{ R-v* })_\varphi \text{ } (\text{ } t_\text{R} \cdots)_\varphi$

Here, the phonological phrase $(\text{C WP})_\varphi$ consists only of functional elements and contains no content word, given that WP is a functional element D. That is, it is an illegitimate phonological phrase. Therefore, (165) is excluded in Φ.

Hence, English does not have a nominative subject WP, probably because apparent "weak" nominative subject pronouns do not cliticize to the neighboring element, unlike the object WPs that cliticize to a verb. Therefore, nominative pronouns in English would be full DPs, which are sometimes pronounced weakly.

4.5.6   Interim summary

In section 4.5, we have discussed some consequences of the proposed theory of phonological interpretations of syntactic objects. The basic idea is that a syntactic object SO is identifiable in the phonological component if an unlabelable element is detectable with minimal search within the SO; this SO is interpreted as a phonological phrase. I have examined unlabelable T, R, TOP, case markers, and Conj, and their contributions to identification of phonological phrases. Unlike previous approaches to phonological phrasing, the proposed theory considers the richness of agreement, which accounts for cross-linguistic variation of phonological phrasing and related phenomena in terms of agreement. The proposed theory further implies that it is X-bar levels rather than XP levels – to use traditional terms – that generally correspond to phonological phrases, as mentioned in endnotes 10 and 26. This contradicts the basic premise of Match Theory: that it is XP, but not X´, that corresponds to a phonological phrase. It remains to be seen whether and/or how we should harmonize the proposed theory with the other basic premise of Match Theory – that syntactic recursion gives rises to prosodic recursion.

In the next section, I will discuss the relation between linearization procedures and prosodic categories.

4.6. Linearization and prosodic hierarchy

I have postponed the discussion of linearization, in order to focus on the proposed mechanism of phonological interpretation in terms of minimal search. Since linear order is not available for syntactic computation, it should be defined on the basis of the materials to be externalized, so that the SM system can interpret them (Chomsky 2013: 39). In this section, I will discuss how linearization procedures apply in the present theory of phonological interpretations, which has dispensed with Spell-Out. Recall that I suggested in section 3.5.2 that phonologically meaningful domains should be attributed to linear ordering, an essential property of externalization, the idea being that basic units or primes for linearization correspond to prosodic domains:

(166) A prime for linearization is a prosodic domain.

I further argued that the following three kinds of linearization are deduced from (166):

(167) a. A prime for Lin(W) is a prosodic word.
b. A prime for Lin(S-O) is a phonological phrase.
c. A prime for Lin(¬S) is an intonational phrase.

Here Lin(W), Lin(S-O), and Lin(¬S) are the linearization of words (syntactic terminal elements), that of Spell-Out domains, and the non-syntactic linearization (affected by information structure), respectively. We have assumed that Lin(W) and Lin(S-O) are parts of the operation Spell-Out. However, since we have abandoned Spell-Out in favor of the interpretive theory, we need to reconsider them.

Let us first consider Lin(W). I have assumed that phonological interpretation proceeds phase by phase, adopting the following condition:

(168) A syntactic object SO receives a phonological interpretation when its containing phase is complete. = (30)

In the absence of Spell-Out, it follows that Lin(W) applies to SOs phase by phase, since it is part of phonological interpretations. Thus, once the phonological component identifies an SO by minimal search for an unlabelable element, Lin(W) linearizes the terminal elements of the SO.

To be more specific, let us consider the linearization of a transitive sentence in English-type languages, schematically shown in (169) below. First, α receives a phonological interpretation when the v*P phase is complete, since the unlabelable t_R is detected with minimal search within α. At this point, Lin(W) applies, as part of the phonological interpretation. Since α involves just one overt item, Lin(W) yields a trivial linear string, as in (170a). Then, δ receives a phonological interpretation when the CP phase is complete, since δ immediately contains unlabelable T. Suppose that T is an overt auxiliary verb. Then, Lin(W) gives a linear order between T and R-v*, as in (170b):

(169)   [F [$_\eta$ R$_\varnothing$ [$_\zeta$ C [$_\varepsilon$ Subj [$_\delta$ T [$_\gamma$ t_{Subj} [$_\beta$R-v* [$_\alpha$ t_R Obj]]]]]]]]]
(170) a. Obj
         b. T < R-v*

Here "<" stands for precedence. Although I will not attempt to construct a full theory of Lin(W), I assume that asymmetric (c-command) relations in syntax are mapped to linear order, in line with Kayne (1994) (see also Collins 2017; Collins and Stabler 2016). Thus, roughly speaking, in (169), T asymmetrically c-commands R-v*, and the former is interpreted as preceding the latter.

Note that this cannot be the end of the linearization procedure at this stage of derivation. We have two linear strings, (170a) and (170b), which need to be linearized in relation to each other.[30] At first glance, this linearization would seem trivial. In the present interpretive framework devoid of the Spell-Out operation, the phonological component can directly look at asymmetric relations in syntax, so it can determine that, for example, R-v* asymmetrically c-commands Obj, and thus (170b) precedes (170a).

However, consider the following example, which we discussed in section 4.1:

(171) [$_\alpha$ The verdict [$_\beta$ that Tom Jones is guilty]] seems to have been reached t_α by the jury.

Details aside, when the syntactic derivation reaches the CP phase β, the linear order is defined for the terminal elements of β. Note that this phonological interpretation applies when α is still in its base position, marked by t_α. If the phonological component looked into syntax before Internal Merge of α and found that terminal elements in β are asymmetrically c-commanded by, say, *reached*, then β would be incorrectly pronounced in the position marked by t_α.[31]

To avoid such a problem, I propose the following linearization procedure, which refers to both syntax and phonology:

(172) Linearization of Linear Strings (Lin(LS)):
        Linear string LS$_1$ immediately precedes LS$_2$ if SO$_1$ corresponding to LS$_1$ immediately contains SO$_2$ corresponding to LS$_2$.

Here, a linear string LS is a string defined by Lin(W). I assume that the correspondence between an LS and a syntactic object SO holds if the elements of the LS are terminals of the SO. Thus, in (171), the linear string *the-verdict* corresponds to α but not to β, the string *that-Tom-Jones-is-guilty* corresponds not only to β but also to α, and the (trivial) string *seems* does not correspond to α or β. I also assume that SO_1 immediately contains SO_2 if there is no such SO between SO_1 and SO_2, which corresponds to the linear string distinct from LS_1 and LS_2. Note that an LS is a phonological object, while containment relations hold between syntactic objects. This is possible in the interpretive approach, because the phonological component has access to the syntax. If we had Spell-Out, the phonological component would just look at the output of Spell-Out, and hence does not have access to the syntax (cf. endnote 30). Note also that the LSs in (172) are primes for linearization and will correspond to prosodic domains, given (166): Lin(LS) will replace Lin(S-O), as we will discuss shortly.

Given the proposed Lin(LS), let us consider (171) in further detail. The internal structure of α is illustrated below:

(173) $[_\alpha$ D$_{the}$ [R$_{verdict}$-n [t$_{Rverdict}$ $[_\beta$ C$_{that}$ [Tom Jones $[_\gamma$ T$_{is}$ [. . . guilty

Here, the nominal root R of *verdict* takes the complement CP (= β), and the R$_{verdict}$ raises to the categorizer n, just like R raising to v*. I assume that DP (= α) is a phase (Citko 2014; Hiraiwa 2005, among others). First, when the CP phase (= β) is reached, γ receives a phonological interpretation since T$_{is}$ is detected with minimal search within γ, and Lin(W) gives the linear string *is* < *guilty* within γ. When the DP phase (= α) is reached, the SO that immediately contains the copy of R$_{verdict}$ (t$_R$*verdict*) receives a phonological interpretation, and Lin(W) gives the linear string *that* < *Tom Jones* within this SO. This SO corresponds to the LS *that* < *Tom Jones* and immediately contains the SO γ, corresponding to the LS *is* < *guilty*. Hence, the former precedes the latter, given Lin(LS). Because these two LSs are primes for Lin(LS), they are now interpreted as phonological phrases:

(174) (that < Tom Jones)$_\varphi$ < (is < guilty)$_\varphi$

When α remains in its original position, the elements at its edge (D$_{the}$ and R$_{verdict}$-n) are not yet phonologically interpreted, since the higher phase is not reached. Therefore, the whole string in (174) has not yet been linearly ordered with respect to any other linear string.

Later in the derivation, α undergoes Internal Merge to the matrix Spec-T. When the matrix CP phase is reached, the phonological interpretation applies:

(175) $[_\zeta$ C $[_\varepsilon$ $[_\alpha$ the verdict $[_\beta$ that Tom Jones $[_\gamma$ is guilty]]] $[_\delta$ T [seems . . .

Here, T is detected with minimal search within δ, and Lin(W) gives the order within δ (trivially, just for *seems*), as in (176a). This string is not interpreted as a phonological phrase at this stage of derivation since it has not yet undergone Lin(LS). At this point, we have the following two strings:

(176) a. seems
　　　 b. (that < Tom Jones)$_\varphi$ < (is < guilty)$_\varphi$

The syntactic objects corresponding to these two strings have no containment relation. So Lin(LS) cannot define a linear order between (176a) and (176b) at this stage. Note that the elements of (176b) are also terminal elements of ε (= "TP" in a traditional term), and ε contains δ, so the string (176b) would be defined as preceding the string (176a) at this stage of derivation. But ε has not yet received a phonological interpretation; nor is it included in an SO that has received a phonological interpretation. Therefore, the precedence relation between (176a) and (176b) cannot be defined at this stage. Lin(LS) refers to both syntax and phonology.

The next phase is an abstract phase FP containing $R_{\o}$, an abstract performative element, which is unlabelable (see (32) in section 3):

(177) [F [$_\eta$ $R_{\o}$ [$_\zeta$ C [$_\varepsilon$ [$_\alpha$ the verdict [$_\beta$ that Tom Jones [$_\gamma$ is guilty]]] [$_\delta$ T [seems . . .

When this phase is reached, $R_{\o}$ is detected with minimal search within η, and Lin(W) applies to the elements within η that have not yet been phonologically interpreted (i.e., *the* and *verdict*), defining the linear string *the* < *verdict*. Now we have the following linear strings:

(178) a. seems   = (176a)
      b. (that < Tom Jones)$_\varphi$ < (is < guilty)$_\varphi$ = (176b)
      c. the < verdict

Given Lin(LS), the string (178c) immediately precedes the string (178b), since the SO α, which corresponds to the string (178c), immediately contains the SO β, which corresponds to the string (178b):

(179) (the < verdict)$_\varphi$ < (that < Tom Jones)$_\varphi$ < (is < guilty)$_\varphi$

Here, *the* < *verdict* is interpreted as a phonological phrase since it has undergone Lin(LS). Lin(LS) also defines the linear order between (179) and (178a). The terminal elements of α and β are also terminal elements of ε; that is, the string (179) corresponds not only to α but also to ε. Since ε immediately contains δ, which corresponds to the string (178a), (179) precedes (178a), and the following linear string is obtained for the derivation of (171):

(180) (the verdict)$_\varphi$ < (that < Tom Jones)$_\varphi$ < (is < guilty)$_\varphi$ < (seems)$_\varphi$ . . .

Here, *seems* is a prime for Lin(LS) and is therefore interpreted as a phonological phrase.

In light of these considerations, let us return to the derivation of a transitive sentence (169), reproduced here:

(181) [F [$_\eta$ $R_{\o}$ [$_\zeta$ C [$_\varepsilon$ Subj [$_\delta$ T [$_\gamma$ t_{Subj} [$_\beta$R-v* [$_\alpha$ t_R Obj]]]]]]]]
(182) a. Obj
      b. T < R-v*

   c. (T < R-v*)$_\varphi$ (Obj)$_\varphi$
   d. Subj
   e. (Subj)$_\varphi$ (T < R-v*)$_\varphi$ (Obj)$_\varphi$

First, α receives a phonological interpretation at the v*P phase because of the unlabelable t_R, and Lin(W) applies to terminal elements in α, giving a trivial string Obj, as in (182a). Second, δ receives a phonological interpretation at the CP phase because of the unlabelable T, and Lin(W) applies, defining T < R-v*, as in (182b). Third, Lin(LS) applies to (182a, b). Since the SO δ corresponding to the linear string T < R-v* immediately contains the SO α corresponding to the (trivial) string Obj, the former precedes the latter, as in (182c). Here, these two strings are interpreted as phonological phrases since they are primes for Lin(LS). Fourth, η receives a phonological interpretation at the root-clause phase (i.e., "FP"), with R_o being detected by minimal search, and Lin(W) applies, giving the string (182d). Then, Lin(LS) applies. Since the SO η corresponding to the string Subj immediately contains the SO δ corresponding to the string (182c), the former precedes the latter, as in (182e). Here, Subj is interpreted as a phonological phrase, since it is a prime for Lin(LS).

Notice that the present cyclic linearization procedures account for the mismatch between syntactic and prosodic constituents (cf. Chapter 2). If we again consider (182b), the linear string is defined for the terminals that correspond to the SO δ, which is identified by minimal search for T. The terminals of δ include T, V-v*, and Obj, but Obj does not receive a phonological interpretation at this stage since it has already been interpreted and linearized, as in (182a), at the previous phase level (i.e., the v*P phase level), where the SO α is identified by minimal search for t_R (see endnote 7 and the discussion near it). Therefore, Lin(W) linearizes only T and V-v*, resulting in the string in (182b). This string then serves as a prime for Lin(LS), as in (182c), and is interpreted as a phonological phrase or prosodic constituent consisting of T and V-v*. This prosodic constituent corresponds to none of the SOs in (181), and the syntax-phonology mismatch is thus accounted for. Hence, the mismatch follows from phase-by-phase phonological interpretations.

Making reference to both syntax and phonology, I have shown that the proposed mechanism of Lin(LS) defines a linear order between the linear strings defined by Lin(W) in the course of phase-by-phase phonological interpretations. Then, (167b) should now be restated as (183b):

(183) a. A prime for Lin(W) is interpreted as a prosodic word.
      b. A prime for Lin(LS) is interpreted as a phonological phrase.
      c. A prime for Lin(¬S) is interpreted as an intonational phrase.

In the previous sections, I have stated that an SO is interpreted as a phonological phrase if an unlabelable element is detected with minimal search within the SO. However, precisely speaking, an SO is interpreted as a phonological phrase because it serves as a prime for the linearization Lin(LS).

Thus, we can maintain the unification of prosodic categories in terms of linearization suggested by Dobashi (2013) (see Chapter 3 for a review). In addition, we can reduce prosodic domains to primes of linearization and can further attribute the hierarchical structure of prosodic categories to the procedures of linear ordering that are essential to externalization. That is, prosodic domains and their hierarchical organization are not stipulated theoretical objects, but are derivable on principled grounds.

4.7. Conclusion

In this chapter, I have argued that the operation Spell-Out is not formulable under the strict internalist concept of language, which takes language to be generation of an infinite array of hierarchically structured expressions mapping to C-I, with the linear property of SM being placed outside the computational system that creates LOT. The processes of externalization are therefore ancillary to language and independent of the mapping to C-I. Consequently, they should be formulated as an interpretive procedure that generates phonological objects, which are eventually interpreted at the SM system, by referring to the computational system. I have described an asymmetry in interpretability between syntax and phonology: syntactically inert (i.e., unlabelable) elements are interpretable in the phonology. Given this asymmetry, the interpretive procedure identifies certain syntactic objects, SOs, as prosodic domains by identifying an unlabelable element, in accordance with the third-factor principle of efficient computation (i.e., minimal search). The phonological interpretation applies cyclically, phase by phase, thereby accounting for the mismatch between syntactic and phonological constituents. I have shown that this approach has more empirical consequences than the Multiple Spell-Out theory of phonological phrasing. In particular, it sheds light on the role of agreement in prosodic domain formation, which, to my knowledge, has never been recognized in the study of phrasal phonology. Moreover, predicted phonological phrases often correspond to X′-level syntactic objects, contrary to the basic premise of Match Theory, which holds that XPs, not X′, match phonological phrases. I will leave a detailed comparison of the proposed theory with Match Theory for future research.

I have also reconsidered the processes of linearization. In Chapter 3, I pointed out that primes for linearization serve as prosodic domains and showed that the three basic prosodic categories (prosodic word, phonological phrase, and intonational phrase) are all reduced to primes for linearization. That is, they are unified in terms of linearization. One linearization procedure was the linearization among Spell-Out domains (Lin(S-O)), which is not available for the system proposed in this chapter. Instead, I have proposed a process of linearization of linear strings (Lin(LS)). Minimal search for an unlabelable element identifies certain SOs, Lin(W) linearizes the terminals of each of these SOs, thereby creating a linear string for each SO, and Lin(LS) then linearizes such linear strings. By replacing Lin(S-O) with Lin(LS), I maintain that the three basic prosodic categories are unified in terms of linearization.

In the next chapter, we will return to intonational phrasing. I argue that a terminated derivation is detectable with zero search and serves as a prime for Lin(¬S), which is interpreted as an intonational phrase.

Notes

1 I will discuss labelable T in detail in section 4.5.2.
2 Here, I assume that R does not raise to Spec-R. I will return to this in section 5.4.1, where I discuss English simple transitive and ECM constructions and their prosodic properties.
3 Since the computation proceeds phase by phase, steps (20a–f) would have to be calculated simultaneously, but I will not consider this issue as it is not relevant to the phonological interpretation of syntactic objects.
4 See Epstein, Kitahara, and Seely (2016) and Chomsky (2015) for IM of the external argument.
5 Here, "visible" is used somewhat metaphorically. The expression "are visible in the processes of externalization" means "can contribute to the post-syntactic phonological processes such as prosodic-domain formation." That is, function words, though invisible in the sense of (25b), receive a phonetic interpretation (i.e., they are pronounced) if they have a phonetic content.
6 I would like to thank Hisatsugu Kitahara for helpful comments on this point.
7 This avoidance of a redundant interpretation could be reduced to the third-factor principle of efficient computation, which I assume to be relevant both to narrow syntax and to broader fields of the cognitive system in general, although I will not pursue this conceptual issue here. See Collins (2017) for related discussions.
8 I will discuss how two phonological phrases are linearized with respect to each other in section 6. I will argue that each string corresponding the syntactic object identified with minimal search by the phonological component (e.g., T<R-v*, Obj) is a prime for linearization and interpreted as a phonological phrase, along the lines of the discussion in section 3.5 (Dobashi 2013).
9 Note that R_{thief} in {n, R_{thief}} is also visible in phonology. As R raises to v*, I assume that R raises to n, forming an amalgam, {R-n, t_R}. Since the copy of R here contains no phonetic content, it does not receive phonological interpretation. Therefore, R-n is included in the phonological phrase corresponding to α in (32). See section 4.5 for a related discussion.
10 It might be theoretically interesting to see that α and γ correspond to T-bar and V-bar (intermediate projections) in the sense of traditional X-bar theory (Chomsky 1986b). They do not seem to receive an interpretation at C-I, nor do they undergo any syntactic operation. Rather, they receive an interpretation in Φ if the current approach is correct. It should also be noted that this result is incompatible with the basic premise of Match Theory that a maximal projection XP corresponds to a phonological phrase.
11 It is not clear if the strong/weak distinction originates in lexical items in the lexicon, or it is "assigned" somewhere between the lexicon and syntactic derivation when, for example, Lexical Array or Numeration is formed. More recent approaches (e.g., Berwick and Chomsky 2011: 37ff.) suggest that parametric variation is entirely reduced to externalization. This entails that parameters do not belong to the lexicon. Then, the strong/weak distinction should also be reduced to externalization, so that T is interpreted as strong in Italian and weak in English. I will leave this issue for future research and continue to assume that the strong/weak distinction is a lexical property.
12 It would be the case that the phonological component can detect TOP as prosodically "stronger" or "higher in the hierarchy" by interacting with the external component of pragmatics/information structure/discourse in the present interpretive approach to the interfaces. I will not further pursue this issue here.

13 Cheng and Downing (2009) and Downing and Mtenje (2011) argue that a prosodic phrase is aligned with the right edge of a phase. They argue that a topic is generated above CP so that it is excluded from the prosodic phrase corresponding to the CP phase.

14 For the lack of complementizer-trace effect in other Bantu languages, see Diercks (2010).

15 This assumption about the verb position departs from my assumption in Chapter 3 that V moves to T. Here, I adopt X as the landing site of V since otherwise we cannot postulate the topic phrase between the subject in Spec-T and V, as we will see directly in (102).

16 Note that Hebrew does not always allow *pro*-drop. Thus, in the present, tense *pro*-drop is not allowed, while the COMP-*t* effect does not occur. See Shlonsky (1988).

17 I have assumed that R is universally weak and unlabelable, following Chomsky (2015). I have also argued that V and Obj are always phrased together in Bantu, on the assumption that Obj raises to Spec-v* (see (42) in this chapter; see also 3.4.2.3). However, Cheng and Downing (2016: 165) argue that this assumption is not well founded and that Obj in fact stays in situ. It is logically possible that Bantu languages have labelable R, because they often show object agreement. Suppose that Obj stays in situ, and that R is labelable in Bantu:

(i)   [C [Subj [R-v*-T [t_{Subj} [$t_{R\text{-}v^*}$ [$_\alpha$ t_R Obj]]]]]]

Then, α is not identified as a phonological phrase since the copy of R is labelable. Given that T is also labelable in Bantu, there is no unlabelable element between the verbal complex R-v*-T and Obj, and hence these are phrased together. I will not pursue this possibility further here, and will continue to assume that R is invariably unlabelable in the following discussions.

18 In their proposed case theory, Neeleman and Weerman (1999) also argue that the matrix verb and ECM subject must appear in the same phonological phrase, for reasons of ECP and case-licensing at PF. See also Richards (2006).

19 As McGinnis (2001: 134) points out, the correlation shown in (123) is not without exception. Chichewa is syntactically an asymmetrical-type language, but its two internal arguments in applicative constructions are phonologically phrased together. McGinnis points out that a Chichewa benefactive has the semantic properties of high applicative and argues that the syntactic asymmetry results because Chichewa does not allow DO-IO order in Specs of ApplHP, unlike other symmetric languages, so that IO cannot move over DO to the subject position.

20 See Cheng and Downing (2016) for the analysis of phonological phrasing in symmetrical languages that is based on phase edges.

21 As I discussed at the beginning of section 4.5, "phonological word (φ)" is a nickname in the sense of Selkirk and Lee (2015). As we will see, the prosodic domains in (132) are identified by minimal search for an unlabelable element and therefore correspond to what we have called "phonological phrases" in previous sections, though they are descriptively called "prosodic words."

22 Here D is usually phonologically null. See Narita (2014: 180 fn.22) and works cited therein for the status of D in Japanese.

23 This problem would not arise if Japanese did not have D (see Fukui 1988; cf. Chierchia 1998; Bošković 2005).

24 The phrasing in (151) could be derived by the restructuring of the basic phonological phrases that are created by minimal search for unlabelable elements:

(i)   (Naomi-no)$_\varphi$ (ane-no)$_\varphi$ (wa'in-o)$_\varphi$ $\rightarrow$ (Naomi-no ane-no wa'in-o)$_\varphi$

The restructuring here is presumably triggered by the absence of lexical accents in the first two phonological phrases, without referring to syntax. Thus, this restructuring is purely phonological in nature. It could also be the case that (151) results from the recursion of phonological phrases, as suggested by Ito and Mester (2012, 2013):

(i)   (Naomi-no)$_\varphi$ (ane-no)$_\varphi$ (wa'in-o)$_\varphi$ → ((Naomi-no)$_\varphi$ (ane-no)$_\varphi$ (wa'in-o)$_\varphi$)$_\varphi$

I will leave this issue open here.

25 As discussed in Yim and Dobashi (2016), the discourse marker -*yo* in Korean, which adds some politeness to the expression, can be attached ubiquitously and optionally, as in the following example:

(i) Ce-A-ka(-yo)   ecey(-yo)   kkaphey-eyse(-yo) Celin-ul(-yo)   mannasse-yo.
    Ce-A-NOM(-yo) yesterday(-yo) café-at(-yo)   Celin-ACC(-yo) met.c-yo
    'Ce-A met Celin at the café yesterday'

                                          (Yim and Dobashi 2016: 214)

They argue that -*yo* is attached to the right edge of a phonological phrase. They observe that -*yo* attachment is not allowed when its host lacks a case marker:

(ii) a. Sonnim*(-i)-yo   wasse-yo.
        guest-nom-yo   came.c-yo.
        'A guest has come.'
    b. Phica*(-lul)-yo   sikhyesse-yo.
        pizza-   acc-yo   ordered.c-yo
        '(I)   ordered a pizza.'

                                          (Yim and Dobashi 2016: 228ff.)

Similarly, certain types of preverbal adverbs that cannot host -*yo* can do so if they accompany a postposition, as in (iii.a), or a predication marker -*key*, as in (iii.b-c) (see also Yim 2004, 2012):

(iii) a. Kapang-i   palo   yeki*(-ey)-yo   isse-yo.
        bag-nom   right   here-in-yo   exist.c-yo
        'The bag is right here.'
    b. Keykho-ka   kkoli-lul ppalli(*-yo)   wumcikyesse-yo.
        gecko-nom   tail-acc   quickly-yo   moved.c-yo
        'The gecko moved its tail quickly.'
    c. Keykho-ka   kkoli-lul ppalu-key-yo   wumcikyesse-yo.
        gecko-nom   tail-acc   quickly-key-yo moved.c-yo
        'The gecko moved its tail quickly.'

                                          (Yim and Dobashi 2016: 236ff.)

If these suffixes are unlabelable, it would be possible to recast Yi and Dobashi's analysis in terms of minimal search for the unlabelable suffixes.

Yim and Dobashi (2016: 231ff.) also discuss how a DP lacking a case marker can host -*yo* when it is interpreted as a topic (the following example is adapted from Yoon 2013):

(iv) Minswu(-nun)(-yo) onul   an wasse-yo.
     Minsu(-top)(-yo)   today not came.c-yo
     'Minsu didn't come today.'

This could be accounted for by assuming that a topic phrase stays in Spec-TOP in Korean and that TOP is too weak to serve as a label, creating a prosodic boundary there, as in the analysis of Italian in section 4.5.3.1.

26 Cf. endnote 10. α in (153)/(154)/(156) also corresponds to an "intermediate projection" in the sense of traditional X-bar theory, contra Match Theory.

27 Thus, in (i) below, *can* cannot form a prosodic word with the subject *John* even though they are adjacent. In contrast, *can* and *swim* form a single prosodic word together since they are in the same phonological phrase.

(i)   John   can swim.
       ((   )ω)$_\varphi$((　　　　)$_\omega$)$_\varphi$

28 Note that a pronominal object can license a floating quantifier, unlike a full DP object (cf. (120b)), indicating that it has moved leftward and stranded the quantifier:

(i) I saw them all yesterday.

(Maling 1976: 709)

This seems to conform to our analysis of WP here. However, a pronominal subject can also license a floating quantifier that immediately follows it, unlike a full DP:

(ii) a. They all are happy.
b. *The soldiers all are happy.

(Postal 1974: 113)

Thus, floating quantifiers associated with pronouns might not be licensed by leftward movement of the pronouns. See Ogawa (1996: 76ff.).

29 The shifted WP D in Spec-R in a simple transitive construction labels the complement of v* (α′ in (161)) as <φ, φ>, just like the full DP object in an ECM construction (see (109)).

30 When we had Spell-Out, as in the framework of Dobashi (2003), the phonological component only had access to the outputs of Spell-Out, so we needed a mechanism that linearizes output strings (which I called the *Assembly Process* in Dobashi (2003); see Chapter 3).

31 Note that if an SO receives a phonological interpretation only at strong phases CP and v*P (that is, if a "phase" in (168) refers to a strong phase), then the problem regarding (171) would not arise. Chomsky (2000, 2001) argues that unaccusative and passive verbs do not constitute strong phases. Then, the terminals in β are not linearized with respect to other terminals such as *reached* and *verdict* in their original position since these other elements do not receive a phonological interpretation until the matrix CP phase or the higher phase (FP, see (177)) is complete. When the matrix CP is complete, α containing β has already undergone IM to Spec-T, and the terminals of β in this derived position are therefore linearized with respect to the other elements.

However, as Legate (2003) argues, unaccusative and passive verbs seem to behave like transitive verbs with respect to phase-hood. If there is no distinction between strong and weak phases, or if a "phase" in (168) is taken to refer to phases in general (weak or strong), then the problem remains. I maintain that (171) poses a problem with linearization, for which we need to develop a fundamental solution.

5 Zero search and intonational phrasing

5.1. Introduction

In this chapter, I attempt to reframe intonational phrasing in accordance with the interpretive approach to syntax-phonology mapping that has been introduced in Chapter 4. Adopting the premise that primes for linearization are interpreted as prosodic domains, I have shown in Chapter 3 that topicalized phrases, shifted heavy NPs, prenominal adjectival modifiers with marked word order, and root clauses are interpreted as intonational phrases since they serve as primes for the non-syntactic linearization $Lin(\neg S)$ (see Chapter 3; Dobashi 2013). In this chapter, I utilize the interpretive approach to externalization to consider what else can serve as a prime for $Lin(\neg S)$. I argue that a terminated derivation, as clarified below, can be detected without search and that it serves as a prime for $Lin(\neg S)$, being interpreted as an intonational phrase.

This chapter is organized as follows. In section 5.2, I examine the Match-Theory approach to intonational phrasing (Selkirk 2009, 2011) and highlight empirical and theoretical problems. In section 5.3, I introduce the notion of termination of a derivation, which is formulated in terms of a workspace of syntactic derivation to which MERGE applies (Chomsky 2017b; Chomsky et al. 2017). In section 5.4, I argue that a terminated derivation can be detected with zero search by the phonological component and show that several instances of intonational phrases do in fact conform to terminated derivations. In section 5.5, I discuss the relation between terminated derivations and $Lin(\neg S)$. I show that a grammatically heterogeneous group of intonational phrases is unified in terms of linearization. In section 5.6, I point out that some instances of $Lin(\neg S)$ need to have direct access to semantics, which is informulable in the Y-model of grammar, where phonology-semantics relations are mediated by the syntax. Such access is allowed in the interpretive approach to the syntax-phonology mapping that is formulated within the I-model of grammar. Section 5.7 concludes this chapter.

5.2. Match clause and intonational phrasing

As I discussed in Chapter 2, prosodic domains are structurally organized (Halliday 1967; Selkirk 1980; Nespor and Vogel 1986). In particular, Ito and Mester (2012,

2013) argue for a very restrictive theory of the prosodic hierarchy, which universally consists of three prosodic categories:

(1)   (   )$_\iota$ Intonational Phrase
      (   )$_\varphi$ (   )$_\varphi$ Phonological Phrase
      (   )$_\omega$ (   )$_\omega$ (   )$_\omega$ Prosodic Word
      Annemarie   can eat   the burger

They argue that these three categories are not just arbitrarily postulated, but rather are provided by the syntactically grounded Match Theory developed by Selkirk (2009, 2011), which assumes that intonational phrases, phonological phrases, and prosodic words correspond to the three types of syntactic units: clauses, phrases, and words, respectively.[1] Selkirk's (2009: 40, 2011: 439) formulation is given below:

(2)   a. Match Clause
         A **clause** in syntactic constituent structure must be matched by a constituent of a corresponding prosodic type in phonological representation, call it ι [intonational phrase].

      b. Match Phrase
         A **phrase** in syntactic constituent structure must be matched by a constituent of a corresponding prosodic type in phonological representation, call it φ [phonological phrase].

      c. Match Word
         A **word** in syntactic constituent structure must be matched by a constituent of a corresponding prosodic type in phonological representation, call it ω [prosodic word].

Among these three Match constraints, let us carefully consider Match Clause (2a), as intonational phrasing is a major concern in this chapter. Selkirk (2011: 452) argues that a clause is the complement of Comp^0 or of Force^0:

(3)   a. [$_{CP}$ Comp^0 [standard clause]]
      b. [$_{ForceP}$ Force^0 [illocutionary clause]]

(3a) accounts for the intonational phrasing of a simple sentence such as *John ate an apple*, which corresponds to a single intonational phrase. However, it would not account for the well-established observation that an intonational phrase corresponds to a root sentence (Downing 1970: 28; Emonds 1976: 44; Nespor and Vogel 1986: 188; see also Selkirk 2009: fn13; Truckenbrodt 2014). For example, in (4), the embedded clause is not separated by comma intonation, a characteristic typical of intonational phrase boundaries:

(4)   You realize (that) the books have already arrived.

                                                    (Emonds 1976: 44)

It seems that (3a) cannot straightforwardly distinguish the root clause from the embedded clause in (4). Moreover, (3a) is a category-specific formulation, referring to a specific category Comp⁰, which would need to be independently motivated on principled grounds. The post-syntactic phonology is generally not specific to a certain syntactic category (see Scheer 2011: 337 and references cited therein). It is not clear then why intonational phrasing can be category-specific.

(3b) seems to be intended to account for the fact that parentheticals, non-restrictive relative clauses, and other semantically similar expressions constitute intonational phrases. Potts (2005: 92) identifies these expressions as "supplements" that do not affect the "at-issue" meaning of their host sentence. Selkirk (2011) argues that these are instances of an "illocutionary clause," and (3b) accounts for the intonational phrasing of *as*-parentheticals and non-restrictive clauses in (5a) and (5b), respectively. The examples are from Nespor and Vogel (1986: 188):

(5)   a. Lions (as you know)ı are dangerous.
      b. My brother (who absolutely loves animals)ı just bought himself an exotic tropical bird.

In addition to these, (3b) seems to account successfully for the intonational phrasing of vocatives and expletive expressions in (6a) and (6b), respectively, which are, again, cited from Nespor and Vogel (1986: 188):

(6)   a. (Clarence)ı I'd like you to meet Mr. Smith.
      b. (Good heavens)ı there's a bear in the back yard.

These expressions are not clauses in a literal sense, but, semantically, they do not affect the at-issue meaning of their host sentences. Thus, their intonational phrase status could be accounted for, with some minor modification of (3b). Moreover, as Potts (2005: 93) points out, the appositives in nominal appositive constructions are also supplements and constitute intonational phrases:

(7)   Chuck, (a confirmed psychopath)ı,

Here, the appositive *a confirmed psychopath* is a supplement and is set off by comma intonation (see also de Vries 2012). This could be accounted for, in the same way as the analysis of (6).

However, as Potts (2005: 92) points out, the intonational phrasing of "slifting" (= sentence lifting) constructions (Ross 1973) and tag questions, respectively illustrated in (8a) and (8b), cannot be accounted for in terms of supplement:

(8)   a. Max, (it seems)ı, is a Martian.
      b. Max is a Martian, (isn't he)ı?

(Potts 2005: 92)

(8a) and (8b) are equivalent to "It seems that Max is a Martian." and "Is Max a Martian?", respectively. In other words, the parenthesized parts in (8a, b) do not provide a secondary proposition that has supplementary semantic content. Nonetheless, they constitute intonational phrases. Furthermore, the dislocated expressions, which do not have a secondary proposition, also correspond to intonational phrases:

(9)   They are so cute (those Australian koalas)$_i$.

(Nespor and Vogel 1986: 188)

In addition to these, the intonational phrases we discussed in Chapter 3 are neither standard nor illocutionary clauses (i.e., topicalized constituents, shifted heavy NPs, and prenominal modifiers with marked word order, to which we return in section 5.5). Thus, Match Clause would require extra devices to accommodate these cases and would not be able to provide a unified treatment of intonational phrases.

In addition to these empirical problems, Match Theory seems to have theoretical shortcomings. First, it is not clear how to formally distinguish a clause from a phrase in (2a) and (2b). A clause CP/TP is just an instance of a general phrase XP. As we discussed in Chapter 4, function words are generally invisible to the post-syntactic computation of phonology (e.g., Selkirk 1984; Truckenbrodt 1999). If so, it would be difficult to distinguish C and T (both functional), or C and v* (both functional, too), for example. Second, in the theory of phrase structure in minimalist syntax, labels and projections are derivative notions that are consulted only by the C-I system, as I discussed in Chapter 4, or may even be undefinable (Collins 2002, 2017). Crucially, Match Theory rests on these concepts, which have no solid basis in the theory of phrase structure.

Therefore, I will attempt to construct an alternative approach to intonational phrasing that accords with the present interpretive architecture of grammar. In section 5.4, I will argue that the notion of termination of a derivation gives a (partial) account of intonational phrasing (a fuller account will be made in terms of linearization in section 5.5). Before moving on to section 5.4, I will introduce in section 5.3 the notions of MERGE, workspace, and termination of a derivation that will form the foundation for the proposed alternative approach.

5.3.   MERGE, workspace, and termination of derivation

Early in the minimalist program, Chomsky (1995: 243) defines the structure-building operation Merge as follows:

(10)   Applied to two objects α and β, Merge forms the new object K, eliminating α and β.

As Chomsky (2017b) points out, it is not explicitly stated here "from what" α and β are eliminated. He argues that they are actually eliminated from a workspace WS, and that Merge is in fact an operation that applies to WS and updates it to a modified workspace WS′ (see also Chomsky et al. 2017). He calls such an operation MERGE. Thus, applied to WS in (10a), MERGE updates it to WS′ in (10b), where α and β have been eliminated:

(11)   a.   WS = [α, β, γ, δ]
       b.   WS′ = [K, γ, δ], where K = {α, β}

Chomsky (2017b) shows that this formulation, along with independently motivated principles, or "desiderata," can successfully restrict the range of possible MERGE operations on principled grounds, thereby excluding illegitimate application of Merge, such as parallel Merge and sideward movement, among others. I will not discuss in detail the workings of MERGE, since they are far beyond the scope of the present study (see, e.g., Goto and Ishii 2018 for further elaboration).

Let us next consider termination of a derivation in the theory of MERGE applying to WS. Early in the minimalist framework, termination is formulated with reference to numeration. Thus, Chomsky (1995: 225ff) states it as follows (see also Chomsky (2000: 106) for the termination in the phase-by-phase computational system):

(12)   Viewing the language L as a derivation-generating procedure, we may think of it as applying to a numeration N and forming a sequence S of symbolic elements $(\sigma_1, \sigma_2, \ldots, \sigma_n)$, terminating only if σ_n is a pair (π, λ) and N is reduced to zero (the computation may go on).

In the framework of MERGE, Chomsky et al. (2017: 20) offer the following definition of termination, which refers to WS but not to numeration:

(13)   A derivation may (but need not) terminate whenever WS contains a single object; if it terminates in any other situation, no coherent interpretation can be assigned.

These definitions imply that a terminated derivation, which is a single object (a pair (π, λ)), may serve as a unit of interpretation at the interfaces.

Given the WS-based definition of termination (13), let us consider the derivation of the following schematic example of a simple transitive construction like *John hit Bill*:

(14)   [$_{CP}$ C [$_{TP}$ Subj T [$_{v*P}$ t_{Subj} v* [$_{VP}$ V Obj]]]]

The first phase of this derivation, i.e., v*P, is derived as follows:

(15)   a.   WS1 = [Subj, v*, V, Obj]
       b.   WS2 = [{V, Obj}, Subj, v*]
       c.   WS3 = [{v*, {V, Obj}}, Subj]
       d.   WS4 = [{Subj, {v*, { V, Obj}}}]

In (15a), WS1 contains four lexical items. MERGE applies to WS1 and updates it to WS2, as in (15b). Here, V and Obj have been eliminated and replaced by {V, Obj}. Then, MERGE applies to WS2 and we then have WS3, where {V, Obj} and v* are replaced by {v*, {V, Obj}}. Finally, Subj and {v*, {V, Obj}} are eliminated from WS3 and we then have WS4, which consists of a single object. Suppose that no new lexical item is introduced into WS4. Then, given the definition of termination in (13), the derivation may terminate here since WS4 contains just the single object {Subj, {v*, {V, Obj}}}. However, if it terminates, the derivation crashes because of the unvalued Case feature of Subj. Suppose instead that the derivation (15) goes on to the next phase level CP:

(15)   e.   WS5 = [{Subj, {v*, {V, Obj}}}, C, T]
     f.   WS6 = [{T, {Subj, {v*, {V, Obj}}}}, C]
     g.   WS7 = [{Subj, {T, {Subj, {v*, {V, Obj}}}}}, C]
     h.   WS8 = [{C, {Subj, {T, {Subj, { v*, {V, Obj}}}}}}]

In (15e), C and T are drawn from the lexicon and added to the WS4, and we have WS5. MERGE updates WS5 to WS6, as in (15f). Here, External Merge has applied to T and {Subj, {v*, {V, Obj}}}. Then MERGE applies to WS6, yielding WS7, where Subj has undergone Internal Merge. Then, MERGE applies to WS7, updating it to WS8, where External Merge has applied to C and {Subj, {T, {Subj, {v*, {V, Obj}}}}}. WS8 completes the CP phase and contains just a single object, where all the uninterpretable features have been valued. Suppose that the derivation terminates at this point. It converges at the interfaces, and the resultant single object may be interpreted by the interface components.

In the next section, I will show that a single object resulting from the termination is interpreted as an intonational phrase in the phonological component.

5.4.   Phonological interpretation of terminated derivations

In Chapter 4, I have argued for the interpretive approach to the syntax-phonology mapping. The phonological component looks into narrow syntax, picks a syntactic object, and uses it in the processes of externalization. Specifically, it identifies a syntactic object as a prime for the linearization Lin(LS) by virtue of the minimal search for a phonologically interpretable (i.e., unlabelable) element, and this prime is then interpreted as a phonological phrase. In line with this approach, let us suppose that it is generally search operations that detect phonologically usable objects in the syntactic derivation, and that the search operations conform to a third-factor principle of efficient computation. Since a terminated derivation is a single object in WS, the phonological component should be able to detect it readily, i.e., with zero search. The phonological component does not even need to search into the syntactic object: a terminated derivation is right there in WS. Then, as a first approx- imation, let us hypothesize that the unit of a terminated derivation corresponds to a prosodic domain. Since this domain is obviously larger than a phonological phrase in the prosodic hierarchy (see (1)), let us suppose that it is an intonational phrase.[2]

(16) A syntactic object SO is interpreted as an intonational phrase if it is a terminated derivation.

I will discuss the relation between (16) and linearization in section 5.5. For the moment, let us determine if (16) holds.

Consider the intonational phrasing of a simple transitive construction (14) and its step-by-step derivation (15), repeated here as (17) and (18), respectively:

(17) $[_{CP}$ C $[_{TP}$ Subj T $[_{v*P}$ t_{Subj} v* $[_{VP}$ V Obj $]]]]$
(18)   a. WS1 = [Subj, v*, V, Obj]
       b. WS2 = [{V, Obj}, Subj, v*]
       c. WS3 = [{v*, {V, Obj}}, Subj]
       d. WS4 = [{Subj, {v*, {V, Obj}}}]
       e. WS5 = [{Subj, {v*, {V, Obj}}}, C, T]
       f. WS6 = [{T, {Subj, {v*, {V, Obj}}}}, C]
       g. WS7 = [{Subj, {T, {Subj, {v*, {V, Obj}}}}}, C]
       h. WS8 = [{C, {Subj, {T, {Subj, {v*, {V, Obj}}}}}}]

As discussed above, this derivation can terminate without crashing only at the stage of (18h). When the phonological component looks into WS8, it can identify the single object there without any search into the structure. Then, (16) correctly predicts that the entire sentence is an intonational phrase. Notice that this approach does not need to stipulate that a specific phrase, say CP, is an intonational phrase, unlike Match Theory. It also accounts for why, for example, another strong phase v*P (the only single syntactic object in WS4) is not an intonational phrase: the derivation will crash due to the unvalued Case feature of Subj if it terminates at the stage of (18d).

Let us next consider the complex sentence (4), repeated in (19):

(19) You realize (that) the books have already arrived.

(Emonds 1976: 44)

Here, the embedded CP does not correspond to an intonational phrase; however, the entire sentence does, as discussed earlier. If the derivation terminates at the embedded CP, the following single object is obtained:

(20) (that) the books have already arrived

This derivation can, in principle, terminate and converge at this stage. However, whether *that* is overt or not, the C of this clause serves to introduce a subordinate clause, unlike the root C, and therefore needs to be selected by a matrix predicate.[3] That is, (20) could terminate but would result in gibberish at the C-I interface. Thus, the derivation should go on to be interpreted appropriately at the interface. When the derivation reaches the root CP, as in (19), it can terminate and converge, and this terminated derivation is interpreted as an intonational phrase. This approach therefore accounts for why only root CPs can be intonational phrases, without any ad hoc stipulation in terms of the interface conditions.

Let us next consider individually the other instances of intonational phrase, which we have discussed in section 5.2. First, consider the parenthetical *as*-clauses and non-restrictive relative (NRR) clauses in (5), repeated in (21):

(21) a. Lions (as you know)$_\iota$ are dangerous.
      b. My brother (who absolutely loves animals)$_\iota$ just bought himself an exotic tropical bird.

Potts (2002a, 2002b) argues that these clauses are similar because they involve operator movement and that their differences are reduced to the semantic types of the gaps (traces) left by the operator movement. In this analysis, *as*-/NRR clauses are associated with their host semantically or post-syntactically through function application. In other words, they are not transformationally related: nothing moves from within the *as*-/NRR clauses into the host sentences; neither does one select the other. Thus, the derivation of these clauses can terminate and converge independently of the host clauses. These clauses thus correspond to an intonational phrase.

Note that the rest of the structure, e.g., *Lions* and *are dangerous* in (21a), also corresponds to intonational phrases, as pointed out by Nespor and Vogel (1986: 189). In accordance with their analysis, I assume that any string that is adjacent to the obligatorily formed intonational phrase automatically forms an intonational phrase on its own. Thus, we actually have three intonational phrases in (21a), as illustrated below:

(22) (Lions)$_\iota$ (as you know)$_\iota$ (are dangerous)$_\iota$.

Here, the *as*-clause obligatorily forms an intonational phrase because of its independent termination, and the adjacent strings, *Lions* and *are dangerous*, automatically form their own intonational phrases. In what follows, though, I will indicate only the relevant intonational phrases, for ease of exposition.

Let us next consider the vocatives and expletive expressions (6a, b), repeated in (23):

(23) a. (Clarence)$_\iota$ I'd like you to meet Mr. Smith.
      b. (Good heavens)$_\iota$ there's a bear in the back yard.

These expressions can terminate and converge on their own, since they only have interpretable features and are not assigned any uninterpretable features such as Case when they enter the WS (see Chomsky 2000: 95 for a relevant discussion on convergence). Thus, they can even be uttered alone, without their "host" sentences, and therefore correspond to intonational phrases.

Let us next consider the appositive nominal construction (7), repeated here in (24):

(24) Chuck, (a confirmed psychopath)$_\iota$,

Again, the appositive can terminate and converge on its own. It is not transformationally related to its host, and there is no selection or feature-checking relation between them, just like the *as-*/NRR clauses. Therefore, the appositive is an independent terminated single object in WS, corresponding to an intonational phrase.

Let us next consider the example of slifting (8a), repeated in (25a). A simpler example of slifting is given in (25b):

(25) a. Max, (it seems)ᵢ, is a Martian.
      b. Max is a Martian, I believe.

(Ross 1973: 131)

Haddican et al. (2014) argue that the two clauses in a slifting construction are generated independently of each other. That is, the slifted clause does not move out of the matrix clause (see also Jackendoff 1972). Adapting Collins and Branigan's (1997) analysis of quotative constructions, they argue that the matrix clause involves movement of a null operator Op that is coindexed with the slifted clause. Thus, in (25b), Op is generated as a complement to the matrix verb *believe*, moving to Spec-CP, where it is coindexed with the slifted clause *Max is a Martian*:

(26) [$_{CP}$ Max is a Martian]ᵢ [$_{CP}$ Opᵢ [$_{CP}$ I believe t_i]]

(adapted from Haddican et al. 2014: 92)

Therefore, the main clause can terminate and converge by itself, just like *as-*/NRR clauses, and corresponds to an intonational phrase. Then, it follows that a matrix clause in the slifting construction serves as a parenthetical intonational phrase when it is linearly integrated into the slifted clause, as in (25a).

Similarly, the intonational phrasing of quotative constructions can be accounted for:

(27) "When on earth," asked Harry, "will the fishing begin again?"

(Collins and Branigan 1997: 10)

According to Collins and Branigan's analysis, a null operator Op is base-generated as a direct speech complement to the verb *ask* in (25). It moves to Spec-CP, and the quote identifies the content of the Op. I will leave aside the technical details of the processes of identification of Op and subject-verb inversion, since they do not affect my argument here:

(28) ["When on earth"]ᵢ [$_{CP}$ Opᵢ [$_{CP}$ asked Harry t_i]] ["will the fishing begin again?"]

Given this analysis, the quote does not move out of the main clause. That is, the CP *asked Harry* is an independent terminated derivation and is interpreted as an intonational phrase when it is linearly integrated between "*When on earth*" and "*will the fishing begin again?*".

Let us consider the tag question (8b), repeated in (29):

(29) Max is a Martian, (isn't he)ₜ

Culicover (1992) points out that tag questions have a pronominal character in that they have a pronominal copy of the main clause subject, a copy of the main clause auxiliary, and the elliptical counterpart of the matrix verb phrase. He thus argues that a tag question involves [+pro] IP (TP, in our terms) and that the interpretive rule takes the tag question as a function and the matrix IP as its argument. This indicates that the relation between the tag and the matrix clause is not transformational. That is, the tag terminates and converges independently of the matrix clause and therefore corresponds to an intonational phrase.

Lastly, let us consider the dislocation (9), repeated in (30):

(30)   They are so cute (those Australian koalas)$_i$.

(Nespor and Vogel 1986: 188)

Ott and de Vries (2013) argue that right dislocation constructions have a biclausal structure and that the second clause has undergone deletion. Thus, the right dislocation construction in Dutch, shown in (31a), has a biclausal structure, as in (31b), where two CPs are juxtaposed and deletion applies to the latter:

(31)   a. Tasman   heeft   ze   gezien,   die   Maori's   [Dutch]
            Tasman   has   them seen   those Maoris
            'Tasman saw them, those Maoris.'
        b. [$_{CP1}$ Tasman heeft ze gezien] [$_{CP2}$ die Maori's$_i$]

(Ott and de Vries 2013: 6)

Here, the "right-dislocated" phrase *die Maori's* is topicalized in CP2, and the residual part undergoes PF-deletion (indicated by strikethrough). Ott and de Vries argue that this analysis dispenses with (often controversial) rightward movement and also accounts for a fuller range of data than do alternative, mono-clausal, analyses. They (p. 29) point out that this analysis can also be taken over to English right-dislocation constructions. If so, the right-dislocated material is included in the independent CP, which terminates and converges on its own, corresponding to an intonational phrase. Furthermore, Ott (2012, 2015) argues for a similar biclausal deletion analysis of left-dislocation, which would allow the present analysis of intonational phrasing to be extended to left-dislocation, since it usually shows comma intonation.

Thus far, I have shown that the proposed hypothesis (16), repeated in (32), is empirically tenable:

(32)   A syntactic object SO is interpreted as an intonational phrase if it is a terminated derivation.

This approach unifies various types of intonational phrases in terms of the notion of termination, without recourse to additional mechanisms of intonational phrasing, such as the COMMA feature of Potts (2005) (see also Selkirk 2005) or par-Merge of de Vries (2012) (see also Dehé 2014), which are proposed to account for intonational phrasing and related phenomena.

It should be noted, however, that (32) does not exhaust all cases of intonational phrasing. As I mentioned in section 5.1, the following elements are also intonational phrases: topicalized constituents, shifted NPs in heavy NP shift constructions, and prenominal adjectival modifiers with marked word order. In the next section, I will argue that these elements and terminated derivations can be further unified in terms of linearization.

5.5. Linearization and intonational phrasing

In Chapters 3 and 4, I argued that prosodic domains are closely tied with primes for linearization and proposed unifying the prosodic domain formations in terms of linearization, which is fundamental to the processes of externalization (Dobashi 2013):

(33)   A prime for linearization is a prosodic domain.

I have argued that the following three kinds of linearization are deduced from (33):

(34)   a. A prime for Lin(W) is interpreted as a prosodic word.
      b. A prime for Lin(LS) is interpreted as a phonological phrase.
      c. A prime for Lin($\neg$S) is interpreted as an intonational phrase.

Among these, let us briefly recapitulate (34c), which is our concern here. It is formulated on the basis of the observation that marked word orders give rise to intonational phrasing. As discussed in section 3.5.3, the basic word order in Chichewa is SVO, but free word order results if subject and object are topicalized, with each constituting an intonational phrase:

(35)   a. SVO: (Njûchi)$_\iota$ (zi-ná-wá-lum-a)$_\iota$ (alenje)$_\iota$
             bees   SM-PST-OM-bite-INDIC hunters
      b. VOS: (Zináwáluma)$_\iota$ (alenje)$_\iota$ (njûchi)$_\iota$
      c. OVS: (Alenje)$_\iota$ (zináwáluma)$_\iota$ (njûchi)$_\iota$
      d. VSO: (Zináwáluma)$_\iota$ (njûchi)$_\iota$ (alenje)$_\iota$
      e. SOV: (Njûchi)$_\iota$ (alenje)$_\iota$ (zináwáluma)$_\iota$
      f. OSV: (Alenje)$_\iota$ (njûchi)$_\iota$ (zináwáluma)$_\iota$
                    (adapted from Bresnan and Mchombo 1987: 744–745)

Likewise, heavy NP shift results in marked word order, and the shifted heavy constituent corresponds to an intonational phrase:

(36)   (Max put in his cár)$_\iota$ (all the boxes of home fúrnishings)$_\iota$.
                                         (Zubizarreta 1998: 148)

Furthermore, prenominal adjectival modifiers are separated by comma intonation if they are in marked order, as in (37b), but do not involve comma breaks in unmarked order, as in (37a):

(37)   a. She loves all those wonderful orange Oriental ivories.
         b. She loves all those Oriental, orange, wonderful ivories.

(Sproat and Shih 1991: 578)

On the basis of these observations, I have argued that the marked word orders result from linearization procedures that are non-syntactic in nature, Lin($\neg$S). Thus, the order of topic phrases in (35) reflects information structure (Lambrecht 1994); the marked order in the heavy NP shift construction in (36) is induced by prosodic balancing (Zubizarreta 1998); and the marked order of adjectives in (37) reflects the structure of parallel modification in the sense of Sproat and Shih (1991: 578), which cannot be ordered by the usual linearization procedure based on asymmetric syntactic relations. Given these considerations, I have suggested (34c) to unify syntactically and semantically heterogeneous intonational phrases in terms of Lin($\neg$S).

Note that it seems impossible to unify the three types of intonational phrases by virtue of termination of a derivation. Topicalized constituents could be terminated derivations: they are semantically coindexed with *pro* in the base-generation analysis explored in Chapter 4 (Frascarelli 2000, 2007) and do not need to be involved in the computation of the host sentence (e.g., feature-checking). However, the shifted heavy NPs are unlikely to be terminated derivations: they are usually accusative NPs that must have been licensed within a single terminated derivation. Moreover, it is unclear whether the prenominal modifiers with marked order are terminated derivations: if something like my speculative analysis of the structure of parallel modification in endnote 28 of Chapter 4 is plausible, the modifiers cannot be independent terminated derivations. Therefore, putting aside technical details of syntactic analyses of these constructions, I maintain that it is linearization, not termination, that ultimately unifies intonational phrasing, as stated in (34c).

Now, let us consider terminated derivations and their linearization. A terminated derivation is, by definition, an independent single syntactic object, which is not syntactically integrated into the associated structure. That is, a terminated derivation is not literally merged with the associated structure in WS. This conforms to de Vries' (2012: 155) observation that c-command relations do not hold across the boundary of parenthetical clauses:

(38)   a. [No climber]$_i$ talked about the mountain he$_i$ conquered last month.
         b. * [No climber]$_i$ talked about the K2, which he$_i$ conquered last month.
(39)   He$_i$ said – this is typical for Joop$_i$ – that he$_{(i)}$ didn't like veggie burgers.

Variable binding into the NRR clause fails, as in (38b), in contrast to the restrictive relative clause, as in (38a). Likewise, Condition C effects do not arise, even if an

R-expression in the parenthetical clause might appear to be bound by the co-referential pronominal subject in the matrix clause in (39). Note in passing that we have not discussed the (39)-kind of parenthetical clause: it is a terminated, convergent derivation, as it has no transformational relation with the rest of the structure, and thus corresponds to an intonational phrase.[4]

Given these considerations, I conclude that terminated derivations are not linearized on the basis of syntactic relations. That is, they are not linearized by Lin(W), which refers to asymmetric c-command, or by Lin(LS), which refers to structural containment relations. In the processes of externalization, however, terminated derivations must be linearly ordered with respect to each other; otherwise, they cannot be interpreted at the SM interface. Although the exact mechanism of the ordering procedure that applies to each of the terminated derivations discussed above is beyond the scope of this study, it is clear that the procedure falls within Lin(¬S), since it does not rely on syntactic relations holding in a single syntactic object. Then, given (33)/(34c), it follows that a terminated derivation is interpreted as an intonational phrase and, thus, that (34c) unifies all intonational phrase types: not only topicalized phrases, shifted NPs in heavy NP shift, and prenominal modifiers with marked order, but also root clauses, (*as-*)parentheticals, NRR clauses, vocatives, expletive expressions, nominal appositives, main clauses in slifting and quotative constructions, tag questions, and right-/left-dislocated constituents. These constitute a semantically and syntactically heterogeneous mixture, but all turn out to be primes for Lin(¬S), which are interpreted as intonational phrases at the SM interface.

5.6. Non-syntactic linearization and the architecture of grammar

As I discussed in Chapter 4, the EST/Y-model of grammar had long been adopted in the study of generative grammar. In this model, a syntactic computation divides into phonology and semantics at some point of derivation. In principle, this model disallows direct phonology-semantics interactions, since the syntax mediates the phonology and semantics (cf. Chomsky 1995: 220). In the (Multiple) Y-model incorporating Spell-Out, the phonological component Φ receives and uses the output of Spell-Out, without looking into the syntax or semantics. That is, Spell-Out mediates the syntax and phonology, and is therefore interposed between the phonology and semantics, thereby disabling direct phonology-semantics interactions.

More recently, from the strict internalist perspective on grammar, Chomsky (2005, *et seqq.*) argues that the hierarchically structured expressions generated by the computational procedure are directly (or perhaps trivially) mapped to C-I and that the processes of externalization are ancillary operations. Given this architecture of grammar (which I called the I-model in Chapter 4), Chomsky (2014: fn9) points out that Φ could in principle have access to C-I. In my formulation, Spell-Out has no place in the I-model appended with the interpretive processes of externalization (see Chapter 4) and therefore nothing is interposed between the phonology on the one hand and the hierarchical linguistic expressions, i.e., the syntax and semantics, on the other. That is, unlike the Y-model, the I-model allows the processes of externalization to have direct access to the semantics. Note that I do not address the question of whether the interactions are mutual, namely, whether the syntax/semantics has access to the phonology.[5]

It should be noted that some instances of the non-syntactic linearization Lin(¬S), which is part of externalization, do need to access semantic information. For example, a tag question is related to its host through function application, so that the former is linearized with respect to the latter but not to some other, arbitrary, terminated derivation: the linearization between the tag and its host refers to the semantics. This, too, is the case with *as-*/NRR clauses, which also involve function application. Likewise, in slifting constructions, the null operator in the main clause is related to the slifted clause through coindexation, and the main clause is linearly ordered with respect to the slifted clause, but not to some other arbitrary clause. Coindexation is supposed to apply in the semantics, since the inclusiveness condition disallows indices in the syntax. That is, the linear ordering for slifting constructions refers to the semantics. The same applies to quotative constructions. Furthermore, topicalized constituents are linearly ordered in relation to information structure: the linearization procedure that applies to topics requires access to the semantics and even pragmatics. These phonology-semantics interactions are possible in the I-model, which has the ancillary interpretive processes of externalization that dispense with Spell-Out. This might be an additional argument for the elimination of Spell-Out, which would make Lin(¬S) informulable by blocking direct access to the semantics.

The interpretive approach also accounts for why intonational phrases often have global properties, unlike phonological phrases (see Chomsky 2004: 108 for relevant discussion; see also Chomsky 2014: fn9). If cyclic Spell-Out were the only operation that connected syntax with phonology, we would expect that prosodic domains would always be local, reflecting syntactic cycles, and that some additional operation would be required in order to recombine the cyclically chunked pieces into a single representation that accounts for a global intonation contour (see Boeckx 2003/2007). In the present interpretive system, Lin(¬S) is independent of syntactic cycles, unlike Lin(LS). For instance, it applies to a unit of function application (i.e., a terminated derivation), which may contain two or more phases, constituting a global intonational domain. Thus, in (21b), reproduced in (40), the NRR clause contains two phases (v*P and CP) but constitutes a single prosodic domain (i.e., an intonational phrase), since it is a unit of Lin(¬S):

(40)   My brother (who absolutely loves animals), just bought himself an exotic tropical bird.

The interpretive approach is free from Spell-Out and hence allows multiple modes of the syntax-phonology connection (i.e., Lin(W), Lin(LS), and Lin(¬S)), thus enabling it to account for the global properties of intonational contour in terms of Lin(¬S), as well as for the local phenomena in prosodic words and phonological phrases in terms of Lin(W) and Lin(LS), respectively.

5.7. Conclusion

In this chapter, I have proposed an interpretive approach to intonational phrasing. In section 5.2, I have shown that Match Theory approaches face empirical and theoretical problems. In section 5.3, I have introduced the notion of termination of a derivation, which is formulated in terms of a workspace to which MERGE applies. In section 5.4, I have pointed out that terminated derivations can be identified by the phonological component with zero search, and shown that they are in fact interpreted as intonational phrases. In section 5.5, I have argued that terminated derivations are instances of primes for the non-syntactic linearization $Lin(\neg S)$, and that $Lin(\neg S)$ unifies intonational phrasing, in line with Dobashi (2013) (see Chapter 3). In section 5.6, I have pointed out that some instances of $Lin(\neg S)$ require direct access to semantic information, which is allowed in the I-model appended with the interpretive processes of externalization, unlike in the previous Y-model.

Although I have critically discussed some aspects of Match Clause (Selkirk 2009, 2011), an important consequence of Match Clause is that it captures recursive phrasing by matching recursive syntactic structure with recursive prosodic structure (see Hamlaoui and Szendrői 2015; Ladd 1996; Szendrői 2001; Frota 2000, among others, for recursive intonational phrases). If we were to account for the effects of recursive intonational phrasing in terms of syntactic recursion, we would need to assume, for example, that a terminated derivation can further undergo MERGE, being embedded within another terminated derivation, and that (a modified version of) $Lin(\neg S)$ linearly and structurally integrates the former into the latter, thereby creating a recursive structure. I will leave unresolved the question of whether and/or how such structural integration can be motivated in the processes of externalization on principled grounds.

Notes

1 Ito and Mester argue that additional prosodic categories are created by the recursion of these three basic categories. See Chapter 2 for a brief review of Match Theory.
2 Here, the term "intonational phrase" should be taken to be a "nickname," just as the term "phonological phrase" is also a nickname in the sense discussed in section 4.5.
3 Here and below, "select" roughly means c-selection or subcategorization, which holds between lexical items within a single syntactic object. That is, selection does not hold across two separate terminated derivations, unlike non-syntactic function application or coindexation, which I assume apply in the semantic component, as we will see below. I would like to thank Masashi Nomura for helpful comments on these ideas.
4 For further ramifications of parentheticals and their prosodic status, see Dehé (2014), Dehé and Kavalova (2007: 1) and works cited therein.
5 See, e.g., Agbayani et al. (2015) for a unidirectional model of syntax-phonology mapping. See, e.g., Richards (2016) for a theory in which phonological information can affect syntactic operations.

6   Summary

I began this book with a chronological review of some previous theories of the syntax-phonology interface, with particular attention to the formation of prosodic domains. Important issues included mismatch between syntactic and phonological constituents, cross-linguistic variation, and a unified account of prosodic categories.

A recent school of thought argues that mismatch naturally follows from cyclic application of Spell-Out: thus, Spell-Out applying at all phases except the first can create a linear string that does not match a syntactic constituent, such as one consisting of an auxiliary verb and main verb but excluding an object. Cross-linguistic variation is largely attributed to the difference in syntactic structure: for example, an object is phrased with a verb if it moves up to Spec-v*P, but is phrased on its own if it stays in situ. However, Multiple Spell-Out approaches fail to account for prosodic categories other than phonological phrases.

Another recent major approach, Match Theory, considers the mismatch to be a superficial phenomenon and argues that prosodic structure reflects recursive syntactic structure and that the apparent mismatch, as well as cross-linguistic variation, results from constraint interactions within the Optimality Theory framework. The basic postulation is that words, phrases, and clauses match prosodic words, phonological phrases, and intonational phrases, respectively, and thus uniformly account for the three basic prosodic categories. However, the distinctions among the notions of words, phrases, and clauses appear rather arbitrary.

Careful reflection on the strict internalist approach to language leads to what I dubbed the I-model of grammatical architecture, in which a computation generating a discrete infinity of hierarchically structured linguistic expressions is mapped to C-I. The processes of sensorimotor externalization are secondary operations, unlike in the EST/Y-model, in which the operation Spell-Out bifurcates a derivation into the SM and C-I interfaces. Spell-Out in its original form cannot be justified in the I-model, since it disrupts the computation to C-I by splitting the derivation. Therefore, the relation between phonology and syntax is formulated as an interpretive procedure in which the phonology looks into the syntax without affecting it. Given these and other considerations, Spell-Out is eliminated from the grammar, and Multiple Spell-Out approaches to the syntax-phonology interface are thus no longer formulable.

Spell-Out functions as the only operation that mediates syntax and phonology in the Y-model, but the I-model appended with the interpretive processes of externalization in principle allows for more than one channel of phonological interpretation. In fact, three modes of phonological interpretations are postulated to give appropriate interpretations of the structured linguistic expressions at the SM interface. These modes are formulated as linearization procedures: namely, Lin(W), Lin(LS), and Lin(¬S).

In the interpretive processes that proceed in parallel with the cyclic computation of syntax, the phonological component identifies local domains to which linearization applies, without recourse to cyclic Spell-Out. Certain syntactic objects SOs are identified with minimal search for phonologically detectable elements, in much the same way as the labeling algorithm. Given the interpretive asymmetry in (1), unlabelable elements such as R and weak T, being syntactically inert, are detected by the phonological component:

(1) *Syntax-Phonology Asymmetry (SPA):*
     Syntactically inert elements are visible in the processes of externalization.

On completion of a phase, the phonological component looks into the syntax and identifies an SO with minimal search for an unlabelable element. Lin(W) linearizes terminal elements (or "words") of the SO by referring to syntactic relations such as c-command, making them interpretable at the SM interface. Because it applies cyclically, Lin(W) usually defines two or more linear strings LSs for a derivation. Lin(LS) orders these LSs by referring to both syntax (i.e., structural containment relations) and phonology (i.e., linear strings already formed), making them additionally interpretable at the SM interface.

In addition to the syntactic cycle, the generative procedure provides another computational block: a terminated derivation. A terminated derivation is a single SO in a workspace and is thus detected with zero search. Terminated derivations, too, must be linearly ordered (sometimes trivially) – otherwise they cannot be interpreted at the SM interface. Because they are not syntactically related, they are linearized by the non-syntactic linearization Lin(¬S). Unlike in the Y-model, where Spell-Out/syntax intervenes between the phonology and semantics, the I-model allows the phonology to have access to the semantics. Thus, Lin(¬S) sometimes linearly orders terminated derivations by referring to semantic information such as coindexation and function application. Lin(¬S) also handles marked word orders induced by non-syntactic factors such as information structure and prosodic weight. Consequently, Lin(¬S) deals with (virtually) all linearization procedures not covered by Lin(W) or Lin(LS), and the three procedures therefore complete the linearization of linguistic expressions required by the SM interface.

Importantly, the linearization procedures have prosodic effects, and each procedure provides its own prosodic category:

(2) a. A prime for Lin(W) is interpreted as a prosodic word.
     b. A prime for Lin(LS) is interpreted as a phonological phrase.
     c. A prime for Lin(¬S) is interpreted as an intonational phrase.

This result entails that prosodic domains and their hierarchical organization (i.e., the prosodic hierarchy) are not stipulated concepts, but rather by-products of linearization. It further conforms to Ito and Mester's (2012, 2013) empirical thesis that there are universally only three prosodic categories. The three interpretive rules in (2) are ultimately unified as follows:

(3)   A prime for linearization is a prosodic domain.

This interpretive approach to prosodic categories, if tenable, is a null hypothesis, in that it does not require any independent mapping algorithms that create prosodic domains and their hierarchical organization. Thus, it is not necessary to specify that a certain level of projection in the phrase structure is matched by a particular prosodic domain.

In this null theory, the mismatch between syntactic and phonological structures follows from a cyclic interpretation/linearization. Lin(W) applying at all but the first cycle can result in a linear string that does not match a syntactic constituent. This linear string serves as a prime for Lin(LS), forming a phonological phrase that does not match a syntactic constituent.

Cross-linguistic variation is partly reduced to the difference in syntactic structure, just like in the Multiple Spell-Out theory of phonological phrasing. In addition to this structural account, richness of agreement affects prosodic domain formation. For instance, English has unlabelable weak T while Chichewa has labelable strong T, and this difference affects phonological phrasing of the subject, since unlabelable T is detectable by the search operation, while labelable T is not.

Remaining issues include a description of what accounts for the syntax-phonology asymmetry (1) on principled grounds; further empirical investigations of the relation between agreement and prosodic domains; recursive prosodic phrasing (a central issue in current Match Theory); and the effect of focus on prosodic phrasing (which I do not discuss in this book but appears to be gaining importance, especially given that the I-model allows the phonology to access the semantics), among others. Moreover, the fact that the interpretive processes are independent of linguistic computation suggests that they also apply to non-linguistic objects in the cognitive system, such as music and math. I leave these issues open for future research.

To conclude, the strict internalist perspective results in a grammatical architecture in which sensorimotor externalization is ancillary to the primary linguistic derivation mapping to C-I. Externalization is a series of interpretive processes that identifies phonologically usable elements in the derivation as sometimes guided by the third-factor principle of efficient computation (embodied as minimal search and zero search), linearly orders them to make them interpretable at the SM interface, and uses them as prosodic domains. It turns out that conceptual advances in the architecture of grammar have significant theoretical and empirical consequences that previous concepts of language could not bring.

References

Abels, Klaus. 2003. *Successive cyclicity, anti-locality, and adposition stranding*. Doctoral dissertation, University of Connecticut, Storrs.

Aboh, Enoch Oladé. 2004. *The morphosyntax of complement-head sequences: Clause structure and word order patterns in Kwa*. Oxford: Oxford University Press.

Ackema, Peter. 2011. Restrictions on subject extraction: A PF interface account. In *Interfaces in linguistics*, ed. by Raffaella Folli and Christiane Ulbrich, 225–241. Oxford: Oxford University Press.

Adger, David. 2003/2007. Stress and phasal syntax. *Linguistic Analysis* 33:238–302.

Agbayani, Brian, Chris Golston, and Toru Ishii. 2015. Syntactic and prosodic scrambling in Japanese. *Natural Language and Linguistic Theory* 33:47–77.

Alexiadou, Artemis, and Elena Anagnostopoulou. 1998. Parametrizing AGR: Word order, V-movement and EPP-checking. *Natural Language and Linguistic Theory* 16:491–539.

Barbosa, Pilar, Maria Eugênia L. Duarte, and Mary K. Kato. 2005. Null subjects in European and Brazilian Portuguese. *Journal of Portuguese Linguistics* 4:11–52.

Beckman, Mary E., and Janet B. Pierrehumbert. 1986. Intonational structure in Japanese and English. *Phonology Yearbook* 3:225–309.

Belletti, Adriana. 1990. *Generalized verb movement: Aspects of verb syntax*. Torino: Rosenberg & Sellier.

Belletti, Adriana. 1994. Verb positions: Evidence from Italian. In *Verb movement*, ed. by David Lightfoot and Norbert Hornstein, 19–40. Cambridge: Cambridge University Press.

Bennett, Ryan, Emily Elfner, and James McCloskey. 2016. Lightest to the right: An apparently anomalous displacement in Irish. *Linguistic Inquiry* 47:169–234.

Berman, Arlene, and Michael Szamosi. 1972. Observations on sentential stress. *Language* 48:304–325.

Berwick, Robert, and Noam Chomsky. 2011. The biolinguistic program: The current state of its development. In *The biolinguistic enterprise*, ed. by Anna Maria Di Sciullo and Cedric Boeckx, 19–41, Oxford: Oxford University Press.

Bickmore, Lee Stephen. 1989. *Kinyambo prosody*. Doctoral dissertation, University of California, Los Angeles, CA.

Bickmore, Lee Stephen. 1990. Branching nodes and prosodic categories: Evidence from Kinyambo. In *The phonology-syntax connection*, ed. by Sharon Inkelas and Draga Zec, 1–17. Chicago: University of Chicago Press.

Bierwisch, Manfred. 1966. Regeln für die Intonation deutscher Sätze. In *Studia Grammatica VII: Untersuchungen über Akzent und Intonation im Deutshen*, 99–201. Berlin: Akademie-Verlag.

Boeckx, Cedric. 2003/2007. Eliminating Spell-Out. *Linguistic Analysis* 33:414–425.

Bonet, Eulàlia, Lisa Lai-Shen Cheng, Laura J. Downing, and Joan Mascaró. 2018. (In) Direct reference in the phonology-syntax interface under phase theory. MS., Universitat Autònoma de Barcelona, Leiden University, and University of Gothenburg. To appear in *Linguistic Inquiry*.

Booij, Geert. 1996. Cliticization as prosodic integration: The case of Dutch. *The Linguistic Review* 13:219–242.

Borer, Hagit. 1984. *Parametric syntax*. Dordrecht: Foris.

Borer, Hagit. 2005a. *In name only: Structuring sense*, volume 1. Oxford: Oxford University Press.

Borer, Hagit. 2005b. *The normal course of events: Structuring sense*, volume 2. Oxford: Oxford University Press.

Borer, Hagit. 2013. *Taking form: Structuring sense*, volume 3. Oxford: Oxford University Press.

Bošković, Željko. 2005. On the locality of left branch extraction and the structure of NP. *Studia Linguistica* 59:1–45.

Bošković, Željko. 2007. On the locality and motivation of move and agree: An even more minimalist theory. *Linguistic Inquiry* 38:589–644.

Bošković, Željko. 2014. Now I'm a phase, now I'm not: On the variability of phases with extraction and ellipsis. *Linguistic Inquiry* 45:27–89.

Bošković, Željko. 2017. Tone Sandhi in Taiwanese and phasal Spell-Out. *Gengo Kenkyu* 152:31–58.

Bowers, John. 1993. The syntax of predication. *Linguistic Inquiry* 24:591–656.

Bowers, John. 2001. Predication. In *The handbook of contemporary syntactic theory*, ed. by Mark Baltin and Chris Collins, 299–333. Oxford: Blackwell.

Brandi, Luciana, and Patrizia Cordin. 1989. Two Italian dialects and the null subject parameter. In *The null subject parameter*, ed. by Osvaldo Jaeggli and Kenneth J. Safir, 111–142. Dordrecht: Kluwer.

Bresnan, Joan. 1971. Sentence stress and syntactic transformations. *Language* 47:257–281.

Bresnan, Joan. 1972. Stress and syntax: A reply. *Language* 48:326–342.

Bresnan, Joan. 1977. Variables in the theory of transformations. In *Formal syntax*, ed. by Peter W. Culicover, Thomas Wasow, and Andrian Akmajian, 157–196. New York: Academic Press.

Bresnan, Joan, and Jonni M. Kanerva. 1989. Locative inversion in Chichewa: A case study of factorization in grammar. *Linguistic Inquiry* 20:1–50.

Bresnan, Joan, and Sam A. Mchombo. 1987. Topic, pronoun, and agreement in Chichewa. *Language* 63:741–782.

Bresnan, Joan, and Lioba Moshi. 1990. Object asymmetries in comparative Bantu syntax. *Linguistic Inquiry* 21:147–185.

Buell, Leston Chandler. 2005. *Issues in Zulu verbal morphosyntax*. Doctoral dissertation, University of California, Los Angeles, CA.

Chen, Matthew. 1987. The syntax of Xiamen tonesandhi. *Phonology* 4:109–150.

Cheng, Lisa Lai-Shen, and Laura J. Downing. 2009. Where's the topic in Zulu? *The Linguistic Review* 26:207–238.

Cheng, Lisa Lai-Shen, and Laura J. Downing. 2012. Prosodic domains do not match Spell-Out domains. *McGill Working Papers in Linguistics* 22.1.

Cheng, Lisa Lai-Shen, and Laura J. Downing. 2016. Phasal syntax = cyclic phonology? *Syntax* 19:156–191.

Cheng, Robert L. 1968. Tone sandhi in Taiwanese. *Linguistics* 6.41:19–42.

Cheng, Robert L. 1973. Some notes on tone sandhi in Taiwanese. *Linguistics* 11.100:5–25.

Chierchia, Gennaro. 1998. Reference to kinds across languages. *Natural Language Semantics* 6:339–405.

Chomsky, Noam. 1965. *Aspects of the theory of syntax*. Cambridge, MA: MIT Press.

Chomsky, Noam. 1970. Remarks on nominalization. In *Readings in English transformational grammar*, ed. by Roderick A. Jacobs and Peter S. Rosenbaum, 184–221. Waltham, MA: Ginn and Co.

Chomsky, Noam. 1981. *Lectures on government and binding*. Dordrecht: Foris.

Chomsky, Noam. 1986a. *Knowledge of language*. New York: Praeger.

Chomsky, Noam. 1986b. *Barriers*. Cambridge, MA: MIT Press.

Chomsky, Noam. 1993. A minimalist program for linguistic theory. In *The view from building 20: Essays in linguistics in honor of Sylvain Bromberger*, ed. by Kenneth Hale and Samuel Jay Keyser, 1–52. Cambridge, MA: MIT Press.

Chomsky, Noam. 1995. *The minimalist program*. Cambridge, MA: MIT Press.

Chomsky, Noam. 1998. Some observations on economy in generative grammar. In *Is the best good enough: Optimality and competition in syntax*, ed. by Pilar Barbosa, Danny Fox, Paul Hagstrom, Martha McGinnis, and David Pesetsky, 115–127. Cambridge, MA: MIT Press and MIT Working Papers in Linguistics.

Chomsky, Noam. 2000. Minimalist inquiries: The framework. In *Step by step*, ed. by Roger Martin, David Michaels, and Juan Uriagereka, 89–155. Cambridge, MA: MIT Press.

Chomsky, Noam. 2001. Derivation by phase. In *Ken Hale: A life in language*, ed. by Michael Kenstowicz, 1–52. Cambridge, MA: MIT Press.

Chomsky, Noam. 2004. Beyond explanatory adequacy. In *Structures and beyond: The cartography of syntactic structures*, volume 3, ed. by Adriana Belletti, 104–131. Oxford: Oxford University Press.

Chomsky, Noam. 2005. Three factors in the language design. *Linguistic Inquiry* 36:1–22.

Chomsky, Noam. 2008. On phases. In *Foundational issues in linguistic theory: Essays in honor of Jean-Roger Vergnaud*, ed. by Robert Freidin, Carlos P. Otero, and Maria Luisa Zubizarreta, 133–166. Cambridge, MA: MIT Press.

Chomsky, Noam. 2013. Problems of projection. *Lingua* 130:33–49.

Chomsky, Noam. 2014. Minimal recursion: Exploring the prospects. In *Recursion: Complexity in cognition*, ed. by Tom Roeper and Margaret Speas, 1–15. Dordrecht: Springer.

Chomsky, Noam. 2015. Problems of projection: Extensions. In *Structures, strategies and beyond: Studies in honour of Adriana Belletti*, ed. by Elisa Di Domenico, Cornelia Hamann, and Simona Matteini, 3–16. Amsterdam: John Benjamins.

Chomsky, Noam. 2016. *What kind of creatures are we?* New York: Columbia University Press.

Chomsky, Noam. 2017a. The language capacity: Architecture and evolution. *Psychonomic Bulletin and Review* 24:200–203.

Chomsky, Noam. 2017b. Reading lecture. Available online at: www.facebook.com/search/top/?init=quick&q=University%20of%20Reading%20chomsky&tas=0.2186655 6606255472

Chomsky, Noam, Ángel J. Gallego, and Dennis Ott. 2017. Generative grammar and the faculty of languages: Insights, questions, and challenges. Ms., MIT, Universitat Autònoma de Barcelona, and University of Ottawa.

Chomsky, Noam, and Morris Halle. 1968. *The sound pattern of English*. New York: Harper & Row.

Chomsky, Noam, and Howard Lasnik. 1977. Filters and control. *Linguistic Inquiry* 8:425–504.

Cinque, Guglielmo. 1982. On the theory of relative clauses and markedness. *The Linguistic Review* 1:247–294.

Cinque, Guglielmo. 1993. A null theory of phrase and compound stress. *Linguistic Inquiry* 24:239–297.

Cinque, Guglielmo. 1999. *Adverbs and functional heads: A cross-linguistic perspective.* Oxford: Oxford University Press.

Citko, Barbara. 2014. *Phase theory: An introduction.* Cambridge: Cambridge University Press.

Clements, George N. 1978. Tone and syntax in Ewe. In *Elements of tone, stress, and intonation*, ed. by Donna Jo Napoli, 21–99. Washington, DC: Georgetown University Press.

Collins, Chris. 1993. *Topics in Ewe syntax.* Doctoral dissertation, MIT Press, Cambridge, MA.

Collins, Chris. 1997. *Local economy.* Cambridge, MA: MIT Press.

Collins, Chris. 2002. Eliminating labels. In *Derivation and explanation in the minimalist program*, ed. by Samuel David Epstein and T. Daniel Seely, 42–64. Oxford: Blackwell.

Collins, Chris. 2004. The agreement parameter. In *Triggers*, ed. by Anne Breitbarth and Henk van Riemsdijk, 115–136. Berlin: Mouton de Gruyter.

Collins, Chris. 2017. Merge(X, Y) = {X, Y}. In *Labels and roots*, ed. by Leah Bauke and Andreas Blümel, 47–68. Berlin: Mouton de Gruyter.

Collins, Chris, and Phil Branigan. 1997. Quotative inversion. *Natural Language and Linguistic Theory* 15:1–41.

Collins, Chris, and Edward Stabler. 2016. A formalization of minimalist syntax. *Syntax* 19:43–78.

Conteh, Pattrick, Elizabeth Cowper, and Keren Rice. 1985. The environment for consonant mutation in Mende. In *Current approaches to African linguistics*, volume 3, ed. by Gerrit J. Dimmendaal, 107–125, Dordrecht: Foris.

Cowper, Elizabeth A., and Keren D. Rice. 1987. Are phonosyntactic rules necessary? *Phonology Yearbook* 4:185–194.

Culicover, Peter W. 1992. English tag questions in Universal Grammar. *Lingua* 88:193–226.

Culicover, Peter W. 1993. The adverb effect: Evidence against ECP accounts of the *that*-trace effect. In *NELS 23: Proceedings of the North East Linguistics Society*, ed. by Amy J. Shafer, 97–111. Amherst: University of Massachusetts, Graduate Linguistic Student Association.

D'Alessandro, Roberta, and Tobias Scheer. 2015. Modular PIC. *Linguistic Inquiry* 46:593–624.

Dehé, Nicole. 2014. *Parentheticals in spoken English: The syntax-prosody relation.* Cambridge: Cambridge University Press.

Dehé, Nicole, Ingo Feldhausen, and Shinichiro Ishihara. 2011. The prosody-syntax interface: Focus, phrasing, language evolution. *Lingua* 121:1863–1869.

Dehé, Nicole, and Yordanka Kavalova, eds. 2007. *Parentheticals.* Amsterdam: John Benjamins.

de Vries, Mark. 2012. Unconventional mergers. In *Ways of structure building*, ed. by Myriam Uribe-Etxebarria and Vidal Valmala, 143–166. Oxford: Oxford University Press.

Diercks, Michael J.K. 2010. *Agreement with subject in Lubukusu.* Doctoral dissertation, Georgetown University, Washington, DC.

Dobashi, Yoshihito. 2003. *Phonological phrasing and syntactic derivation.* Doctoral dissertation, Cornell University, Ithaca, NY.

Dobashi, Yoshihito. 2009. Multiple Spell-Out, assembly problem, and syntax-phonology mapping. In *Phonological domains: Universals and deviations*, ed. by Janet Grijzenhout and Bariş Kabak, 195–220. Berlin: Mouton de Gruyter.

Dobashi, Yoshihito. 2010. Computational efficiency in the syntax-phonology interface. *The Linguistic Review* 27:241–260.

Dobashi, Yoshihito. 2013. Autonomy of prosody and prosodic domain formation: A derivational approach. *Linguistic Analysis* 38:331–355.

Dobashi, Yoshihito. 2014. Prosodic domains and the syntax-phonology interface. In *The Routledge handbook of syntax*, ed. by Andrew Carnie, Yosuke Sato, and Daniel Siddiqi, 365–387. London: Routledge.

Downing, Bruce T. 1970. *Syntactic structure and phonological phrasing in English*. Doctoral dissertation, University of Texas, Austin.

Downing, Laura J. 2011. The prosody of 'dislocation' in selected Bantu languages. *Lingua* 121:772–786.

Downing, Laura J. 2013. Issues in the phonology-syntax interface in African languages. In *Selected proceedings of the 43rd annual conference on African linguistics*, ed. by Olanike Ola Orie and Karen W. Sanders, 26–38. Somerville, MA: Cascadilla Proceedings Project.

Downing, Laura J., and Al Mtenje. 2011. Un-WRAP-ing prosodic phrasing in Chichewa. *Lingua* 121:1965–1986.

Drury, John. 1999. The mechanics of π-derivations: An alternative 'direction' for syntactic theory. In *University of Maryland working papers 8*, ed. by Sachiko Aoshima, John Drury, and Tuomo Neuvonen, 180–212. College Park: University of Maryland, Department of Linguistics.

Elordieta, Gorka. 2007. Segmental phonology and syntactic structure. In *The Oxford handbook of linguistic interfaces*, ed. by Gillian Ramchand and Charles Reiss, 125–177. Oxford: Oxford University Press.

Elfner, Emily. 2012. *Syntax-prosody interactions in Irish*. Doctoral dissertation, University of Massachusetts, Amherst MA.

Elfner, Emily. 2013. Recursivity in prosodic phrasing: Evidence from Conamara Irish. In *Proceedings of the 40th annual meeting of the North-East Linguistic Society*, volume 1, ed. by Seda Kan, Claire Moore-Cantwell, and Robert Staubs, 191–204. Amherst: University of Massachusetts, Graduate Linguistic Student Association.

Elfner, Emily. 2015. Recursion in prosodic phrasing: Evidence from Connemara Irish. *Natural Language and Linguistic Theory* 33:1169–1208.

Emonds, Joseph E. 1976. *A transformational approach to English syntax*. New York: Academic Press.

Emonds, Joseph E. 1978. The verbal complex V′-V in French. *Linguistic Inquiry* 9:151–175.

Epstein, Samuel David, Erich M. Groat, Ruriko Kawashima, and Hisatsugu Kitahara. 1998. *A derivational approach to syntactic relations*. Oxford: Oxford University Press.

Epstein, Samuel David, Hisatsugu Kitahara, and Daniel Seely. 2016. Phase cancelation by external pair-merge of heads. *The Linguistic Review* 33:87–102.

Epstein, Samuel David, and T. Daniel Seely. 2002. Rule applications as cycles in a level-free syntax. In *Derivation and explanation in the minimalist program*, ed. by Samuel David Epstein and T. Daniel Seely, 65–89. Oxford: Blackwell.

Erteschik-Shir, Nomi. 2007. *Information structure: The syntax-discourse interface*. Oxford: Oxford University Press.

Erteschik-Shir, Nomi, and Lisa Rochman, eds. 2010. *The sound patterns of syntax*. Oxford: Oxford University Press.

Féry, Caroline. 2011. German sentence accents and embedded prosodic phrases. *Lingua* 121:1906–1922.

Féry, Caroline. 2017. *Intonation and prosodic structure*. Cambridge: Cambridge University Press.

Féry, Caroline, and Shinichiro Ishihara, eds. 2016. *Handbook of information structure*. Oxford: Oxford University Press.

Fodor, Jerry. 1975. *Language of thought*. New York: Crowell.

Fortuny, Jordi. 2008. *The emergence of order in syntax*. Amsterdam: John Benjamins.

Frascarelli, Mara. 2000. *The syntax-phonology interface in focus and topic constructions in Italian*. Dordrecht: Kluwer.

Frascarelli, Mara. 2007. Subjects, topics and the interpretation of referential *pro*: An interface approach to the linking of (null) pronouns. *Natural Language and Linguistic Theory* 25:691–734.

Frota, Sónia. 2000. *Prosody and focus in European Portuguese: Phonological phrasing and intonation*. New York: Garland.

Fuß, Eric. 2003/2007. Cyclic Spell-Out and the domain of post-syntactic operations: Evidence from complementizer agreement. *Linguistic Analysis* 33:267–302.

Fuß, Eric. 2008. *Word order and language change: On the interface between syntax and morphology*. Frankfurt am Main: Habilitationsschrift, der Johann-Wolfgang-Goethe Universität.

Fukui, Naoki. 1986. *A theory of category projection and its applications*. Doctoral dissertation, MIT, Cambridge, MA. Published as Fukui 1995.

Fukui, Naoki. 1988. Deriving the differences between English and Japanese. *English Linguistics* 5:249–270.

Fukui, Naoki. 1995. *Theory of projection in syntax*. Tokyo: Kuroshio.

Fukui, Naoki. 2011. Merge and bare phrase structure. In *The Oxford handbook of linguistic minimalism*, ed. by Cedric Boeckx, 73–95. Oxford: Oxford University Press.

Fukui, Noaki, and Hiromu Sakai. 2003. The visibility guideline for functional categories: Verb raising in Japanese and related issues. *Lingua* 113:321–375.

Ghini, Micro. 1993. Φ-formation in Italian: A new proposal. *Toronto Working Papers in Linguistics* 12:41–78.

Goto, Nobu, and Toru Ishii. 2018. Some consequences of MERGE and determinacy. Ms., Toyo University, Tokyo, and Meiji University, Tokyo.

Grohmann, Kleanthes K., and Michael T. Putnam. 2003/2007. Dynamic stress assignment. *Linguistic Analysis* 33:337–374.

Guéron, Jacquline. 1980. On syntax and semantics of PP extraposition. *Linguistic Inquiry* 11:637–678.

Gussenhoven, Carlos. 1992. Sentence accents and argument structure. In *Thematic structure: Its role in Grammar*, ed. by Iggy M. Roca, 79–106. Berlin: Foris.

Gussenhoven, Carlos. 2004. *The phonology of tone and intonation*. Cambridge: Cambridge University Press.

Gussenhoven, Carlos. 2005. Procliticized phonological phrases in English: Evidence from rhythm. *Studia Linguistica* 59:174–193.

Haddican, William, Anders Holmberg, Hidekazu Tanaka, and George Tsoulas. 2014. Interrogative slifting in English. *Lingua* 138:86–106.

Haik, Isabelle. 1984. Indirect binding. *Linguistic Inquiry* 15:185–223.

Halliday, M.A.K. 1967. *Intonation and grammar in British English*. The Hague: Mouton.

Hamlaoui, Fatima, and Kriszta Szendrői. 2015. A flexible approach to the mapping of intonational phrases. *Phonology* 32:79–110.

Hashimoto, Shinkichi. 1934. *Kokugoho Yosetsu* [The outlines of Japanese grammar]. Tokyo: Meiji Shoin.

Hauser, Marc D., Noam Chomsky, and W. Tecumseh Fitch. 2002. The faculty of language: What is it, who has it, and how did it evolve? *Science* 298:1569–1579.

Hawkins, John A. 1994. *A performance theory of order and constituency*. Cambridge: Cambridge University Press.

Hayes, Bruce. 1982. Extrametricality and English stress. *Linguistic Inquiry* 13:227–276.

Hayes, Bruce. 1989. The prosodic hierarchy in meter. In *Phonetics and phonology 1: Rhythm and meter*, ed. by Paul Kiparsky and Gilbert Youmans, 201–260. Orlando: Academic Press.

Henderson, Brent Mykel. 2006. *The syntax and typology of Bantu relative clauses*. Doctoral dissertation, University of Illinois, Urbana-Champaign, IL.

Hiraiwa, Ken. 2005. *Dimensions of symmetry in syntax: Agreement and clausal architecture*. Doctoral dissertation, MIT, Cambridge, MA.

Idsardi, William, and Eric Raimy. 2013. Three types of linearization and the temporal aspects of speech. In *Challenges to linearization*, ed. by Theresa Biberauer and Ian Roberts, 31–56. Berlin: de Gruyter.

Inkelas, Sharon. 1989. *Prosodic constituency in the lexicon*. Doctoral dissertation, Stanford University, CA.

Inkelas, Sharon, and Draga Zec, eds. 1990. *The phonology-syntax connection*. Chicago: University of Chicago Press.

Inkelas, Sharon, and Draga Zec. 1995. Syntax-phonology interface. In *The handbook of phonological theory*, ed. by John A. Goldsmith, 535–549. Oxford: Blackwell.

Irurtzun, Aritz. 2009. Why Y: On the centrality of syntax in the architecture of grammar. *Catalan Journal of Linguistics* 8:141–160.

Ishihara, Shinichiro. 2003. *Intonation and interface conditions*. Doctoral dissertation, MIT, Cambridge, MA.

Ishihara, Shinichiro. 2005. Prosody-scope match and mismatch in Tokyo Japanese *wh*-questions. *English Linguistics* 22:347–379.

Ishihara, Shinichiro. 2007. Major phrase, focus intonation, Multiple Spell-Out (MaP, FI, MSO). *Linguistic Review* 24:137–167.

Ishihara, Shinichiro. 2015. Syntax-phonology interface. In *Handbook of Japanese phonetics and phonology*, ed. by Haruo Kubozono, 569–618. Berlin: De Gruyter.

Ito, Junko, and Armin Mester. 1992/2003. Weak layering and word binarity. In *A new century of phonology and phonological theory: A festschrift for Professor Shosuke Haraguchi on the occasion of his sixtieth birthday*, ed. by Honma Takeru, Masao Okazaki, Toshiyuki Tabata, and Shin-ichi Tanaka, 26–65. Tokyo: Kaitakusha.

Ito, Junko, and Armin Mester. 2007. Prosodic adjunction in Japanese compounds. In *Formal Approaches to Japanese Linguistics* 4, *MIT Working Papers in Linguistics 42*, ed. by Yoichi Miyamoto and Masao Ochi, 97–111. Cambridge, MA: MIT Press, MIT Press Working Papers in Linguistics.

Ito, Junko, and Armin Mester. 2009. The extended prosodic word. In *Phonological domains: Universals and deviations*, ed. by Janet Grijzenhout and Bariş Kabak, 135–194. Berlin: Mouton de Gruyter.

Ito, Junko, and Armin Mester. 2012. Recursive prosodic phrasing in Japanese. In *Prosody matters: Essays in honor of Elisabeth Selkirk*, ed. by Toni Borowsky, Shigeto Kawahara, Tokahito Shinya, and Mariko Sugahara, 280–303. London: Equinox.

Ito, Junko, and Armin Mester. 2013. Prosodic subcategories in Japanese. *Lingua* 124:20–40.

Ito, Junko, and Armin Mester. 2016. Unaccentedness in Japanese. *Linguistic Inquiry* 47:471–526.

Jackendoff, Ray. 1972. *Semantic interpretation in generative grammar*. Cambridge, MA: MIT Press.

Jackendoff, Ray. 1977. *X-bar syntax: A study of phrase structure*. Cambridge, MA: MIT Press.

Jackendoff, Ray. 1997. *The architecture of the language faculty*. Cambridge, MA: MIT Press.

Johnson, Kyle. 1991. Object positions. *Natural Language and Linguistic Theory* 9:577–636.

Julien, Marit. 2002. *Syntactic heads and word formation*. Oxford: Oxford University Press.

Jun, Sun-Ah. 1998. The accentual phrase in the Korean prosodic hierarchy. *Phonology* 5:189–226.

Kabak, Barış, and Anthi Revithiadou. 2009. An interface approach to prosodic word recursion. In *Phonological domains: Universals and deviations*, ed. by Janet Grijzenhout and Barış Kabak, 105–133. Berlin: Mouton de Gruyter.

Kager, René, and Wim Zonneveld. 1999. Phrasal phonology: An introduction. In *Phrasal phonology*, ed. by René Kager and Wim Zonneveld, 1–34. Nijmegen: Nijmegen University Press.

Kahnemuyipour, Arsalan. 2004. *The syntax of sentential stress*. Doctoral dissertation, University of Toronto.

Kahnemuyipour, Arsalan. 2009. *The syntax of sentential stress*. Oxford: Oxford University Press.

Kaisse, Ellen M. 1985. *Connected speech: The interaction of syntax and phonology*. New York: Academic Press.

Kalivoda, Nicholas. 2018. *Syntax-prosody mismatches in Optimality Theory*. Doctoral Dissertation, University of California, Santa Cruz, CA.

Kandybowicz, Jason. 2006. Comp-trace effects explained away. In *Proceedings of the 25th West coast conference on formal linguistics*, ed. by Donald Baumer, David Montero, and Michael Scanlon, 220–228. Somerville, MA: Cascadilla Proceedings Project.

Kandybowicz, Jason. 2009. Embracing edges: Syntactic and phono-syntactic edge sensitivity in Nupe. *Natural Language and Linguistic Theory* 27:305–344.

Kanerva, Jonni M. 1990. Focusing on phonological phrases in Chichewa. In *The phonology-syntax connection*, ed. by Sharon Inkelas and Draga Zec, 145–161. Chicago: University of Chicago Press.

Kayne, Richard. 1994. *The antisymmetry of syntax*, Cambridge, MA: MIT Press.

Kenesei, István, and Irene Vogel. 1995. Focus and phonological structure. Ms., University of Szeged and University of Delaware. Available online at: www.nytud.hu/eng/kenesei/publist.html

Kidima, Lukowa. 1990. Tone and Syntax in Kiyaka. In *The phonology-syntax connection*, ed. by Sharon Inkelas and Draga Zec, 195–216. Chicago: University of Chicago Press.

Kidima, Lukowa. 1991. *Tone and accent in KiYaka*. Doctoral Dissertation. University of California, Los Angeles, CA.

Kim, No-Ju. 1997. *Tone, segments, and their interaction in North Kyungsang Korean: A correspondence theoretic account*. Doctoral dissertation, The Ohio State University, Columbus, OH.

Kishimoto, Hideki. 2017. Case marking. In *Handbook of Japanese syntax*, ed. by Masayoshi Shibatani, Shigeru Miyagawa, and Hisashi Noda, 447–495. Berlin: Mouton de Gruyter.

Kisseberth, Charles W. 1994. On domains. In *Perspectives in phonology*, ed. by Jennifer Cole and Charles W. Kisseberth, 133–166. Stanford, CA: CSLI.

Kisseberth, Charles W., and Mohammad Imam Abasheikh. 1974. Vowel length in Chi-Mwi:ni: A case study of the role of grammar in phonology. In *Papers from the parasession on natural phonology*, ed. by Anthony Bruck, Robert A. Fox, and Michael W. LaGaly, 193–209. Chicago Linguistic Society.

Kisseberth, Charles W., and Mohammad Imam Abasheikh. 2011. Chimwiini phonological phrasing revisited. *Lingua* 212:1987–2013.

Kratzer, Angelika, and Elizabeth Selkirk. 2007. Phase theory and prosodic spellout: The case of verbs. *The Linguistic Review* 24:93–135.

Kula, Nancy C., and Lee S. Bickmore. 2015. Phrasal phonology in Copperbelt Bemba. *Phonology* 32:147–176.

Ladd, D. Robert. 1986. Intonational phrasing: The case for recursive prosodic structure. *Phonology Yearbook* 3:311–340.

Ladd, D. Robert. 1996. *Intonational phonology*. Cambridge: Cambridge University Press.

Lakoff, George. 1972. The global nature of the nuclear stress rule. *Language* 48:285–303.

Lambrecht, Knud. 1994. *Information structure and sentence form: Topic, focus and the mental representations of discourse referents*. Cambridge: Cambridge University Press.

Lasnik, Howard. 1972. *Analyses of negation in English*. Doctoral dissertation, MIT Press, Cambridge, MA.

Lasnik, Howard. 1999. Chains of arguments. In *Working minimalism*, ed. by Samuel Epstein and Norbert Hornstein, 189–215. Cambridge, MA: MIT Press.

Lasnik, Howard, and Mamoru Saito. 1991. On the subject of infinitives. In *Papers from the twenty-seventh regional meeting of the Chicago linguistic society*, ed. by Lise Dobrin, Lynn Nichols, and Rosa Rodrigues, 324–343. Chicago: Chicago Linguistic Society.

Legate, Julie Anne. 2003. Some interface properties of the phase. *Linguistic Inquiry* 34:506–516.

Maling, Joan. 1976. Notes on quantifier postposing. *Linguistic Inquiry* 7:708–718.

Marantz, Alec. 1997. No escape from syntax: Don't try morphological analysis in the privacy of your own lexicon. *University of Pennsylvania Working Papers in Linguistics* 4.2:201–225.

Marvin, Tatjana. 2002. *Topics in the stress and syntax of words*. Doctoral dissertation, MIT Press, Cambridge, MA.

May, Robert. 1985. *Logical form*. Cambridge, MA: MIT Press.

McCarthy, John, and Alan Prince. 1986. *Prosodic morphology*. Amherst and Waltham, MA: University of Massachusetts and Brandeis University.

McCarthy, John, and Alan Prince. 1993. Generalized alignment. In *Yearbook of morphology 1993*, ed. by Geert Booij and Jaap van Marle, 79–153. Dordrecht: Kluwer.

McCarthy, John, and Alan Prince. 1995. Faithfullness and reduplicative identity. In *Papers in optimality theory, University of Massachusetts occasional papers in linguistics 18*, ed. by Jill Beckman, Laura Walsh Dickey, and Suzanne Urbancxyk, 249–384. Amherst, MA: University of Massachusetts, Graduate Linguistic Student Association.

McCawley, James D. 1968. *The phonological component of a grammar of Japanese*. The Hague: Mouton.

McGinnis, Martha. 2001. Variation in the phase structure of applicatives. In *Linguistic variation yearbook 1*, ed. by Pierre Pica and Johan Rooryck, 105–146. Amsterdam: John Benjamins.

Mchombo, Sam. 2004. *The syntax of Chichewa*. Cambridge: Cambridge University Press.

Myrberg, Sara. 2013. Sisterhood in prosodic branching. *Phonology* 30:73–124.

Nagahara, Hiroyuki. 1994. *Phonological phrasing in Japanese*. Doctoral dissertation, University of California, Los Angeles.

Nakamura, Masaru. 1994. Topicalization, neg-preposing, and locative preposing. In *Current topics in English and Japanese*, ed. by Masaru Nakamura, 151–177. Tokyo: Hituzi Syobo.

Nakanishi, Ryota. 2016. A Label-based account for the *that*-trace effect. *Gengo Bunka Kyoodoo Kenkyuu Purojekuto 2016* [Cooperative research project on language and culture 2016], 49–58, Osaka: Osaka University.

Napoli, Donna Jo, and Marina Nespor. 1979. The syntax of word-initial consonant gemination in Italian. *Language* 55:812–841.

Narita, Hiroki. 2012. Phase cycles in service of projection-free syntax. In *Phases: Developing the framework*, ed. by Ángel J. Gallego, 126–172. Berlin: Mouton de Gruyter.

Narita, Hiroki. 2014. *Endocentric structuring of projection-free syntax*. Amsterdam: John Benjamins.

Nasukawa, Kuniya, and Phillip Backley. 2015. Heads and complements in phonology: A case of role reversal? *Phonological Studies* 18:67–74.

Neeleman, Ad, and Fred Weerman. 1999. *Flexible syntax: A theory of case and arguments*. Dordrecht: Kluwer.

Nespor, Marina, and Irene Vogel. 1982. Prosodic domains and external sandhi rules. In *The structure of phonological representations (part 1)*, ed. by Harry van der Hulst and Norval Smith, 225–255. Dordrecht: Foris.

Nespor, Marina, and Irene Vogel. 1986. *Prosodic phonology*. Dordrecht: Foris.

Newman, Stanley. 1946. On the stress system of English. *Word* 2:171–187.

Obata, Miki. 2010. *Root, successive-cyclic and feature-splitting internal merge: Implications for feature-inheritance and transfer*. Doctoral dissertation, University of Michigan, Ann Arbor, MI.

O'Connor, Kathleen M., and Cédric Patin. 2015. The syntax and prosody of apposition in Shingazidja. *Phonology* 32:111–145.

Odden, David. 1987. Kimatuumbi phrasal phonology. *Phonology* 4:13–36.

Odden, David. 1990. Syntax, lexical rules, and postlexical rules in Kimatuumbi. In *The phonology-syntax connection*, ed. by Sharon Inkelas and Draga Zec, 259–278. Chicago: University of Chicago Press.

Odden, David. 1996. *The phonology and morphology of Kimatuumbi*. Oxford: Oxford University Press.

Ogawa, Yoshiki. 1996. Word order, object shift and multiple specifiers. *English Linguistics* 13:63–92.

Ogawa, Yoshiki. 2001. *A Unified theory of verbal and nominal projections*. Oxford: Oxford University Press.

Ott, Dennis. 2012. Movement and ellipsis in contrastive left-dislocation. In *Proceedings of the 30th West coast conference on formal linguistics*, ed. by Nathan Arnett and Ryan Bennett, 281–291. Somerville, MA: Cascadilla Press.

Ott, Dennis. 2015. Connectivity in left-dislocation and the composition of the left periphery. *Linguistic Variation* 15:225–290.

Ott, Dennis, and Mark de Vries. 2013. Right-dislocation as deletion. Ms., University of Groningen.

Pak, Marjorie. 2008. *The postsyntactic derivation and its phonological reflexes*. Doctoral dissertation, University of Pennsylvania.

Perlmutter, David M. 1968. *Deep and surface structure constraints in syntax*. Doctoral dissertation, MIT, Cambridge, MA.

Pereltsvaig, Asya. 2004. Topic and focus as linear notions: Evidence from Italian and Russian. *Lingua* 114:325–344.

Pesetsky, David. 2017. Complementizer-trace effects. In *The Wiley Blackwell companion to syntax*, 2nd edition, ed. by Martin Everaert and Henk C. van Riemsdijk, 993–1026. Oxford: Wiley Blackwell.

Pollock, Jean-Yves. 1989. Verb movement, Universal Grammar, and the structure of IP. *Linguistic Inquiry* 20:365–424.

Poser, William John. 1984. *The phonetics and phonology of tone and intonation in Japanese*. Doctoral dissertation, MIT Press, Cambridge, MA.

Postal, Paul. 1974. *On raising: One rule of English grammar and its theoretical implications*. Cambridge, MA: MIT Press.

Potts, Christopher. 2002a. The lexical semantics of parenthetical-*as* and appositive-*which*. *Syntax* 5:55–88.

Potts, Christopher. 2002b. The syntax and semantics of *as*-parentheticals. *Natural Language and Linguistic Theory* 20:623–689.

Potts, Christopher. 2005. *The logic of conversational implicatures*. Oxford: Oxford University Press.

Prieto, Pilar. 2005. Syntactic and eurhythmic constraints on phrasing decisions in Catalan. *Studia Linguistica* 59:194–222.

Prince, Alan, and Paul Smolensky. 1993/2004. *Optimality theory: Constraint interaction in generative grammar*. Oxford: Blackwell.

Pyle, Charles. 1972. On eliminating BM's. In *Papers from the Eighth regional meeting: Chicago linguistic society*, ed. by Paul M. Peranteau, Judith N. Levi, and Gloria C. Phares, 516–532. Chicago, IL: Chicago Linguistic Society.

Pylkkänen, Liina. 2008. *Introducing arguments*. Cambridge, MA: MIT Press.

Revithiadou, Anthi, and Vassilios Spyropoulos. 2009. A Dynamic approach to the syntax-phonology interface: A case study from Greek. In *InterPhases: Phase-theoretic investigations of linguistic interfaces*, ed. by Kleanthes K. Grohmann, 202–233. Oxford: Oxford University Press.

Revithiadou, Anthi, and Vassilios Spyropoulos. 2011. Syntax-phonology interface. In *The continuum companion to phonology*, ed. by Nancy C. Kula, Bert Botma, and Kuniya Nasukawa, 225–253. London: Continuum.

Rice, Keren D. 1990. Predicting rule domains in the phrasal phonology. In *The phonology-syntax connection*, ed. by Sharon Inkelas and Draga Zec, 289–312. Chicago: University of Chicago Press.

Richards, Marc D. 2004. *Object shift and scrambling in North and West Germanic: A case study in symmetrical syntax*. Doctoral dissertation, University of Cambridge, Cambridge.

Richards, Marc D. 2006. Weak pronouns, object shift and multiple spell-out: Evidence for phases at the PF-interface. In *Minimalist essays*, ed. by Cedric Boeckx, 160–181. Amsterdam: John Benjamins.

Richards, Norvin. 2016. *Contiguity theory*. Cambridge, MA: MIT Press.

Riedel, Kristina. 2009. *The syntax of object marking in Sambaa: A comparative Bantu perspective*. Doctoral dissertation, University of Leiden.

Riemsdijk, van Henk, and Edwin Williams. 1981. NP-structure. *The Linguistic Review* 1:171–217.

Ritter, Elizabeth Ann. 1988. *A case study in the syntax of agreement: Hebrew noun phrases and Benoni verb phrases*. Doctoral dissertation, MIT Press, Cambridge, MA.

Rizzi, Luigi. 1982. *Issues in Italian syntax*. Berlin: De Gruyter Mouton.

Rizzi, Luigi. 1997. The fine structure of the left periphery. In *Elements of grammar*, ed. by Liliane Haegeman, 281–337. Dordrecht: Kluwer.

Rochemont, S. Michael, and Peter W. Culicover. 1990. *English focus constructions and the theory of grammar*. Cambridge: Cambridge University Press.

Ross, John Robert. 1967. *Constraints on variables in syntax*. Doctoral dissertation, MIT Press, Cambridge, MA. Published as *Infinite syntax!* Norwood, NJ: Ablex (1986).

Ross, John Robert. 1970. On declarative sentences. In *Readings in English transformational grammar*, ed. by Roderick A. Jacobs and Peter S. Rosenbaum, 222–277. Waltham, MA: Ginn.

Ross, John Robert. 1973. Slifting. In *The formal analysis of natural languages*, ed. by Maurice Gross, Morris Halle, and Marcel-Paul Schützenberger, 133–169. The Hague: Mouton.

Rotenberg, Joel. 1978. *The syntax of phonology*. Doctoral dissertation, MIT Press, Cambridge, MA.

Rugemalira, Josephat M. 1993a. *Runyambo verb extensions and constraints on predicate structure*. Doctoral dissertation, University of California, Berkeley.

Rugemalira, Josephat M. 1993b. Bantu multiple 'object' constructions. *Linguistic Analysis* 23:226–252.

Rugemalira, Josephat M. 2005. *A grammar of Runyambo*. Dar es Salaam: Language of Tanzania (LOT) Project, University of Dar es Salaam.

Sabel, Joachim, and Jochen Zeller. 2006. Wh-question formation in Nguni. In *Selected proceedings of the 35th annual conference on African linguistics*, ed. by John Mugane, John P. Hutchison, and Dee A. Worman, 271–283. Somerville, MA: Cascadilla Proceedings Project.

Safir, Ken. 1985. Binding in relatives and LF. *Glow Newsletter* 14:77–79.

Saito, Mamoru. 2016. (A) case for labeling: Labeling in languages without φ-feature agreement. *The Linguistic Review* 33:129–175.

Saito, Shogo. 2019. A phonological analysis of VP-ellipsis. To appear in *JELS* 36: *Proceedings of the English Linguistic Society of Japan*.

Samek-Lodovici, Vieri. 2005. Prosody-syntax interaction in the expression of focus. *Natural Language and Linguistic Theory* 23:687–755.

Samuels, Bridget D. 2009. *The structure of phonological theory*. Doctoral dissertation, Harvard University, Cambridge, MA.

Samuels, Bridget D. 2011. *Phonological architecture: A biolinguistic perspective*. Oxford: Oxford University Press.

Samuels, Bridget D., and Hiroki Narita. 2013. Phasing out projection: Considerations from the syntax-phonology interface. *Linguistic Analysis* 38:357–391.

Sandalo, Filomena, and Hubert Truckenbrodt. 2002. Some notes on phonological phrasing in Brazilian Portuguese. In *Phonological answers (and their corresponding questions), MIT Working Papers in Linguistics 42*, ed. by Anikó Csirmaz, Zhiqiang Li, Andrew Nevins, Olga Vaysman, and Michael Wagner, 285–310. Cambridge, MA: MIT Press, MIT Press Working Papers in Linguistics.

Sato, Yosuke. 2009. Spelling out prosodic domains: A Multiple Spell-Out account. In *InterPhases: Phase-theoretic investigations of linguistic interfaces*, ed. by Kleanthes K. Grohmann, 234–259. Oxford: Oxford University Press.

Sato, Yosuke, and Yoshihito Dobashi. 2016. Prosodic phrasing and the *that*-trace effect. *Linguistic Inquiry* 47:333–349.

Scheer, Tobias. 2008. Why the prosodic hierarchy is a diacritic and why the interface must be direct. In *Sounds of silence: Empty elements in syntax and phonology*, ed. by Jutta M. Hartmann, Veronika Hegedüs, and Henk van Riemsdijk, 145–192. Amsterdam: Elsevier.

Scheer, Tobias. 2011. *A guide to morphosyntax-phonology interface theories*. Berlin: De Gruyter Mouton.

Scheer, Tobias. 2012a. Chunk definition in phonology: Prosodic constituency vs. phase structure. In *Modules and interfaces*, ed. by Maria Bloch-Trojnar and Anna Bloch-Rozmej, 221–253. Lublin: Wydawnictwo KUL.

Scheer, Tobias. 2012b. *Direct interface and one-channel translation: A non-diacritic theory of the morphosyntax-phonology interface*. Berlin: Mouton de Gruyter.

Seidl, Amanda. 2001. *Minimal indirect reference: A theory of the syntax-phonology interface*. London: Routledge.

Selkirk, Elisabeth. 1972. *The phrase phonology of English and French*. Doctoral dissertation, MIT Press, Cambridge, MA.

Selkirk, Elisabeth. 1974. French liaison and the X' notation. *Linguistic Inquiry* 5:573–590.

Selkirk, Elisabeth. 1980. Prosodic domains in phonology: Sanskrit revisited. In *Juncture*, ed. by Mark Aronoff and Mary-Louise Kean, 107–129. Saratoga, CA: Anma Libri.

Selkirk, Elisabeth. 1984. *Phonology and syntax: The relation between sound and structure*. Cambridge, MA: MIT Press.

Selkirk, Elisabeth. 1986. On derived domains in sentence phonology. *Phonology Yearbook* 3:371–405.

Selkirk, Elisabeth. 1996. The prosodic structure of function words. In *Signal to syntax: Bootstrapping from speech to grammar in early acquisition*, ed. by James L. Morgan and Katherine Demuth, 187–213. Mahwah, NJ: Lawrence Erlbaum.

Selkirk, Elisabeth. 2000. The interaction of constraints on prosodic phrasing. In *Prosody: Theory and experiment*, ed. by Merle Horne, 231–261. Dordrecht: Kluwer.

Selkirk, Elisabeth. 2001. The syntax-phonology interface. In *International encyclopedia of the social and behavioral sciences*, ed. by David L. Sills, 15407–15412. Amsterdam: Elsevier.

Selkirk, Elisabeth. 2005. Comments on intonational phrasing in English. In *Prosodies: With special reference to Iberian languages*, ed. by Sónia Frota, Marina Vigário, and Maria João Freitas, 11–58. Berlin: Mouton de Gruyter.

Selkirk, Elisabeth. 2009. On clause and intonational phrase in Japanese: The syntactic grounding of prosodic constituent structure. *Gengo Kenkyu* 136:35–73.

Selkirk, Elisabeth. 2011. The syntax-phonology interface. In *The handbook of phonological theory*, 2nd edition, ed. by John Goldsmith, Jason Riggle, and Alan C. L. Yu, 435–484. Oxford: Wiley-Blackwell.

Selkirk, Elisabeth, and Seunghun J. Lee. 2015. Constituency in sentence phonology: An introduction. *Phonology* 32:1–18.

Shaked, Amit. 2007. Competing syntactic and phonological constraints in Hebrew prosodic phrasing. *The Linguistic Review* 24:169–199.

Shiobara, Kayono. 2009. A phonological view of phases'. In *InterPhases: Phase-theoretic investigations of linguistic interfaces*, ed. by Kleanthes K. Grohmann, 182–201. Oxford: Oxford University Press.

Shiobara, Kayono. 2010. *Derivational linearization at the syntax-prosody interface*. Tokyo: Hituzi Syobo.

Shiobara, Kayono. 2011. Significance of linear information in prosodically constrained syntax. *English Linguistics* 28:258–277.

Shiobara, Kayono. 2019. XP-YP kozo-no superu auto: Toi-kozo o chushin-ni [Spelling-Out the Spell-Out of an XP-YP structure: A case of coordinate structure]. To appear in *JELS 36: Proceedings of the English Linguistic Society of Japan*. Tokyo Woman's Christian University, Tokyo.

Shlonsky, Ur. 1988. Complementizer-cliticization in Hebrew and the empty category principle. *Natural Language and Linguistic Theory* 6:191–205.

Simpson, Andrew, and Zoe Wu. 2002. IP-raising, tone sandhi and the creation of S-final particles: Evidence for cyclic Spell-Out. *Journal of East Asian Linguistics* 11:67–99.

Smith, Jennifer L. 2011a. [+wh] complementizers drive phonological phrasing in Fukuoka Japanese. *Natural Language and Linguistic Theory* 29:545–559.

Smith, Jennifer L. 2011b. Category-specific effects. In *The Blackwell companion to phonology*, ed. by Marc van Oostendorp, Colin J. Ewen, Elizabeth V. Hume, and Keren Rice, 2439–2463. Malden, MA: Wiley-Blackwell.

Sobin, Nicholas. 2000. Minimal CP and the adverb effect. In *Kansas working papers in linguistics 25*, ed. by John Kyle and Stacey Stowers, 15–38. Lawrence: University of Kansas, Linguistic Graduate Student Association.

Sobin, Nicholas. 2002. The comp-trace effect, the adverb effect and minimal CP. *Journal of Linguistics* 38:527–560.

Sportiche, Dominique. 1988. A theory of floating quantifiers and its corollaries for constituent structure. *Linguistic Inquiry* 19:425–449.

Sproat, Richard, and Chilin Shih. 1991. The cross-linguistic distribution of adjective ordering restrictions. In *Interdisciplinary approaches to language: Essays in honor of S.-Y. Kuroda*, ed. by Carol Georgopoulos and Roberta Ishihara, 565–593. Dordrecht: Kluwer.

Szendrői, Kriszta. 2001. *Focus and the syntax-phonology interface*. Doctoral dissertation, University College London.

Taglicht, Josef. 1998. Constraints on intonational phrasing in English. *Journal of Linguistics* 34:181–211.

Takano, Yuji. 1996. *Movement and parametric variation in syntax*. Doctoral dissertation, University of California, Irvine, CA.

Takano, Yuji. 1998. Object shift and scrambling. *Natural Language and Linguistic Theory* 16:817–889.

Takano, Yuji. 2014. A comparative approach to Japanese postposing. In *Japanese syntax in comparative perspective*, ed. by Mamoru Saito, 139–180. Oxford: Oxford University Press.

Taraldsen, K. Tarald. 1978. On the NIC, vacuous application and the *that-trace* filter. Ms., MIT Press, Cambridge, MA.

Tenny, Carol L. 1994. *Aspectual roles and the syntax-semantics interface*. Dordrecht: Kluwer.

Tokizaki, Hisao. 2005. Prosody and phrase structure without labels. *English Linguistics* 22:380–405.

Tokizaki, Hisao. 2008. *Syntactic structure and silence*. Tokyo: Hituzi Syobo.

Truckenbrodt, Hubert. 1995. *Phonological phrases: Their relation to syntax, focus, and prominence*. Doctoral dissertation, MIT Press, Cambridge, MA.

Truckenbrodt, Hubert. 1999. On the relation between syntactic phrases and phonological phrases. *Linguistic Inquiry* 30:219–255.

Truckenbrodt, Hubert. 2005. A short report on intonation phrase boundaries in German. *Linguistische Berichte* 203:273–296.

Truckenbrodt, Hubert. 2007. The syntax-phonology interface. In *The Cambridge handbook of phonology*, ed. by Paul de Lacy, 435–456. Cambridge: Cambridge University Press.

Truckenbrodt, Hubert. 2014. Intonation phrases and speech acts. In *Parenthesis and ellipsis: Cross-linguistic and theoretical perspectives*, ed. by Marlies Kluck, Dennis Ott, and Mark de Vries, 301–349. Berlin: de Gruyter Mouton.

Truckenbrodt, Hubert, and Caroline Féry. 2015. Hierarchical organisation and tonal scaling. *Phonology* 32:19–47.

Ura, Hiroyuki. 2000. *Checking theory and grammatical functions in universal grammar*. Oxford: Oxford University Press.

Uriagereka, Juan. 1999. Multiple spell-out. In *Working minimalism*, ed. by Samuel Epstein and Norbert Hornstein, 251–282. Cambridge, MA: MIT Press.

Uriagereka, Juan. 2012. *Spell-Out and the minimalist program*. Oxford: Oxford University Press.

Vance, Timothy J. 1993. Are Japanese particles clitics? *Journal of the Association of Teachers of Japanese* 27:3–33.

Vogel, Irene. 2009a. Universals of prosodic structure. In *Universals of language today*, ed. by Sergio Scalise, Elisabetta Magni, and Antonietta Bisetto, 59–82. Dordrecht: Springer.

Vogel, Irene. 2009b. The status of clitic group. In *Phonological domains: Universals and deviations*, ed. by Janet Grijzenhout and Bariş Kabak, 15–46. Berlin: Mouton de Gruyter.

Wagner, Michael. 2005. *Prosody and recursion*. Doctoral dissertation, MIT Press, Cambridge, MA.

Wagner, Michael. 2010. Prosody and recursion in coordinate structures and beyond. *Natural Language and Linguistic Theory* 28:183–237.

Wasow, Thomas. 1997. Remarks on grammatical weight. *Language Variation and Change* 9:81–106.

Wasow, Thomas. 2002. *Postverbal behaviour*. Stanford, CA: CSLI Publications.

Watson, Duane, and Edward Gibson. 2004. The relationship between intonational phrasing and syntactic structure in language production. *Language and Cognitive Processes* 19:713–755.

Yahya, Yusra. 2013. *An integrated approach to the syntax-phonology interface: A cross-linguistic study*. Doctoral dissertation, The English and Foreign Languages University (EFL-U), Hyderabad.

Yim, Changguk. 2004. *The EPP and nominal/predicational PPs in English and Korean*. Doctoral dissertation, Cornell University, Ithaca, NY.

Yim, Changguk. 2012. Fragment answers containing-*yo* in Korean: New evidence for the PF deletion theory of ellipsis. *Linguistic Inquiry* 43:514–518.

Yim, Changguk, and Yoshihito Dobashi. 2016. A prosodic account of -*yo* attachment in Korean. *Journal of East Asian Linguistics* 25:213–241.

Yoon, Sangseok. 2013. Interactive nature of the Korean honorific marker -*yo*. In *Studies in Korean linguistics and language pedagogy: Festschrift for Ho-min Sohn*, ed. by Sung-Ock Sohn, Sungdai Cho, and Seok-Hoon You, 206–221. Seoul: Korean University Press.

Zec, Draga. 2005. Prosodic differences among function words. *Phonology* 22:77–112.

Zec, Draga, and Sharon Inkelas. 1990. Prosodically constrained syntax. In *The phonology-syntax connection*, ed. by Sharon Inkelas and Draga Zec, 365–378. Chicago: University of Chicago Press.

Zec, Draga, and Sharon Inkelas. 1991. The place of clitics in the prosodic hierarchy. In *Proceedings of the tenth west coast conference on formal linguistics*, ed. by Dawn Bates, 505–519. Stanford CA: CSLI Publications.

Zeller, Jochen. 2004. Left dislocation in Zulu. Ms., University of KwaZulu-Natal, Nurban, South Africa. Available online at: www.jzeller.de/pdf/LDZuluSep04.pdf

Zeller, Jochen. 2014. Three types of object marking in Bantu. *Linguistische Berichte* 239:347–367.

Zerbian, Sabine. 2006. *Expression of information structure in the Bantu language Northern Sotho*. Doctoral dissertation, Humboldt University, Berlin.

Zubizarreta, Maria Luisa. 1998. *Prosody, focus, and word order*. Cambridge, MA: MIT Press.

Zwicky, Arnold M. 1982. Stranded *to* and phonological phrasing in English. *Linguistics* 20:3–57.

Index

Printed in the United States
by Baker & Taylor Publisher Services